DYNASTY RESTORED

DYNASTY RESTORED

*How Larry Bird and the 1984 Boston Celtics
Conquered the NBA and Changed Basketball*

THOMAS J. WHALEN

ROWMAN & LITTLEFIELD
Lanham • Boulder • New York • London

Published by Rowman & Littlefield
An imprint of The Rowman & Littlefield Publishing Group, Inc.
4501 Forbes Boulevard, Suite 200, Lanham, Maryland 20706
www.rowman.com

86-90 Paul Street, London EC2A 4NE, United Kingdom

British Library Cataloguing in Publication Information Available

Library of Congress Cataloging-in-Publication Data
Names: Whalen, Thomas J., 1964– author.
Title: Dynasty restored : how Larry Bird and the 1984 Boston Celtics conquered the NBA and changed basketball / Thomas J. Whalen.
Description: Lanham, MD : Rowman & Littlefield, [2024] | Includes bibliographical references and index. | Summary: "Dynasty Restored takes a detailed historic look at the fabled 1984 NBA championship showdown between the LA Lakers and Boston Celtics. Related issues of ethnicity, politics, class, and economics are also explored, along with colorful portraits of the players, owners, and coaches involved"—Provided by publisher.
Identifiers: LCCN 2024015528 (print) | LCCN 2024015529 (ebook) | ISBN 9781538159712 (cloth) | ISBN 9781538159729 (epub)
Subjects: LCSH: NBA Finals (Basketball) 1984. | Boston Celtics (Basketball team)—History. | Los Angeles Lakers (Basketball team)—History. | Bird, Larry, 1956–
Classification: LCC GV885.515.N37 W45 2024 (print) | LCC GV885.515.N37 (ebook) | DDC 796.323/640973—dc23/eng/20240509
LC record available at https://lccn.loc.gov/2024015528
LC ebook record available at https://lccn.loc.gov/2024015529

In loving memory of my parents

Contents

ACKNOWLEDGMENTS

A special thank-you to my undergraduate research assistants, Andrea Ventura and Michael DuPre. Andrea, in particular, provided invaluable support over the past three years in helping me conduct interviews and spending countless hours researching sections of this book. I wish her well in what I'm sure will be a very successful postgraduate career. An equal debt of gratitude is due to Dan Hammond, who reviewed an early draft of the manuscript and offered helpful comments. He is one of my oldest and most valued friends. Jeff Twiss of the Boston Celtics, as well as the staffs of the Naismith Memorial Basketball Hall of Fame, Boston Public Library, Boston University's Mugar Library, and the Beverly and Salem Public Libraries, were all especially helpful and cooperative. Christen Karniski once again proved what a consummate professional she is by guiding this manuscript through the publication process.

Finally, I want to pay a special tribute to my late aunts Catherine (Dion) Connors and Laurien (Dion) Fitzgerald. Products of the Greatest Generation, they were always the glue that held my extended family together. I miss them dearly.

INTRODUCTION

My first impression was that he did not look like much of a superstar. For there, slumped semi-naked before me on a locker room stool within the crumbling innards of ancient Boston Garden, sat Larry Bird. Bird was quietly fielding questions from the media following a 131–108 blowout win over the wretched San Diego Clippers on a rainy Sunday afternoon in late January of 1980. I was 15 years old and a rookie sportswriter for my high school newspaper, who on a lark had managed to convince a bemused local newspaper columnist to have me accompany him to the game. I was particularly impressed by the spiffy-looking club press pass I was issued featuring a cartoonish Lucky the Leprechaun leaning on a shillelagh and spinning a basketball on his right forefinger. Truth be told, though, I was not much of a hoops fan at the time. When I was not thinking about lettering as a varsity runner, asking a girl out on a date, or members of the opposite sex in general, I was most concerned about the fortunes of the hapless Red Sox. They were my favorite hometown team growing up, forever in pursuit of their first World Series title since George Herman "Babe" Ruth had knocked homers out of Fenway Park in 1918.

My beloved hardworking father—two years away from unexpectedly dying of a brain abscess—used to tease me about my over-the-top loyalties to the local nine, hinting, I suspect, that there were other worthier teams in town to root for. But I failed to grasp the point—that is, until I witnessed the Celtics demolish the Clippers. There was just something indescribably singular about the whole experience, whether it was looking up at all the green-and-white championship banners hanging from the Garden rafters, hearing the chatter of players on the parquet floor, or just the sheer fun of being in a rarified environment where an awkward, freckle-faced teenager like me struggling with a stutter somehow felt welcomed.

That perhaps explains why I was initially underwhelmed when I had my first up close and personal encounter with Bird, despite the fact that the soon-to-be crowned Rookie of the Year had just dropped 36 points on the visitors from California. Bird on the court was a sight to behold—effortlessly sinking outside jump shots, making crisp, bullet-like passes to teammates, and repeating the endearing habit of wiping his hands on the back soles of his old-school high tops whenever there was a break in the action. Yet, facing a scrum of television, radio, and newsprint reporters on deadline within the cramped, smelly Boston locker room afterward, he seemed quite different from the brash, superbly talented, and confident figure I had observed during the contest. His pinched, pie-shaped face with a slight hint of a blond mustache above the upper lip betrayed a sense of weariness and exhaustion. He kind of reminded me of Bill Bixby before he turned into that rage-filled title character on *The Incredible Hulk*, the popular 1980s sci-fi network television series that millions of Americans watched on Friday nights every week.

I debated with myself whether it would be worth asking him for an interview. After all, if the self-described "Hick from French Lick" could hardly muster much enthusiasm for individuals who actually did this sort of thing for a living, how would he respond to me? Drawing upon an inner reserve of personal courage (or foolhardiness?) that even this typist scarcely knew existed, I cautiously approached the great forward. In an unintentionally high-pitched voice that probably sounded like a cross between Mickey Mouse and the late great Pee-wee Herman, I spat out my request for a Q&A; and to my everlasting gratitude, Bird graciously said yes. The intervening years have dimmed my memories of what was actually said during that encounter, but I think I asked him for an assessment of the Celtics bench that year along with some other fairly banal inquiries. Bird patiently answered every one of them and when our brief exchange was over, I thanked him.

Returning to my high-school routine of class, track practice, and homework the next day, I found myself less interested in following the usual trials and tribulations of the Red Sox and more engrossed in the collective fates of Bird and his teammates. They rewarded me for my increased ardor in the onrushing decade ahead by appearing in five National Basketball Association World Championship Series, or Finals as they were soon to be officially known, as I went away to college and began my writing career after graduation. Yet if I had to select a single season that best exemplified how special this remarkable group of athletes were, it would have to be 1984 when they overcame several on- and off-court struggles to win the championship by besting Magic Johnson and a great Los Angeles Lakers team in an epic seven-game playoff showdown.

This book recounts the story of their heroic deeds and the amazing year that produced them.

CHAPTER ONE

Why 1984 Wasn't Like *1984*

RONALD REAGAN ALWAYS LIKED TO TELL A GOOD JOKE. IT WAS A WAY for the former acting legend of screen and television to win over audiences. So, it was completely in character for the 40th president of the United States to crack wise before a room full of aides and reporters as he waited to give his weekly radio address to the nation from his ranch near Santa Barbara, California, on August 11, 1984. "My fellow Americans," he said, "I'm pleased to tell you today that I've signed legislation that will outlaw Russia forever. We begin bombing in five minutes."[1] Unfortunately for Reagan, his irreverent remarks were captured on a live microphone and leaked to the public, causing an international row. For the leadership of the Russian Communist Party ruling what was then known as the Soviet Union took the 72-year-old president and devout anticommunist at his word. They put their military forces on high alert and issued an official statement condemning the "irresponsible old man" for his "unprecedented and hostile attack."[2] Only when it became clear that Reagan wasn't serious did tensions die down.

Welcome to 1984, where the decades-long Cold War rivalry between the United States and Russia was still raging and where any minor diplomatic misunderstanding or military miscalculation threatened to escalate into World War III. Just such a nightmare scenario had almost played out months earlier when the United States and its North Atlantic Treaty Organization (NATO) allies participated in an annual war game exercise known as Able Archer in Western Europe. As British historian and author Taylor Browning writes, "It was a communications game in which

NATO's Allied Command Europe (ACE) could practise and refine their signals communications along with the command-and-control procedures to be used in the event of war" with the Soviets.[3] On this occasion, however, the latter interpreted the exercise as the real thing. "It was a time of peak tension," remembered Russian rocket force commander Ivan Yesin. "We had to stay extra vigilant so as not to overlook the moment when a nuclear strike might have been delivered against the Soviet Union."[4] Yesin was told to remain in his bunker indefinitely and await orders from above to launch a devastating counterattack. "There was precious little time for decision-making," he said.[5] Fortunately, cooler heads prevailed in the Kremlin and the "Soviet War Scare" entered the history books as a close call, perhaps too close a call for the normally unflappable Reagan, who had once condemned his communist adversaries for overseeing what he called "an evil empire."[6] Now he confided in his private diary that he believed a more constructive dialogue with Russia was needed to prevent any future Able Archers. "I feel the Soviets," Reagan wrote, "are so defense minded, so paranoid about being attacked that without being in any way soft on them we ought to tell them no one has any intention of doing anything like that."[7]

Avoiding Armageddon was not the only pressing item on Reagan's agenda. The year 1984 was a presidential election year, and none of his predecessors had managed to serve a full two terms in the White House since 1960. The popular Republican intended to end this trend starting with a convincing electoral victory in November. But standing in his way was Walter "Fritz" Mondale, the former vice president from Minnesota who had secured his party's nomination after vanquishing civil rights activist Jesse Jackson and Colorado Senator Gary Hart in the Democratic primaries. Mondale wasted no time going on the offensive, accusing Reagan of possessing a "trigger-happy attitude toward nuclear war" and irresponsibly running up the national debt with his conservative tax-cutting policies favoring the wealthy.[8] Neither of these punches landed as the president's aw-shucks, carefully honed Teflon political image precluded any serious engagement on the issues. "Reagan was holding one perfect campaign event after another and steadily gaining momentum," Mondale recalled in his illuminating 2010 autobiography, *The Good Fight: A Life in*

Liberal Politics. "He seldom held big rallies or gave substantive speeches. It was all perfect miniatures, carefully scripted visits that produced thirty seconds of great television and made people feel good."[9]

Not even Mondale's bold selection of New York Congresswoman Geraldine Ferraro to be the first woman vice presidential candidate in history did much to move the political needle. Reagan enjoyed a commanding lead in the polls heading into the first of two nationally televised presidential debates on October 7. Then things surprisingly went awry. Submitting one of the worst political performances of his career, Reagan raised concerns about his continued fitness for office by coming off as doddering, confused, and uninformed. "This was a Ronald Reagan I had never seen before," First Lady Nancy Reagan candidly admitted in her memoirs. "It was painful to watch. There was no way around it, that debate was a nightmare."[10] Suddenly Reagan no longer appeared an easy lock for reelection; voters had too many questions about his mental acuity.

But he managed to put to bed these reservations in the second debate two weeks later by brilliantly turning the tables on Mondale. Asked pointedly by one of the panelists whether his advanced years should be an issue in the race, Reagan quipped, "I am not going to exploit, for political purposes, my opponent's youth and inexperience."[11] Mondale immediately felt all the air rush from his campaign: "The joke completely disarmed people's doubts about his age and his capacities and allowed them to think, 'He's okay.' They wanted Reagan to be okay and now they could believe it."[12] Reagan went on to claim a landslide victory on election day, capturing 49 states with an impressive 59 percent of the popular vote.

Contributing to Reagan's historic triumph was a booming national economy that had only recently emerged from a recession-plagued decade of runaway inflation, crippling unemployment, and low productivity. "Things look a heck of a lot better than people were saying several months ago," noted one pleased economist.[13] Indeed, the gross domestic product, which is a measurement of the country's total goods and services, grew by a whopping 6.8 percent in 1984.[14] Prosperity had returned; and with extra money now lining their pockets, Americans—especially young urban professionals, or Yuppies, as they were called—went on a spending spree, buying expensive new homes, trendy clothing, luxury cars, and new must-have electronic devices like mobile phones and personal computers. "Not in decades," journalist-historian Haynes Johnson later concluded, "perhaps not in the century, had acquisition and flaunting of wealth been celebrated so publicly by so many."[15]

A poster boy for this new age of soulless materialism was a brash, profane, and narcissistic real estate mogul from Queens, New York, named Donald J. Trump. Dubbed "the ego that ate Manhattan" by *People* magazine, Trump craved fame and celebrity the way Yogi Bear feasted on picnic baskets.[16] Nothing was ever enough. In fact, a popular joke of the day went that the self-promoting 38-year-old would attend the opening of an envelope.[17] "He was the rare billionaire who shunned privacy, who invited cameras to focus on the ego wall in his office," noted his perceptive biographers Michael Kranish and Marc Fisher in *Trump Revealed: An American Journey of Ambition, Ego, Money, and Power*. "He flaunted his wealth, spent ostentatiously, worked the media to keep himself on the gossip pages and the business pages and the sports pages and the front pages."[18] Put another way, "The Donald" was well on his way to a future run for high political office.

Whereas Trump luxuriated in his own notoriety, Michael Jackson had difficulty adjusting to his. The year 1984 was a big one for the ubiquitous singer and dancer as his best-selling *Thriller* album remained firmly ensconced at No. 1 on the charts despite having been released more than a year before. His music videos were in heavy rotation on the popular MTV cable network, and there was a run on red leather jackets and sequined gloves by avid fans hoping to emulate the Motown product's signature fashion style. "Oh my god, I loved Michael Jackson," recalled Rozonda "Chilli" Thomas, a Grammy Award-winning recording artist who was a teenager at the time. "When his videos came on, I'd run over and kiss the TV."[19] The public adoration aside, all was not well with the "King of Pop." He had grown weary of life in a fishbowl, where how much money he earned in a single day made national and international headlines. Introspective and shy by nature, Jackson approached media appearances the way an average person would a root canal. "I really do hate this," he confessed to a *Rolling Stone* interviewer.[20] Yet there was no escaping the attention. He had become a 1980s version of Elvis complete with overzealous admirers mobbing him at every turn. "You feel like you're spaghetti among thousands of hands," he said. "They're ripping you and pulling your hair. And you feel that at any moment you're gonna just break."[21]

The toll on his mental health proved enormous as Jackson's behavior grew increasingly more bizarre. He took to sleeping in a hyperbolic oxygen chamber at night to ward off the aging process while preferring the company of young children and a pet chimpanzee named Bubbles to adults.[22] "In some ways," observed Hollywood actress and friend Jane Fonda, "Michael reminds me of the walking wounded. He's an extremely fragile person. I think that just getting on with life, making contact with people, is hard enough, much less to be worried about whither goest the world."[23] And things were about to get even more complicated for the conflicted megastar. While filming a soft drink commercial featuring an elaborate pyrotechnic display in late January, Jackson's scalp accidentally caught fire, leaving him with second- and third-degree burns. "Something went wrong and it exploded and Michael's hair caught on fire," recounted an eyewitness.[24] Jackson would never be the same. While recovering from the painful injury, he developed an addiction to painkillers that ultimately claimed his life at 50 in 2009.

"I always want to know what makes good performers fall to pieces," Jackson once said.[25] Tragically, he found out.

And 1984 proved no kinder to patrons and workers at a crowded McDonald's restaurant in San Diego, California, on July 18. A heavily armed gunman named James Huberty entered the popular fast-food establishment during the early evening dinner rush and proceeded to mow down 21 people, five of whom were under 12. Nineteen others were also wounded in the onslaught, which represented the largest mass shooting in U.S. history up to that point. "The suspect was firing everywhere, at anything that moved," said Arthur Velasquez, a San Diego police officer arriving on the scene. "I saw bodies lying outside, adults and children. Some were still alive. I sadly witnessed [the shooter] killing a man laying next to his wife who had already been shot."[26] Huberty, who was carrying a 12-gauge shotgun and a pair of semiautomatic weapons when he committed the atrocities, was later killed by a police sharpshooter with a single bullet to the chest. As to why the 41-year-old—described by neighbors and coworkers as a gun-loving loner with a bad temper—went on the killing spree, his motive remained unclear. Huberty had recently been fired from his job as a security guard and was said to be "somewhat despondent."[27] Whether that was enough to push him over the edge has long puzzled survivors and investigators. "We may never know," the *Boston Globe* said.[28]

In popular culture, audiences lined up at cinemas to see *Ghostbusters*, an offbeat supernatural comedy directed by Ivan Reitman and starring *Saturday Night Live* alumni Bill Murray and Dan Aykroyd. Originally conceived as a vehicle for the late actor and comedian John Belushi, who died from a drug overdose in 1982, the film follows the misadventures of three swashbuckling parapsychologists (Murray, Aykroyd, and costar Harold Ramis in a memorable turn) in trying to save New York City from a host of demonic forces, including a giant marshmallow man dressed in a sailor suit that has nothing on King Kong. "Shit happens, someone has to deal with it, who you gonna call?" asks Murray's sardonic lead character, Dr. Peter Venkman.[29] Unusual for a movie of this nature, *Ghostbusters* was a huge hit globally, raking in $295 million at the box office. This became a major surprise to Reitman, no stranger to success with a string of blockbuster comedies such as *Meatballs* (1979) and *Stripes* (1981) already under his producing belt. "Nothing was like *Ghostbusters*," he told author Nick de Semlyen shortly before his death in 2022. "It really exploded all over the world and became central to the culture for a year."[30]

On television *The Cosby Show* and *Miami Vice* debuted to strong ratings. Cocreated and starring a pre-sex scandal Bill Cosby, *Cosby* was a heartwarming situation comedy about the daily goings-on of the Huxtables—a well-to-do African American family from Brooklyn, New York. Critics fell over themselves in offering praise. "If nothing else," wrote Howard Rosenberg of the *Los Angeles Times*, "*The Cosby Show* is a modern TV rarity, a comedy featuring black kids whose parents aren't white. What's more, the first half-hour is a belly laugher that respects its audience. The kids are cute but not *cute*; the parents bothered but not berserk or predictable. These are rational characters and predicaments that you can believe and understand."[31] *Miami Vice* delved into the gritty underworld of the Miami drug trade as seen through the eyes of a pair of hip young undercover detectives played by Don Johnson and Philip Michael Thomas. Shot on location with stylish élan and featuring a propulsive 1980s pop musical soundtrack, the show popularized Ray-Ban sunglasses, face stubble, pastel jackets, and the sockless look. "It was the Eighties, man," Johnson reflected many years later. "It was all about what it looked like."[32]

As popular as these programs were, they failed to match the buzz generated by a highly unconventional, if visually arresting commercial that aired during the third quarter of the Super Bowl XVIII telecast on Sunday, January 22. Directed by future Academy Award nominee Ridley Scott, the 60-second spot began with the image of a stern-faced blonde woman in a white tank top and red shorts racing through a bleak futuristic setting grasping a large sledgehammer in her hands. In a clear nod to the dystopian themes raised by George Orwell's classic 1949 novel *1984*, she is pursued by a horde of club-wielding "thought police" who seem intent on doing her harm.[33] When she reaches her appointed destination—a packed assembly hall dominated by a large video screen—the nameless runner hurls her hammer Thor-like toward the image of the bespectacled "Big Brother" figure on display. The screen then explodes into a miasma of blinding white light and swirling smoke. Cue the voiceover: "On January 24th, Apple Computer will introduce Macintosh. And you'll see why 1984 won't be like *1984*."[34] The commercial ran only that one time nationally but made a huge impression. The new sleek, cube-shaped Mac personal computer became a runaway best seller and popularized PCs as indispensable items to have in American offices and households. Its bold launch also helped establish Steve Jobs—the visionary Apple cofounder who pushed for the ad over the objections of his board of directors—as a hi-tech industry legend. Jobs had said he wanted something "that will stop people in their tracks."[35] His got his wish.

In sports, 1984 saw the Soviet Union pull out of the Summer Olympic Games in Los Angeles due to stated public concerns over the alleged safety of their athletes and "hostile anti-Soviet propaganda."[36] The real reason, though, had to do with payback for the United States boycotting the Moscow games four years earlier. Regardless, American athletes dominated the competition with 174 medals, the host country's biggest haul since 1904. Track and field standout Carl Lewis led the way with four gold medals in four events—the 100- and 200-meter runs, the 4 x 100-meter relay, and the long jump. Only the legendary Jesse Owens from the 1936 Berlin Olympics had ever accomplished that singular feat. "This has been the time of my life," Lewis said.[37] He was not alone. Mary Lou Retton made history by becoming the first American woman to capture the all-around gold in gymnastics while future LGBTQ+ activist Greg Louganis garnered record margins of victory in the three-meter and 10-meter diving events.

The biggest accolades, however, were reserved for Michael Jordan, who dazzled crowds with his death-defying moves on the basketball court while lifting the men's team to an easy triumph over Spain in the gold medal round. Earlier that spring, the still amateur guard had been selected by the Chicago Bulls in the first round of the NBA draft, and his Olympic performance served as a tantalizing preview of what was to come. Even the normally hard-to-please Bobby Knight, the future Hall of Fame coach from Indiana University who called the shots for the American squad, had been taken aback by the jaw-dropping talent he witnessed. "He's going to be the greatest damn basketball player that ever lived," he predicted.[38]

Turning to the pros, the perpetually snakebitten Chicago Cubs stunned the baseball world by winning the National League East division and qualifying for the postseason for the first time since the end of the Second World War. They managed to do so courtesy of an MVP performance by second baseman Ryne Sandberg (.314 batting average with 19 homers and 84 runs batted in) and the pitching heroics of veteran right-handed starter Rick Sutcliffe, a crucial midseason trade pickup who went 16–1 down the stretch to earn Cy Young Award honors. Long suffering Cubs fans like Illinois native and White House press secretary James Brady had difficulty believing their good fortunes. "We'll all just have to go back into the jungle . . . for education and retraining," he joked.[39]

Yet, as unexpectedly glorious as the regular season was, the league playoffs proved a different matter as the Chicagoans reverted to their losing ways. After building a seemingly insurmountable two games to none lead over the San Diego Padres in the best-of-five series to determine who would go on to play the American League champion Detroit Tigers in the World Series, the Cubs managed to drop the next two contests. But that was just a warm-up for the deciding game in which the usually sure-handed Chicago first baseman Leon "Bull" Durham made a critical late-inning error to hand over victory to the Padres. "What's it like in Chicago?" San Diego reliever Rich "Goose" Gossage speculated afterward. "It's got to be . . . like finding out the day before Christmas there's no presents."[40] He would have gotten no argument from Cubs diehards.

Neither would Edmonton Oilers fans have thought to question the transcendent play of Wayne Gretzky. Only 24 at the start of the 1983–84 season, the tall, thin, sandy-haired center from Ontario, Canada, had already established himself as one of the all-time greats in the National Hockey League, averaging an unprecedented 177 points per season along with winning the Hart Memorial Trophy as MVP four consecutive years. "There's not enough adjectives," Oilers coach Glen Sather said of the lofty heights Gretzky had achieved on the ice.[41] But it wasn't as easy as it looked. Lacking exceptional speed and upper body strength, Gretzky had to make do with his preternatural intuition and guile. "He can sense the gaps," Hall of Fame winger Gordie Howe said. "And that's the key to his game. People who don't know hockey watch the guys with all the hustle and bustle and The Kid doesn't seem to have anything extra. . . . But the real thing is he's one of the few players today who knows where all 12 men are on the ice, and what they're going to do. You can't get the puck past him—even from behind."[42]

For sure, Gretzky broke down the permutations of a contest like a supercomputer processing complex data sets. And this analytical approach, in combination with a deadly accurate shot from the left side, invariably left opponents throwing their arms up in despair. As one teammate said, "If you take your eye off Gretzky, he'll bank [the puck] off your skate, your back, your helmet, your wife. I could hang a nickel in the net, and he'd hit it every time."[43] Despite Gretzky's primacy, "The Great One" did lack one important item on an otherwise flawless hockey resume: a Stanley Cup championship. That glaring omission would be remedied in late May when the Oilers bulldozed their way to the final round of the playoffs and defeated the four-time defending champion New York Islanders in five games to claim their first title. "It's exciting to win individual awards," a misty-eyed, champagne-soaked Gretzky said after the victory. "But there's no feeling like this. Nothing compares."[44]

On the gridiron, the Los Angeles Raiders crushed the Washington Redskins in the Super Bowl, 38–9, behind the explosive offense of All-Pro running back Marcus Allen, who scored two touchdowns and rushed for a game-high 191 yards. But the real high-stakes drama occurred off the field as the fledgling United States Football League had announced that it would abandon its spring schedule of games for a fall one starting in 1986, thus challenging head-on the more established National Football League. The driving impetus for the move was New Jersey Generals owner Donald Trump who declared, "If God wanted football to be played in the spring, he wouldn't have created baseball."[45] The impetuous billionaire had purchased the Generals the previous August and made immediate waves by ponying up big money to sign away All-Pro linebacker Lawrence Taylor from the NFL's New York Giants. Trump "didn't give a shit [that he had several years remaining on his Giants contract]," Taylor told *Esquire* writer Drew Jubera in 2016. "He had me call my bank, and sure as shit, thirty minutes later he wired me a million dollars in my account. I was like, 'Thanks Don.' I respected that he put his money where his mouth is."[46] The deal ultimately fell through, though, and Taylor ended up returning the money.

The setback did not deter Trump from successfully pursuing other high profile NFL stars like former MVP quarterback Brian Sipe from the Cleveland Browns. But the rest of the USFL was not as resilient or well-heeled. After playing one more spring season, the financially shaky league ran out of money, precluding the planned move to autumn. A last ditch $1.7 billion antitrust lawsuit to force a merger with the NFL had also been pursued but to no avail. "It all happened in a flash," remembered broadcaster Charles Steiner, who called the plays for the Generals on the radio.[47] Like so many other dubious enterprises Trump had embraced over the course of his long, checkered business career—a casino, a passenger airline, a mortgage firm, and a private university—the USFL proved a bust.

A bust is how many would have described the NBA in the years leading up to 1984. Tarnished by numerous incidents of on-court violence that made basketball games resemble professional wrestling matches, the league's popularity plummeted to the point where the CBS television network felt compelled to broadcast seven NBA Finals contests on a tape-delayed basis to the East Coast from 1979 to 1981.[48] That would have been unthinkable for a Super Bowl or World Series. If this wasn't bad enough, a series of well-publicized drug scandals rocked the sport, further alienating fans and derailing the careers of once-promising young standouts such as Spencer Haywood and Michael Ray Richardson. "So much coke is snorted in the NBA, that if 10 players sneezed at once you could bet one or two of them were losing money," wrote Bill Russell, the former Celtics great turned network broadcaster, in his frank 1979 memoir, *Second Wind*.[49]

Adding to the NBA's woes was a dearth of leadership at the top. Larry O'Brien—a former top adviser to Presidents John F. Kennedy and Lyndon B. Johnson—had been installed as league commissioner in 1975, but he demonstrated little aptitude or enthusiasm for the job, treating it as another political sinecure. Revealingly, O'Brien called the position the "easiest" he ever had, even though, by his own admission, he had to deal with a hard-to-please group of owners whom he derided as "the biggest bunch of assholes you'll ever want to meet."[50] The contempt was mutual. Ownership collectively viewed O'Brien, as David Halberstam wrote in *The Breaks of the Game*, his critically acclaimed book on the troubled state of the NBA in the late 1970s, as "slow and ineffective and virtually incompetent in dealing with the media."[51] Nor was O'Brien spared criticism from underlings who worked closely with him in the league office. "I think all of us had a sense that there was more show to Larry than there was substance," related attorney Harvey Benjamin.[52]

Indeed, the supremely confident, nattily dressed O'Brien liked to project an air of aloof superiority over those he came in contact with, including emerging superstars like Larry Bird during his rookie season.

"I figured you couldn't even *talk* to him, that it was like getting through to the President of the United States or something," Bird later wrote in his 1989 autobiography with Bob Ryan.[53]

Little did Bird realize how things were about to change dramatically when O'Brien stepped down as commissioner at the start of 1984 and was succeeded by David Stern. A then relatively unknown figure outside of NBA circles, Stern had toiled several years as the league's first general counsel before being promoted to executive vice president for business and legal affairs in 1980. In that latter capacity, the affable, down-to-earth Columbia Law School graduate earned plaudits for skillfully negotiating a landmark 1983 labor agreement with NBA Players Association head Larry Fleisher that imposed a salary cap of $3.6 million on each team for the 1984–85 season.[54] The purpose of the cap—the first of its kind for any major professional sports league—was to bring a measure of financial stability to the NBA as the majority of clubs had been operating in the red for several years. It would certainly succeed on that front, as overall franchise revenues and values soon rose to record levels of profitability. "Teams can now plan their futures better and have some projections on where they're going," said longtime Washington Bullets owner Abe Pollin.[55] In spite of the accomplishment, Stern refused to rest on his laurels. When he assumed the top job, he let it be known that he envisioned the league becoming a global entertainment brand along the lines of Disney. As Stern explained to *Sports Illustrated*, "They have theme parks and we have theme parks. Only we call them arenas."[56] What the NBA lacked moving forward, however, was the same kind of iconic characters and compelling story lines to attract mass audiences.

Larry Bird and the Boston Celtics would provide some of those missing essentials during their epic 1983–84 championship run.

CHAPTER TWO

The Rise, Fall, and Rebirth of an NBA Dynasty

THE GREATEST BASKETBALL DYNASTY IN HISTORY WAS THE BRAINCHILD of Walter Brown, an unassuming, avuncular Phillips Exeter Academy graduate who ran the Boston Garden, a premier New England sporting and entertainment venue that hosted heavyweight boxing matches, rodeos, professional hockey games, three-ring circuses, and college basketball showdowns. In June of 1946, Brown spearheaded a drive with other major arena owners around the country to form the Basketball Association of America, later to be rebranded the National Basketball Association in 1950. The main impetus behind Brown's move was to create a major new attraction to keep people coming to the Garden during the long winter months when hockey—the main draw—was not in session. As he once explained, "I felt we needed to add dates. We had a building which cost a million dollars a year to run, and was being used less than half the nights of the year. Taxes and assessments were spiraling, and ten different unions were annually negotiating for increased contracts."[1] But what to call the local hoop entry? "Wait, I've got it— the Celtics," Brown reportedly told his publicist Howie McHugh after briefly considering other nicknames. "We'll call them the Boston Celtics! The name has a great tradition. And besides, Boston's full of Irishmen. We'll give them green uniforms and call them the Celtics."[2]

If only the rest of that inaugural 1946–47 season had gone as smoothly. For the team got off to a rocky start and never recovered, losing more games than it won and failing to make the playoffs. Coach John "Honey" Russell, who had guided the Seton Hall University Pirates to national prominence in the late 1930s, found the pro game a tad more challenging, especially with an undersized starting lineup that had trouble putting points on the board. As eccentric center Kevin "Chuck" Connors later joked, "Anyone who knows anything about the Boston Celtics knows when they started they were the strongest team in the league—in the cellar holding everyone else up. Yes, sir, we were the *worst*." The future star of *The Rifleman* television series had contributed to this sorry state of affairs with his own inept and undisciplined play. But he forever earned a special place in Celtics history when he unintentionally delayed the start of the team's first home opener by an hour on November 5, 1946. "During warm ups I took a set shot—a harmless set shot—and *crash*, the glass backboard shattered," he said.[3] Honey Russell lasted only one more season in Boston before returning to the college game. His successor— former minor league baseball player Alvin "Doggie" Julian—fared no better, churning out two more losing campaigns. The idea that the Celtics would become a standard of excellence to which all other pro basketball teams would compare themselves in the coming decades seemed about as probable as then Hollywood B-movie actor Ronald Reagan ascending to the White House.

Apart from the on-court failure, Brown also faced personal bankruptcy as he had sunk most of his life savings into keeping the troubled franchise afloat financially. All told, the team had lost close to half a million dollars over the previous four years, a staggering sum in those days. "Things were so bad that even my wife wanted me to get out of the business," Brown said. "I remember her telling me: 'we've had a lot of teams that have lost—but they were trying to win.'"[4] Brown needed to turn things around quickly, and on the advice of a fellow NBA owner, he hired Arnold "Red" Auerbach as his new head coach on April 27, 1950. "This is an opportunity that makes me very happy," Auerbach told reporters at the team press conference announcing his hiring. "I know the crying need for immediate success, and I fully intend to do everything within my power to give Boston the best basketball team that can possibly be put together."[5] Equal parts intelligent, vain, demanding, loud ,and profane, Auerbach was just what the hoops doctor ordered in terms of setting the Celtics down a winning path.

Only 32, the Brooklyn-born immigrant's son had already experienced some NBA success, leading the short-lived Washington (D.C.) Capitols to a divisional championship in 1947. A great deal more success followed in the early 1950s as Auerbach built a highly competitive Celtics squad around the singular gifts of playmaking guard Bob Cousy. "The Cooz" was a fellow New York City native who had dazzled college basketball audiences with his no look behind-the-back passes and buzzer-beating shots with the Holy Cross Crusaders from the nearby central Massachusetts industrial town of Worcester. Ironically, Auerbach had stubbornly refused to draft Cousy, dismissing him as a "local yokel" when he became available as a territorial pick after graduation.[6] "I just wasn't too impressed," Auerbach later wrote in his first autobiography with Paul Sann.[7] He believed Cousy was more the creation of exaggerated media hype than a bona fide hoops standout. Fortunately for Auerbach and the Celtics, the Hall of Fame guard fell into their laps when the Chicago Stags—the NBA team holding Cousy's contractual rights—suddenly folded, and he was assigned to the Celtics in a special dispersal draft. The unusual circumstances of his acquisition notwithstanding, Cousy emerged as the team's first superstar, leading the league in assists several times and averaging 20 points. "I was blessed with long arms and big hands, which helped me when it came to passing and dribbling behind the back," Cousy reflected decades later. "Really, they're moves you see 12-year-old kids doing on the playground today, and some of those kids are smoother than I was as a pro. But my vision was my greatest gift. People would say, 'You have eyes behind your back.' What I'm blessed with is great peripheral vision. That was what gave me a tremendous sense of where everyone was on the court."[8] Even the usually intractable Auerbach had to admit that he had badly misjudged Cousy. "Cousy was better than I thought he was," he conceded. "He was such a competitor."[9]

Although Auerbach had transformed the Celtics into a consistent winner, the team could never quite get over the hump in the playoffs, failing to advance beyond the second round during the brash young coach's first six seasons. Sure, they could score points in bunches, but they were soft defensively and lacked rebounding. Enter Bill Russell. The late-blooming, former board-crashing University of San Francisco center had led his team to two consecutive NCAA titles and captained the U.S. Olympic men's basketball squad to a gold medal-winning performance at the 1956 Summer Olympics in Melbourne, Australia. "His defensive presence altered the basic flow of the game," author Jeff Greenfield later observed. "All of the traditional scoring methods—the lob pass to the big center, the penetration of a guard posting a smaller opponent, the back-door play—were subject to instant nullification by the presence of Russell."[10] Indeed, even though Russell was a mediocre shooter with few offensive moves to speak of, he invariably dominated games. Word soon reached Auerbach from his network of contacts in the sport that the future Hall of Famer was someone to set his sights on. Russell "can't hit the broad side of a barn," former Celtic Don Barksdale informed him, "but he can get you 18 rebounds a game, his passing ability for a big man is better than any college player I've ever seen, and he can block shots with such finesse that he can swat the ball directly to a teammate . . . [H]e can play against anybody in the NBA and come out the winner."[11] Auerbach was sold, and he cagily maneuvered to acquire Russell's drafting rights.

Slated to pick seventh overall in the 1956 NBA draft, Auerbach knew the team would have to trade up several places to have a realistic shot. So, he dealt All-Star starting center Ed Macauley along with the rights to forward Cliff Hagan of the University of Kentucky to the St. Louis Hawks for their number two pick. It was a steep price and one that might have cost Auerbach his job if Russell turned out a bust, but Auerbach was confident he had done his homework. "You had to remember why you were doing it," he said. "You had to feel it was worth it or why bother? We thought [Russell] was worth it."[12] As added insurance, Auerbach also prevailed upon Walter Brown to promise Lester Harrison, the financially strapped owner of the Rochester Royals and possessor of the number one choice, that he would schedule the Ice Capades at the latter's arena if he agreed to pass on Russell. Brown was in the position to grant the favor because he was the president of the popular skating show. Harrison "felt indebted to Walter," Auerbach explained.[13]

All the behind-the-scenes maneuverings paid off for Auerbach and the Celtics. Russell's subsequent performance on the court exceeded all expectations as the goateed Louisiana native not only elevated the team's play but that of the entire game of basketball. "Before Russell," the pioneering basketball writer Leonard Koppett posited, "the NBA was a vertical game—nearly all the guys went directly to the basket. Russell made basketball a horizontal game because his shot blocking took away the layup. He forced teams to pass the ball from side to side to set up the medium-range jump shot, and that meant outside shooting became more important."[14] In the eyes of teammates like fellow rookie first round pick Tommy Heinsohn, a burly shoot-the-lights out forward who later in life developed a passion for landscape painting, Russell came off as an artist in his own right. "Russell was like a Cezanne on defense, a craftsman who perceived his art form in a unique way that led to a whole new school of thought," he wrote. "Cezanne, the great French postimpressionist, did it with geometric forms. Russell did it with timing, with great leaping ability, with blocked shots, and . . . with a particular delight in the psychology of it all."[15]

For sure, mind games became a signature staple in Russell's defensive arsenal. "Look, I can block shots," he confided to Jeremiah Tax of *Sports Illustrated*. "But if I tried to block all the shots my man takes, I'd be dead. The thing I got to do is make my man *think* I'm gonna block every shot he takes. How can I do it? O.K., here. Say I block a shot on you. The next time you're gonna shoot. I know I can't block it, but I act exactly the same way as before. I make exactly the same moves. I'm confident. I'm not thinking anymore, but I got you thinking. You can't think and shoot— nobody can. You're thinking, Will he block this one or won't he? I don't even have to block it. You'll miss."[16] Opponent Tom Hawkins coined the phrase "Russell-phobia" to describe the unique phenomena. He recalled witnessing players on several occasions breaking toward the hoop for uncontested layups and suddenly freeze in panic. They would invariably look over their shoulder for Russell to swoop in and swat the ball away. "It's a thing that happens to people when they play the Celtics," he said.[17]

Russell was not without his individual quirks. An inveterate practical joker with an ear-piercing laugh likened to that of a giraffe, he could be found nervously vomiting in the locker room before every game as his teammates solemnly stood at attention for the playing of the national anthem. Once he called a timeout at the end of a close contest to set up a play and started to cackle uncontrollably. When puzzled teammates asked what was the matter, he responded thusly: "Hey, this is something. Here I am a grown man . . . running around semi-nude in front of thousands of people in Baltimore, playing a game and yelling about killing people. How's that?"[18] These idiosyncrasies aside, Russell was an intensely serious man who did not suffer fools gladly, often coming off as cold and aloof to outsiders. He routinely refused to sign autographs and rankled sports traditionalists by claiming he was no role model for anyone's children except his own. But he reserved his most trenchant comments on how people of color like himself were traditionally discriminated against by ingrained societal structures of racism and inequality. "Here's the way I look at it," he said. "A lot of places I go now I'm acceptable because—well, look, I play golf. I don't belong to a country club, but I play a lot of them as a guest. As Bill Russell of the Celtics. I'm acceptable. If I tried to go as Bill Russell, citizen, I'd have no chance. I'd have to be awful foolish to believe in what is fondly known as 'The American Dream.'"[19]

Although such frank statements earned Russell pariah status in many corners of the country, including Boston, they had no discernible impact on how the Celtics went about their business on the basketball floor. The team became an unstoppable force, winning nine championships between 1957 and 1966, including an unheard of eight in a row from 1959 and 1966. Apart from Russell, the starting lineup positively brimmed over with Hall of Fame talents like Heinsohn, Sam Jones, Frank Ramsey, Tom "Satch" Sanders, and K. C. Jones. "They did everything they could to win a game," said Willie Naulls, a former All-Star small forward from New York who joined the team in 1963. "They *lived* basketball. They were thinking players who outsnookered you all the time. I would learn more in my first year with them than I learned in my first seven years in the league, and I was a damned good player."[20] The bench wasn't too shabby either, with 1962 first-round draft pick John Havlicek helping pioneer the unsung "sixth man" role in basketball—a top reserve who entered contests playing upwards to thirty minutes a night while providing fresh legs over the competition. "One thing I learned from Red Auerbach was that it's not who starts the game, but who finishes it [that's important], and I was generally around at the finish," declared Havlicek, a fastidious Ohio State graduate with a well-deserved reputation for hustle.[21]

With the unexpected death of Walter Brown in 1964, Auerbach found it increasingly difficult to balance his coaching duties with those he already had in the front office. As a result, he decided to retire from the bench and become a full-time general manager at the conclusion of the 1965–1966 season. As to who would be filling his coaching shoes, Auerbach entertained several possibilities, including bringing in Bob Cousy, who had established himself at the collegiate level as a highly successful coach with the Boston College Eagles. Ultimately, though, the cigar chomping Celtics leader decided on Russell, concluding that the five-time league Most Valuable Player needed a new challenge to keep his competitive juices flowing over the long haul of an NBA season. "As the years went on, motivation was tough for Bill," Auerbach explained. "But as coach, he had to motivate himself and the team."[22] Russell was initially hesitant to take on the added responsibilities. "I kept thinking," he recalled, "'Do I think I could do a good job? Would I be the best man?'"[23] He also had witnessed firsthand the intense pressure the job had exerted on Auerbach, who saw his hair turn prematurely gray during his years in charge. "But," Russell noted, "being somewhat of a nut myself, I finally decided it might be fun."[24]

The move was nothing less than historic. Russell became the first African American in history to helm a major professional sports franchise. Immediately, comparisons were made to Jackie Robinson of the old Brooklyn Dodgers, who integrated Major League Baseball in 1947. Russell went out his way to squelch such talk. "This doesn't even come close to the Robinson case," he said. "At the time there were no Negroes in any big league sports. Now there are so many, you don't even know who they are. But this is part of the thing Robinson did. It is part of the same story. Now maybe there will be some more Negro coaches and managers in sports."[25] Reaction to Russell's appointment was overwhelmingly positive. "This was a smart move by the Celtics," *Boston Globe* sports columnist Bud Collins wrote. "Does Arnold Auerbach make any other kind? It was eminently bright because Russell the coach will never allow Russell the player to retire. Russell the coach—loose jointed enough to kick Russell the player in the fanny—will be able to yell at his No. 1 player: 'Listen No. 6—start hustling. It's my job you're fooling with.'"[26]

The 1966–67 Celtics responded well to their new coach, winning 61 games—seven more than they had under Auerbach the previous season. Unfortunately, the Philadelphia 76ers—paced by the prolific offense of all-time scoring great Wilt Chamberlain—had an even better year, finishing with a then record NBA mark of 68–13. In the postseason, the 76ers proved equally adept, requiring only five games to get by the Celtics in the Eastern Division Finals. They then demolished the San Francisco Warriors in the final playoff round to secure their first league title in franchise history. "When Philadelphia eliminated us," John Havlicek remembered ruefully, "their fans were chanting 'The Celtics are dead, the Celtics are dead.' That made a lasting impression on me and I said, 'Right now, we are dead for only one year.'"[27] Havlicek knew what he spoke of, for the Celtics came roaring back the next two seasons to capture back-to-back NBA crowns.

The 1969 championship posed the toughest challenge. Having barely made the playoffs due to an assortment of debilitating injuries and an aging veteran nucleus, the team surprised everyone by qualifying for another Finals appearance that spring against the Los Angeles Lakers, who had fortified themselves in the offseason by acquiring Chamberlain in a trade. "That Celtics team was so old and beaten up, when it took to the court it needed only a fife and drum to look like the Spirit of '76," longtime NBA referee Earl Strom later joked. "Russell was hunched over and everyone was taped up like mummies."[28] Regardless, these underdog Celtics had enough left in the tank to force a Game 7 where they gutted out a 108–106 victory. The key play was an improbable foul line jumper made by veteran journeyman forward Don Nelson in the closing moments of the contest that deflected high in the air off the back rim before finally dropping straight down into the hoop. "I rushed the shot to beat the clock," Nelson remembered. "It didn't 'feel' good and I didn't think it would go in. I was just hoping it'd hit the rim in time and we'd have a chance at the rebound."[29] An exhausted Russell could barely muster the energy required to speak with reporters after the game. "I wouldn't trade this bunch of guys for any other bunch of guys in the world," he said. "We see each other as men and we judge a man by his character, not how well he plays, or anything like that.

"You can see things we've achieved as a group and it's definitely thrilling."[30]

The dynasty came to an abrupt end not long afterward when Russell officially announced his retirement from the game in an exclusive *Sports Illustrated* cover story titled "I'm Not Involved Anymore." "Since 1943, when I first saw a basketball," he attempted to explain, "I've played approximately 3,000 games, organized and otherwise. I think that's enough." He categorically denied that money had anything to do with the decision. "If you're looking for a reason why I feel I've played enough, I'll tell you this. There are professionals and there are mercenaries in sports. The difference between them is that the professional is involved. I was never a mercenary. If I continued to play, I'd become a mercenary because I'm not involved anymore . . . I played because I enjoyed it—but there's more to that than that. I played because I was dedicated to being the best. I was part of a team, and I dedicated myself to making that team the best. To me, one of the most beautiful things to see is a group of men coordinating their efforts toward a common goal—alternately subordinating and asserting themselves to achieve real teamwork in action."[31]

The news did not surprise his teammates. They had witnessed up close the grinding daily toll that being a player-coach had taken on him. "Bill just ran out of gas, physically and mentally," Larry Siegfried later told author Terry Pluto. "He had played under pressure his whole life— the only thing acceptable was a championship, and winning a title was expected rather than appreciated. When you were a member of those Celtics teams, you were not supposed to have an off night. With Russell being a coach, it was a double burden on him; he couldn't have a bad night on the court or with his coaching. He spent his whole career like the top gunfighter with all these guys gunning for him, wanting to knock him off. Bill wanted to leave on top, and to leave on his own terms."[32] Red Auerbach tried to talk Russell out of leaving, knowing how difficult it would be for him to walk away from a $300,000-a-year paycheck. "Hey, you can sell [*Sports Illustrated*] another story called 'Why I Changed My Mind,'" Auerbach said. But Russell held firm in his decision, and Auerbach backed off. He had too much respect for his star player to press any further. "How could I have told him he owed me or owed the Celtics anything? He owed nothing," Auerbach said. "That's the way I honestly felt. I think I knew Russell as well as any man alive. He played with tenacity or purpose and conducted his private life the same way. He'd make up his mind to do something, and as long as it made sense to him he would have the balls to do it, whether it made sense to anybody else or not."[33]

Russell's exit left a gaping hole at the team's center position, which Auerbach tried to partially fill by acquiring 7-foot veteran journeyman Hank Finkel in a trade with the San Diego Rockets. A former All-American with the University of Dayton Flyers, Finkel could score points but lacked anything approaching the menacing defensive presence of Russell. Opponents now had a relative unobstructed pathway to the basket, and they took advantage. "We expected [Finkel] to do a job like Russell did, and that wasn't fair," Havlicek said. "But the fact is, when Russ left we went from being one of the best defensive teams to one of the lesser defensive teams. And that's where the games are won: defense."[34] Indeed, the Celtics lost 11 of their first 14 games and dropped to the bottom of the standings. Only the lowly Detroit Pistons prevented them from finishing in last place. It was a trying season for everyone, especially Tommy Heinsohn, who took over the coaching reins from Russell. Since retiring as a player in 1965, Heinsohn had remained in the New England area, working as a top executive in the insurance industry. But he missed basketball and relished the challenge of leading his old team. The only problem was that the core of the club's roster, outside of Havlicek, was well past its prime. "I knew the Celtics," an opponent said. "They were nice guys. They wanted to win. . . . But everything in sports goes in circles. Finally, it was just someone else's turn to win."[35]

The Celtics went into full rebuilding mode and reemerged a few seasons later as serious title contenders with a new cast of talented young players led by center Dave Cowens. The fourth overall pick in the 1970 NBA draft, the fleet-footed, red-haired Florida State University product had caught Auerbach's eye the first time he scouted him. "He was so good I kept hoping he would make a mistake," Auerbach said. "There were some scouts from other teams there and I figured if they saw the same potential that I did, we were dead."[36] The latter did not happen, and the Celtics found themselves with a cornerstone franchise player who averaged more than 18 points and 13 rebounds per contest. "He could either start a fast break or lead one, pounding down-court like a runaway stallion—legs pumping, nostrils flaring, eyes bright as high-beam headlights," author and sports columnist Ray Fitzgerald wrote. "No Boston Garden floorboard escaped a Cowens knee-bone. To watch him dive after a loose ball was to see fury unleashed. Such moments, and they came often, were clinics on hustle, intensity, concentration, and all those buzz words that seldom escape the guidebooks they're imprisoned on."[37] Cowens's aggressiveness, however, came with a price. Referees were less inclined to give him the benefit of the doubt on close plays around the basket. "I make a lot of stupid fouls, but there are a lot called that I never really understand," Cowens said. "I think they have to learn your game. They see me block a shot, maybe, and they think to themselves, 'He couldn't have done that without fouling,' and they call one." In one memorable game against the Houston Rockets, Cowens became so upset with the officiating that he knocked guard Mike Newlin down to the floor to make a point. "NOW THAT'S A FUCKING FOUL!" he roared to referee Bill Jones.[38]

Cowens, along with hard-nosed veteran forward Paul Silas, whom Auerbach managed to pry away from the Phoenix Suns in a trade, provided a formidable front-court tandem that powered the Celtics to NBA titles in 1974 and 1976. "Me and Dave just began to just wear teams out," Silas remembered. "I mean *wear* them out."[39] The second championship was perhaps the sweetest as it came against Phoenix in six hard fought contests, including a memorable 128–126 triple-overtime thriller in Game 5. Although Cowens came up big with 26 points before fouling out in the second OT, it was his little-used backup, 6–10, 230-pound journeyman Jim Ard—who took home game honors. He stepped in and calmly sank the go-ahead free throws with 31 seconds remaining. Fellow benchwarmer Glenn McDonald also was another improbable contributor. The bearded swingman from Long Beach State scored six clutch points in the final overtime, easily the highlight of his three seasons in a Boston uniform. "Everybody poured their guts out," Heinsohn said. "That's the only way we won. With spunkiness. We knew what we had to do."[40]

The Celtics failed to recapture that winning formula the following year. Although the team did reach the Eastern Conference semifinals before losing out to the high-flying Philadelphia 76ers of Julius "Dr. J." Erving and George McGinnis in seven games, the club was roiled by a series of setbacks and controversies. Unable to come to contract terms with Silas by the end of training camp, Auerbach dealt him to the Denver Nuggets in a three-way deal that netted Boston former first round draft pick and All-Star forward Curtis Rowe from Detroit. The move was not popular in the Celtics locker room. Silas had been a consummate pro and teammate in his four seasons in Boston. He had earned NBA All-Defensive First Team honors twice while averaging double figures in points and rebounds. "When I first got here, I really believed all of that stuff about tradition and so on was a lot of bullshit," he once said. "But I know better now. It's real, all right, and I'm awfully proud to be part of it."[41] Then the unthinkable happened. "All year Red was telling Silas, 'You're my man,'" said Joseph Henry "Jo Jo" White, the team's brainy point guard who set a franchise record in durability by playing in 488 consecutive games. "Silas was one of those guys the Celtics were famous for having. He was a guy who did all the dirty work and never said a word. Red knew Silas's worth to the team. That's why he worked on his head all year. 'You're my man.' But when it came time for the dollars, they did the moon walk."[42]

Auerbach was unapologetic. He thought Silas's salary demands, which would have made him the highest paid player on the roster, were unreasonable, and in Rowe the team had a more than adequate replacement. Heinsohn privately disagreed, believing the wingman's departure would affect Cowens's game in a negative way. "Silas had taken a lot of the rebounding load off Dave, who did not relish the prospect now having to fight the battle alone," Heinsohn later wrote.[43] Indeed, convinced that the Celtics had thrown away any realistic shot of repeating as champions and feeling emotionally drained, Cowens notified Auerbach that he was taking an indefinite leave of absence eight games into the new campaign. "I just lost my enthusiasm for the game," he informed John Papanek of *Sports Illustrated*. He claimed the decision had been in the works for some time. "I'd been thinking about it for three months," Cowens said. "I even thought seriously about quitting before the season started, but I figured, I'd try it and see how it was. And I just didn't have it." His competitive fire was simply gone. "When somebody drives right by you and you shrug your shoulders and say, 'Aw, what the hell,' when you go down and make a basket like a robot, when you win or lose a ball game and it doesn't matter either way, when you can't even get mad at the refs, then something's wrong. I couldn't do anything about it. When there's nothing left, there's no use making believe there is." To do otherwise, Cowens explained, would be dishonest. "I don't want to take their money if I'm not earning it," he said.[44]

Auerbach was taken aback by the decision. "What could I say?" he said. "I've had other guys come to me and say the fun had gone out of it, but that usually happens when they're 33 or 34. Dave's such a fine kid. I didn't try to use my personality on him in any way. I understand. He made it very clear that he was unhappy playing, and after that I never said another word to dissuade him."[45]

Auerbach, however, knew Cowens could not stay away from basketball long, and the fiery 28-year-old did return to the team after two months. In the interim Cowens had occupied himself working at a harness racing track in the nearby town of Foxboro, a move that had greatly irritated Auerbach. "For him to be in the race-track business while we're playing basketball in all probability was a violation of his contract," Auerbach told *Washington Post* reporter John Schulian. "We're in competition with the track, and I told him of the conflict."[46]

None of this mattered to Cowens, who could be as stubbornly individualistic as Russell. He was just happy to be back doing what he loved most. "My enthusiasm has returned and I'm anxious to get started playing again," Cowens said.[47] And the Celtics desperately needed him. The team was only one game over .500 when he rejoined them, but he provided enough of a competitive spark to get them back into the playoffs and defeat a tough San Antonio Spurs squad led by shooting guard George "The Ice Man" Gervin in the first round. "They come out, look at you and know they're going to win," said San Antonio coach Doug Moe afterward. "When a team knows it's going to win, it wins, the Celtics have always known."[48] True to form, Cowens's unpredictable personality continued to draw attention. After the Celtics upended the Spurs in the series home opener, Cowens was seen moonlighting as a cabdriver in the Chinatown section of Boston. "I had six fares and made good tips," the career eight-time NBA All-Star boasted to a local reporter.[49]

The 1977–78 Celtics got off to a poor start and never recovered, finishing with an abysmal 32–50 record and out of the playoffs for the first time since 1971. "I'm confused," Cowens said. "I lie awake nights thinking. I try to think back to other teams I've been on, other situations, but I've never been part of a situation like this."[50] For sure, the club boasted several All-Stars on its roster including Havlicek, White, and Sidney Wicks. Yet as newly signed veteran guard Dave Bing later pointed out, they were all *"former* All-Stars."[51] Put another way, they were near washed up and no longer possessed the legs or playmaking skills needed to lift the team at crucial moments. If this wasn't bad enough, the players became increasingly turned off by Heinsohn's old-school coaching ways, which involved a lot of yelling and personal put-downs. "You can't be a dictator now," Heinsohn complained. "The Knute Rockne era, the Vince Lombardi era, the Red Auerbach era are all dead now. You're the Henry Clays now, the Great Compromisers. You can't yell at these ballplayers. You can't stand up and scream like Red used to. There's nobody who walks in as a dictator. You are trying to find a way to have a workable relationship and a workable system. You devise a program, and then you present it. But sometimes it comes in conflict with what other people think ought to be done."[52]

Heinsohn did not last the season. He was unceremoniously shown the door after 34 games and replaced by former teammate Satch Sanders, who went 21–28 for the remainder of the schedule. "I didn't really enjoy playing against them," admitted Paul Silas, now in a Seattle Superson-ics uniform. "The fight, the spirit, it wasn't there. When you played the

Celtics, you'd be in a battle and you enjoyed it. You hoped it would always be that way. This year, it was almost like they were a laughingstock."[53]

The sole highlight from that dismal campaign came from John Havlicek, who had announced at the midway point of the season his intention to retire. Playing in his last game on April 9, Hondo had arrived at Boston Garden wearing a rented tuxedo because, he said, "you should wear special clothes on special occasions."[54] After receiving an eight-minute standing ovation from the sold-out crowd before tipoff, the 38-year-old Hondo, who had posted relatively pedestrian numbers (for him) on the year, turned back the clock and pulled out a vintage performance against the Buffalo Braves. He scored 29 points and dished out eight assists in a resounding 131–114 Boston victory. "There goes a man who demanded perfection from himself," Johnny Most told his radio audience. "And many nights he was indeed perfection personified. It's difficult to say goodbye to Johnny Havlicek, a man who gave his heart and soul to this team every time he stepped onto the court."[55]

Most was not the only observer on the day to be impressed. Hollywood screen legend and former collegiate athletic standout John Wayne happened to be in town for a medical procedure and chose to convey his congratulations ["HONDO IS WATCHING"] in a telegram.[56] Clearly moved by the gesture, Havlicek indicated to reporters after the game that he was proud to have shared the same nickname with Wayne over the years. "He's been a big part of my life," he said.[57]

More turmoil awaited the Celtics in the offseason. Team owner Irving H. Levin, a suntanned Hollywood movie producer who had purchased the club in 1975, decided to swap franchises with owner John Y. Brown of the Buffalo Braves. Not long afterward, the Braves received league approval to move to the West Coast to become the new San Diego Clippers. The main impetus behind the deal was Levin's desire to operate a ballclub nearer to his home base in the Sunshine State. But Levin almost certainly knew that he would have been blocked by his fellow owners if he uprooted the Celtics for that purpose. There was simply too much history and tradition associated with the team. He faced no such obstacle with the Braves, however, a nondescript franchise that had only been in existence since 1970. Brown's own motives for agreeing to the unusual exchange were less nuanced. A native Kentuckian, the former encyclopedia salesman had made his fortune building Kentucky Fried Chicken into a lucrative national restaurant chain before selling his stake in the company for $284 million in 1971. Brown had added the Braves to his expanding portfolio in 1976 after having been a part owner of the ABA Kentucky Colonels the prior three seasons. He lived for the next deal; and when the Celtics became available, he knew it was too good a business opportunity to pass up. The team was an established NBA brand representing a city with a sizable national television market. "I'm your consummate entrepreneur," Brown once boasted. "I'll try anything. I'm not afraid of failure."[58]

From the start there was concern whether Brown could coexist with Auerbach. Both were voluble, headstrong individuals with their own ideas on how to run things. Brown did not dampen such speculation in his comments to the media. "[Auerbach] is the Celtics, but at the same time, if he wants total control—which pretty much he's been given—I've got to ask myself, 'Why should I have the team?' I don't want to own a team and just be a fan in the stands. I want to be responsible for my own destiny. If we fail, I want to be part of that failure, and if we succeed, I want the self-satisfaction that I made the contribution. Hopefully, we can both be part of it. If we can't, then I think we might as well face up to it and say it doesn't make sense for what we both want out of life."[59] Auerbach was less than pleased, but what irritated him most was a related trade that Brown had worked out with Levin, sending Wicks and three lesser players to San Diego for the services of power forward Marvin "Bad News" Barnes, point guard Nate "Tiny" Archibald, and swingman Billy Knight. Brown had not even bothered to consult him about the transaction. "We were like the Japanese ambassador who was meeting with Roosevelt while Pearl Harbor was being bombed," then team vice president Jan Volk said. "We were absolutely in the dark."[60]

A humiliated Auerbach seriously considered leaving the Celtics. The New York Knicks, winners of two championships earlier in the decade, had hit the skids and expressed strong interest in bringing the 60-year-old Brooklynite back home to turn things around. Intrigued, Auerbach made arrangements to fly to the Big Apple to hear their pitch in the apartment of Sonny Werblin, president of the Madison Square Garden Corporation. "I was there with my lawyer, Bob Richards and I got unbelievable treatment from them," Auerbach told the *New York Times*.[61] He was offered the team presidency and practically anything else he wanted, including a hefty salary and long-term job security. Prior to the Werblin meeting, Most tried to talk his old friend out of going. "You can't do this," he pleaded. "If you leave, I couldn't stay in Boston. Do you think Cowens would stay if you left? Do you think Havlicek or Heinsohn or KC or any of your players would ever want to be associated in any fucking way with this organization again?" Auerbach appeared unmoved. "I'm not going to be a stooge for John Y. Brown, a guy who obviously thinks he knows more basketball than I do," he responded. "I respect Werblin. I know he'll give me the power to run the team my way, without any interference."[62] In point of fact, Auerbach all but had his bags packed for New York when his wife, Dorothy, made a timely intervention. "How can you leave 13 championship flags," she asked. "Some day you're going to want to retire, so why do you want to make an intermediate stop?"[63] It also had not hurt that wherever he traveled in Boston during this uncertain time, ordinary people approached him on the street about staying. "It was all so goddamn flattering," Auerbach said.[64]

Brown publicly voiced support for Auerbach's decision to remain in the Celtics fold. "I really don't think he would have felt comfortable with the Knicks," he said. "They always have been his adversary."[65] Yet the tensions between the two remained. "The way it works up there," Brown bitterly complained, "is that whatever goes right Red did. Whatever goes wrong, the owner did."[66] Auerbach voiced an equally unflattering take on Brown. "He had a tremendous ego, like he knew it all," Auerbach told *Harvard Business Review* managing editor Alan M. Webber in 1987. "He used to call up different general managers around the league to pick their brains, and they'd lie to him. They'd feed him all this information and then they'd call me back and ask, 'Hey, what does that guy really want?' And he'd make deals. Well, he made one great big deal that could have destroyed the team."[67] The transaction involved the Celtics acquiring All-Star big man Bob McAdoo from the Knicks for three first-round draft picks that Auerbach had painstakingly amassed to rebuild the club.

Equally disconcerting was the rumor that Brown's then fiancée, former Miss America Phyllis George, had been the main driving force behind the deal. George was a huge McAdoo fan, and Brown reportedly wanted to win her favor. "What a goddamn joke," Auerbach confided to Most. "I have absolutely nothing against McAdoo but how the hell is he going to help Cowens' game? David's still going to have to do most of the rebounding. McAdoo's smooth, but he's not the effort-type player David is. He's an excellent jump shooter and scorer, but David gives us those things, too. Plus, David likes the contact inside. McAdoo is a finesse player."[68]

The deal failed to improve the Celtics' prospects on the basketball court as the team compiled an even worse record (29–53) than the year before. Sanders, whose low-key approach to coaching proved about as effective as Heinsohn's volatile style had been in his last season, was fired after the team stumbled out of the gate. "When things aren't going well," Sanders said, "somebody must pay the price—usually the coach. And that was me."[69] Cowens stepped in to replace Sanders, making him only the second player-coach in Celtics history. But unlike Russell, Cowens did not inherit a championship-caliber roster. He had more of a dumpster fire on his hands. Marvin Barnes was a leading reason why. A brilliantly talented player who had the ability to take over games with his prodigious shooting and rebounding skills, "Bad News" had all the makings of a superstar. He had been the ABA Rookie of the Year in 1975 while scoring 24 points a game. But when Barnes reached the NBA in 1976, the flamboyant 6–8, 230-pound power forward proved wildly inconsistent due to rampant personal drug use and an overactive night life. "I loved the limelight, and I loved the high I got playing basketball, that emotional lift, and it was hard to get that after the game was over," he said. "It was like, the game's over, come down now, and I didn't want to come down. So the drugs were a way to get back up there, mentally."[70]

His reckless behavior did not change with the Celtics. If anything, it reached alarming new depths. Remembered Barnes, "I became so hooked that while I was sitting at the end of the bench during a game at the Garden, I put a towel over my head, reached into the pocket of my warm-ups, pulled out a vial filled with coke, and snorted up."[71] Shortly thereafter,

Barnes looked down and noticed he was dripping blood out of his nose onto the parquet floor. "He was just a free spirit," Cowens said. "He was on his own wavelength. He was a decent guy with a decent heart. He just couldn't control whatever it was controlling him."[72] Barnes was given his release by the team before the season ended.

The Celtics became relevant again with the arrival of rookie sensation Larry Bird during the 1979–80 season. All the acrobatic passing Indiana native did was average 21 points, 10 rebounds, and 4.5 assists per game at small forward while lifting the club to instant title contention with an NBA-best 61–21 regular season mark. New Celtics head coach Bill Fitch, a no-nonsense disciplinarian who had taken over the team when Cowens opted to go back to being a full-time player, nicknamed Bird "Kodak" for his ability to take "an instant picture" of the whole court with his mind's eye. "He sees the creative possibilities," Fitch explained. "Larry can create off a set play, and in the context of that play he can invent something that's never been done."[73] Auerbach was equally fulsome in his praise. "We never had a corner man who can do the things he can," he said. "[Bird's] intensity reminds me of Havlicek. Sanders was a great rebounder and Heinsohn a great shooter, but here's a guy who can do both of those things and is also a great passer with great hands. This kid is in their class at this point. He's in the Celtic mold as we used to know it."[74] Auerbach had taken a huge gamble in selecting Bird with the team's sixth overall pick in the 1978 NBA draft. For the Indiana State star had a year of college eligibility remaining, and if the Celtics had been unable to sign him before the following spring's draft, the team would have been left empty-handed. Auerbach plowed ahead anyway. The potential upside involved was simply too enticing to pass over. "Larry Bird showed me what I wanted to see the first time I laid eyes on him," he said. "He was a damn good player who could put some points on the board and move the ball around."[75]

Bird ultimately signed with the Celtics for $3.25 million over five years, a record amount for a rookie in any sport up to that point. But contract negotiations had been unusually acrimonious. Auerbach and Bird's agent, pioneering Boston sports attorney Bob Woolf, did not see eye to eye. Woolf, who preferred using "friendly persuasion" over personal confrontation, felt that Auerbach was going out of his way in trying to intimidate him, comparing the unpleasant experience to the former coach working a referee during a game.[76] "He's more of a dictator than a negotiator," Woolf complained.[77] Auerbach did not care. He felt that Bird did not deserve the kind of money he was asking. "It's been proven," he snarled. "A cornerman can't dominate the game. A big man, occasionally even a guard. But one man playing a corner can't turn a franchise around."[78] The contractual impasse was only broken when new Celtics owner Harry Mangurian injected himself into the stalled talks. An accomplished horse breeder and longtime John Y. Brown business partner, Mangurian had bought out Brown's controlling interest in the club the previous spring when the latter left to launch a successful political career in Kentucky. Unlike the combative Auerbach, who Woolf claimed "goes through life like hot lava," Mangurian was a more measured man.[79] He believed in the art of compromise and was able to hammer out a mutually satisfactory agreement with Bird's camp. "Red never really appreciated spending a lot of money," Mangurian quipped afterward.[80]

Bird proved he was worth every penny of the historic deal as he captured NBA Rookie of the Year honors that season, beating out the equally heralded Earvin "Magic" Johnson of the Los Angeles Lakers. But he was not the only reason for the Celtics revival. Veteran floor general Tiny Archibald experienced a career renaissance at age 30, overcoming a debilitating Achilles tendon injury and averaging 14.1 points and 8.4 assists a game. "We had a bunch of guys who loved to rebound and take off," Archibald said. "That made my job easy because, as the point person, I had a lot of options."[81] Among his options was all-purpose swingman Michael Leon "M. L." Carr, a tenacious defender and disruptive force on the boards who held his teammates to exacting standards, even if their last name was Bird. "He was good-natured, but if he felt you weren't doing the job on the court, he'd let you know about it," Bird recalled. "Coaches might sometime beat around the bush, but "Hey,' M. L. would say, 'Why don't you tell the coach to take you out of the game? You're lousy tonight.'"[82] Carr had been signed away from the Detroit Pistons as a restricted free agent, which meant at that time the Celtics were required to make compensation. After some hemming and hawing on both sides, the final agreement worked out involved the Celtics shipping three-time league scoring champion Bob McAdoo, who never wanted to be in Boston, to the Pistons. Given McAdoo's superior star status, Auerbach was also able to induce then Detroit coach and future college basketball television commentator Dick Vitale to hand over two 1980 first round draft picks that eventually yielded Hall of Famers Kevin McHale and Robert Parish. "You've got to be loyal to your organization," Vitale told Steve Bulpett of the *Boston Herald* in 2018. "[S]o what am I going to do? Am I going to stand in the press conference and say 'I don't want to do this?' You take the shots. But the bottom line is that it worked out beautifully for Boston. It didn't work out for us."[83] Indeed, McAdoo would play only one full season in Detroit before being waived, his days as a productive league starter over.

Although the Celtics accomplished the greatest single-season turn-around in NBA history by winning 34 more games than they had the previous season, the team came up short in the playoffs. After sweeping the Houston Rockets in the opening round, they lost in five games to Dr. J's more experienced Philadelphia crew in the Eastern Conference Finals. "I suppose we didn't play very well," Cowens confessed afterward. "We just couldn't get anything going for any length of time. The fine points weren't there. It's sort of a shock, because I don't think anyone on this team thought we were going to lose." Bird, who scored a lackluster 12 points on 5-for-19 shooting in the deciding game, put himself at the top of the list of those expecting more. "We were considered the best team," he said, "but they put us away like we were nothing."[84] The whole episode left a bitter taste in his mouth. Losing, especially after enjoying such a great regular season, was deemed unacceptable. The only way to make amends was to win it all the following year. Interestingly enough, that is exactly what happened.

But the 1980–81 title run did not get off to an auspicious start. Cowens, the mainstay of two Celtics championship squads, called it quits at the end of training camp. Pro basketball's version of "Charlie Hustle" claimed that his body was no longer up to the demands of playing a full NBA schedule. "I have sprained my ankle at least 30 times over the duration of my career, broken both legs and fractured a foot," he said.

"Two years ago a team of foot and bone specialists said they were amazed I could play up to that point without sustaining serious injuries. I am basically playing on one leg and my left ankle is so weak that I can best describe it as saying I have a sponge for an ankle."[85] Bird took the news particularly hard. "Dave *had* been acting a bit funny in practice," he later recalled. "It did seem as if he really wasn't into it. We had all worked hard the year before and we all knew we would be working hard again and we felt Dave had probably been through so much that he thought it was time for him to get out. I was sad because I was looking forward to playing with him that year."[86]

Fortunately, Cowens's successor at center was already in place. Robert Parish was a lanky, shot-blocking big man who had compiled underwhelming statistics with the Golden State Warriors the previous four seasons. Although he did show flashes of brilliance on the floor, his reputation around the league suggested that he lacked consistency and personal drive. *Boston Globe* sports columnist Ray Fitzgerald alluded to this fact when he sarcastically noted that Parish had not reminded him of Kareem Abdul-Jabbar or even lumbering backup center Rick Robey the last time he saw him playing in a Golden State uniform. "He lah-de-dahed through a television game from the Coast, a 7-foot invisible man," Fitzgerald wrote. "Phlegmatic is a good word, and also disinterested, and lethargic makes three. A change of scenery and a chance to play for a contender and join the Celtics' 'family' will change all that. Sure it will."[87] Fitzgerald would be forced to eat his words as Parish became an All-Star that season with an 18.9 scoring average.

Parish had been part of an earlier blockbuster deal orchestrated by Auerbach sending Boston's first and thirteenth picks in the entire 1980 NBA Draft to Golden State for the former Centenary College star and the third pick, which the Celtics used to select University of Minnesota center-forward Kevin McHale—"the second-best low post player of all time, after Jabbar," according to future teammate and Hall of Fame center Bill Walton.[88] Golden State, in turn, took consensus First Team All-American center Joe Barry Carroll at number one. In the years to follow, the trade would rank as one of the biggest heists in Boston sports history. For although Carroll would go on to enjoy a 12-year NBA career, his good but not great production numbers were dwarfed by those of Parish and McHale, who combined with Bird to form "The Big Three," the most dominant basketball frontcourt of the 1980s. "What can I tell you?" a grinning Bill Fitch told reporters when the deal was officially announced. "Red has done it again."[89]

The franchise-altering move almost never came to pass. That's because Auerbach originally intended to use the team's number one pick on Ralph Sampson, a highly prized 7–4 freshman center from the University of Virginia. Auerbach viewed Sampson as Russell 2.0 but with a greater range of offensive skills. "I see no reason for him not to turn pro now," Auerbach said at the time. "What would be the purpose of attending Virginia one more year, or, at best two? He would never be able to make up, in money, experience, later what he would be passing up right now."[90] To demonstrate how serious he was, Auerbach flew to Sampson's home in Harrisonburg, Virginia, to personally sell his parents on the idea. "My pitch was simple and direct: this was a chance that would never come again," Auerbach told best-selling author John Feinstein in 2004. "We were a good team, a team that was going to contend for championships as soon as Ralph arrived. If he stayed in school, the chances were good he'd end up with a bad team where he had to be the Man from day one. We already had Bird, that would take the pressure off. Plus, if he got hurt while he was still in college, all the money he was counting on was out the window."[91] Auerbach received a polite hearing, but ultimately Sampson decided to stay in school where he became a three-time collegiate National Player of the Year. Auerbach voiced no regrets. "I gave it my best shot," he said.[92]

With McHale and Parish added to the mix, the Celtics cut a swath through their competition all the way to the NBA Finals in which they upended the Houston Rockets (now in the Western Conference) in six games. The only hiccup in their title quest occurred in the Eastern Conference Finals when the team squared off against Philadelphia in a playoff rematch from the year before. The Sixers held a commanding three games to one advantage until the Celtics launched a furious comeback and took the series in seven. "And so the astounding two-year frog-turned prince metamorphosis of the embarrassing, oft-despicable Boston Celtics team of 1978–79 is now complete," enthused Bob Ryan in the pages of the *Globe*. "Now they have the official championship, back where the Boston hoop *cognoscenti* realizes it belongs."[93] Curiously, Finals MVP honors did not go to either Bird, Parish, or McHale—all big-time contributors—but to forward Cedric "Cornbread" Maxwell, a breakout four-year veteran who had been drafted by the Celtics out of the University of North Carolina at Charlotte. Maxwell led the club in field goal percentage (.568) and scoring average (17.7) against Houston while also providing solid rebounding and flypaper defense. In the pivotal fifth contest, when Bird's scoring touch temporarily deserted him, Maxwell picked up the slack with 10 for 13 shooting from the field. He also added 15 rebounds on the evening. "It was the most fired up I've ever seen him," Bird wrote in his autobiography. "He could smell it. He was getting great position underneath and we were all feeding him."[94]

The 1981–82 Celtics won 63 games and seemed poised to repeat, that is until they crossed paths with Philadelphia again in the playoffs. This time around, it was Boston's turn to fall in seven after they lost Tiny Archibald to a shoulder injury early in the series. Without the services of their penetrating starting point guard, the Celtics offense bogged down and never really recovered. "Very depressing," Archibald recalled. "I couldn't raise my shooting arm. I even practiced shooting righty, but I knew I couldn't help the team."[95] Former Brigham Young University star Danny Ainge, acquired from Major League Baseball's Toronto Blue Jays after a nasty legal battle, had been pressed into action as a backcourt replacement, but a combination of inexperience and inconsistent outside shooting neutralized the rookie's effectiveness. "It hurts," Bird said of the missed opportunity.[96]

The next season proved just as disappointing. Despite making the postseason for the fourth straight year, the Celtics got swept in the second round by an inferior Milwaukee Bucks squad. "There was no fire!" exclaimed M. L. Carr. "No anger, just a resigned acceptance of defeat. That wasn't the Boston Celtics."[97] A big problem was that several veterans on the team, including McHale and Parish, had grown tired of Fitch's acerbic, authoritarian style of leadership. They tuned him out, and that led to a highly dysfunctional locker-room atmosphere. "Bill was what you might call a dominant figure as a coach," Fitch assistant and future Celtics head coach Jimmie Rodgers told the *Los Angeles Times* years later. "His approach was [initially] needed because we were rebuilding. But sometimes, when you reach a certain level, like win a championship, you may have to alter that approach."[98] Yet Fitch stubbornly refused to do so, leaving even staunch supporters such as Bird scratching their heads. "I think Bill wondered if he could get the guys to play the way they did for him before," Bird said.[99] Something had to give, and when Harry Mangurian announced after the playoffs he was selling the team, Fitch knew it was time to tender his resignation. Mangurian had treated him well, but he was unwilling to take his chances with a new ownership. "That's when it all clicked," Fitch said.[100]

His replacement on the bench was K. C. Jones, an old Auerbach favorite who had labored as an assistant under Fitch for several seasons. Jones had never felt his input was valued, however, and on one occasion vented his frustration by uncharacteristically getting into a physical altercation with Fitch. "I was wrong when I went after Bill," Jones admitted afterward. "But I have my pride."[101]

Whether Jones could instill a similar fighting spirit in the underachieving Celtics remained an open question entering the 1983–84 campaign.

CHAPTER THREE

Out of the Blocks

K. C. JONES HAD ALWAYS BEEN A MAN OF FEW WORDS. WHEN HE WAS assigned as Bill Russell's undergraduate roommate at the University of San Francisco in the fall of 1952, Russell recalled that his future Boston teammate and lifelong friend did not utter a single word to him for an entire month. "Not a *word*," Russell wrote. "He'd slap my bunk on the way out of the room in the mornings, and he'd nod at the salt or sugar during the silent meals we ate in the school cafeteria. That was the extent of our communication."[1] But Jones displayed no such reticence when he learned that the Celtics had acquired four-time All-Star guard Dennis Johnson from the Phoenix Suns for backup center Rick Robey and a first-round draft pick in a blockbuster trade on June 27, 1983. Johnson "can bring the ball up court, he can stuff someone on a blocked shot and he can play a forward position as a defensive guard," Jones enthused to the media. "Mainly, though, he can play defense and put the ball in the hoop."[2]

For sure, the acquisition of Johnson, or "DJ" as he was better known to teammates and fans, addressed a major deficiency in the Celtics backcourt. Tiny Archibald, the Hall of Fame playmaker and vital contributor for the 1981 champions, had gone into steep decline due to an assortment of injuries and the fact that his slender 6–1, 150-pound frame could no longer withstand the pounding of a full NBA season. He received his perfunctory release from the team in July. "It wasn't the way I hoped to go out," he said, "but I had a great career doing what I loved."[3]

Meanwhile, unproven youngsters Gerald Henderson and Danny Ainge had shown promise but hardly seemed suitable candidates to replace Archibald at the No. 1 guard position. They lacked offense and turned the ball over too much. Slow-footed veteran Quinn Buckner—acquired the previous season as trade compensation for Dave Cowens when the latter decided to unretire and join the Milwaukee Bucks—was strictly backup material. Ditto for Carlos Clark, a 6–4 rookie shooting guard from Ole Miss, who had averaged 15.4 points in 118 games for the Rebels. Johnson, though, checked all the right boxes. As Red Auerbach said, "Johnson fills one of our most important needs. We got a strong defensive guard who also averaged 14.2 points a game last season. We now have a big guard who can play the big guards like Magic Johnson." For his part, the 29-year-old Johnson expressed delight at the prospect of joining a serious playoff contender. "You're never happy leaving one place, but that's not my choice," he said. "I feel good about going to the Celtics. I'm going to a team that has a championship tradition behind them and hopefully ahead of them. I know their needs and I think I can fit in."[4]

The Johnson trade would not by any means be the only newsworthy item coming out of Celtics camp that turbulent offseason. Kevin McHale flirted with going to the New York Knicks as a free agent, setting off howls of protest from the Boston front office. "Let the Knick lawyers come up with any contract they want," Red Auerbach huffed to reporters. "They're just wasting their time. McHale won't play for the Knicks, you can bet on that."[5] To bolster this defiance, Auerbach, working in tandem with lame duck Celtics owner Harry Mangurian, devised a clever strategy: signing New York free agents Marvin Webster, Sly Williams, and Rory Sparrow to offer sheets, thus forcing Knicks management to choose between throwing a load of cash at McHale or risk losing all three valuable players. They could not afford to do both due to the financial constraints imposed by the NBA's new salary cap structure that was coming into effect. "If the Knicks got to their cap number, they couldn't make a deal for Kevin," recalled Jan Volk, Auerbach's top lieutenant and former team legal counsel. "We didn't know when that was going to happen, so we decided to help the process along."[6] The Knicks were blindsided by the move, maintaining that it was unnecessarily vindictive. "We are in a tough situation," admitted Hubie Brown, the team's loud and outspoken head coach.[7] This was music to Auerbach's churlish ears as he could not resist twisting the knife further. "They were the first ones to go after one of my Boston players. We just move faster than other people do," the cigar-chomping Celtics boss commented gleefully.[8]

Weary of parlaying any further, New York withdrew from the McHale sweepstakes, thereby clearing a path for the Celtics to sign McHale to a hefty four-year deal worth $4 million on July 21, making the Minnesotan temporarily the highest paid player in club history. "I'm extremely glad it's over," he said. "It took too long. I'm sorry that Boston fans had to be subjected to the nonsense." Whereas McHale expressed relief, Larry Bird grew agitated. The $3.25 million contract he had signed as a rookie was due to expire at the conclusion of the upcoming season when he could theoretically become the most prized free agent in the league. And Bird and his agent Bob Woolf were looking for a big payday. "The signing of McHale makes it more urgent for the Celtics to resolve the Bird problem," Wolff said. "We'd like to work out an agreement. We're ready, willing and able at any time." The one catch was that Bird refused to haggle over terms of a new agreement once the regular season began. "Larry wants it that way," Wolff explained. "He does not want any negotiations to interfere with his playing."[9]

Unlike their negotiation four years earlier when Wolff and Auerbach went at it hammer and tongs like Obi-Wan Kenobi and Darth Vader in a light saber duel, this time the deliberations went relatively smoothly and without acrimony. "I never had to sell Red on the worth and value of Larry Bird," Wolff later said. "I felt he should be the highest paid player in the game. Every Hall-of-Famer and former coach will tell you he's the best all-around player ever. Red didn't need much coaxing."[10] The final terms of the deal awarded Bird a total of $12.6 million spread out over seven years, making him the third-highest-paid player in the NBA, behind only Philadelphia 76ers center and reigning MVP Moses Malone and Magic Johnson of the Lakers. "Of course no one is worth that kind of money," Celtics Hall of Famer and team broadcaster Bob Cousy said, "but if Moses is going to get $2 million a year, then Larry certainly should. He is a genuine superstar in a sport where there are a lot of great players."[11] Typically, Bird appeared almost embarrassed to be discussing his newfound financial windfall. "Money has never really bothered me," he told the media. "You still have to go out and produce. Just because I got the big contract, I'm not gonna lie down and say, 'OK, guys, go do the work.' This just makes me want to try harder than ever . . . I hope I don't change."[12]

What, in fact, did change was the person signing Bird's paychecks. On August 9, Harry Mangurian ended months of speculation about who would succeed him as Celtics owner by selling the club for $17 million to an investment group headed by Don F. Gaston, the former executive vice president of Gulf and Western Industries. "Outside of Gulf & Western [which owned the Knicks], these guys have more money than any other team in the NBA," Mangurian said. "They don't even have to go to the bank for a loan. They just bring the money right in."[13]

Nonetheless, the Gaston group was something of a dark horse as most league watchers had tabbed prosperous Boston area businessman Steve Belkin to be at the top of the list of prospective team buyers. But reports emerged suggesting that Belkin had had inappropriate connections with a pair of convicted bookmakers through a former business partner. A subsequent investigation conducted by the NBA cleared Belkin of any wrongdoing, but it was too late to save his bid for ownership of the Celtics. "I really feel bad for him," Mangurian said. "There was never any doubt in my mind that the league report on him would turn up positive. But the bad publicity about some of his associates just became a killer."[14]

Gaston himself faced questions about his prior business dealings. While still on the board of Gulf and Western, the Texas native had been the focus of a 1979 Securities and Exchange Commission investigation concerning alleged misuse of company funds "for purposes unrelated to business and of obtaining personal banks loans from institutions that hoped to do business with Gulf & Western."[15] A settlement was reached with the SEC two years later, but a perception lingered that Gaston had been caught, as acerbic *Boston Globe* sports columnist Will McDonough put it, "with his fingers still in the cookie jar."[16]

All the same, Gaston appeared infinitely preferable to many other suitors who had lined up to make a bid on the NBA's most decorated franchise, including a controversial young business tycoon who went on to become the 45th president of the United States. Having already purchased the New Jersey Generals of the USFL, Donald Trump sought to add the Celtics to his expanding sports entertainment portfolio. There was only one problem: Red Auerbach. Having already endured the likes of John Y. Brown, Auerbach had no desire to deal with another slick, large-ego owner whose natural inclination was to call all the shots. "Red wouldn't have anything to do with him," said Jan Volk, Auerbach's long-time administrative right arm.[17] Auerbach biographer and longtime basketball beat writer Dan Shaughnessy agreed. "Red would not have eaten any shit from that guy. No way," he maintained.[18] And without Auerbach's approval, any potential sale was dead in the water as Mangurian had essentially given him veto power. Gaston and his two business partners, Alan Cohen and Paul Dupee, were more to the Celtics godfather's liking anyway. They were perfectly content to sit back and let Auerbach run things. "When I want to do something like make a deal," Auerbach said, "all I have to do is call one of these three guys and tell him what I am doing. That's the arrangement we have. I don't have to go chasing all three of them around the country to take a vote."[19]

As eventful as the summer had been, more drama awaited K. C. Jones and Co. at the start of October when the team opened training camp at the Pappas Gymnasium on the leafy campus of Hellenic College in suburban Brookline, Massachusetts. Robert Parish, upset that he was the lowest-paid member of the Big Three at $650,000 per annum, demonstrated his displeasure by storming out of camp, telling club trainer Ray Melchiorre simply that he would not be available to play.[20] The move took his new head coach and fellow Celtics by surprise, especially since the All-Star center had been in active talks with the Boston front office for a lucrative extension to his contract, which had three years to run. "It bothers me that he isn't here, in that he's a fine person and we miss him," Jones said. "I hope it works out. But whatever happens, I've left it alone. Red (Auerbach) will call me when something happens."[21] Larry Bird was less diplomatic, no doubt stewing over the team potentially being without the 19 points and 11 rebounds a game Parish had provided the season before. "If Robert doesn't want to be here, he doesn't want to be here," Bird said. "We've got enough talent on the bench. That will hurt, but we'll get by somehow."[22] M. L. Carr disagreed, saying, "We absolutely need him. When you analyze a team, you start in the middle. Like Kareem with the Lakers and Moses [Malone] with the Sixers. You start in the middle and go from there."[23]

Parish's work stoppage lasted the entirety of eight days. He and team management reached an accord on October 13 that gave Parish more money by adding another year to his existing deal and moving up some deferred compensation payments the club already owed him. As Volk recounted, "The negotiations dealt as much with a human sense as a financial sense. Because I think there was a perception there that Robert felt he wasn't respected or appreciated. And that was not the case. But [the contract dispute] was resolved. We told him yes, there would be an extension."[24] Word of the settlement was met with a huge sigh of relief from Parish's teammates, none louder than Kevin McHale, who had been given the unenviable task of filling in at the number 5 spot for four exhibition games. "I'm glad Robert got squared away," McHale said. "This means I won't be having as much time at center, which is probably just as well. I wasn't really comfortable playing 25 minutes at center."[25]

As for the possibility of any ill will spilling over from the episode into the locker room, the Celtics to a man dismissed the notion out of hand. "I'm sure if the players thought he didn't deserve [the money], there would be some dissension among the guys," Gerald Henderson said. "But there's no question that the guys know Robert deserves it. This wasn't very good timing for us, but he had to do what he thought was right." Besides, Danny Ainge joked, given how poorly McHale had shot from the floor during their last exhibition contest without Parish—a woeful 3 for 16—the third-year guard could go back to "working on my outside shot instead of my post moves."[26]

Such flippancy was absent when the Celtics crossed swords with the Philadelphia 76ers during an October 16 preseason clash at Boston Garden. "I thought this might be the first Game in NBA history called because of violence," Cedric Maxwell said.[27] Indeed, although the Celtics prevailed 99–86, the headlines emerging from the showdown concerned the assorted brawls and physical standoffs that broke out between the two archrivals on the floor, including one involving Red Auerbach. The 65-year-old GM raced down from his box seat to confront 6–10, 255-pound Moses Malone after the Hall of Fame center put Celtics forward Cedric Maxwell into a headlock under the boards in the first quarter. "Hit me, you big SOB," screamed Auerbach. "Go ahead. I'm not big, hit me you SOB."[28] Although greatly agitated, Malone had the presence of mind not to take up Auerbach's offer. "If Moses had hit Red, Harold Katz [the 76ers owner] would be paying Red, not Moses," M. L. Carr told reporters afterward. "Moses' money would be referred instead of deferred."[29]

Auerbach, who would be fined $2,500 by the league for his vituperative outburst, also took the opportunity to point his stubby finger at Philadelphia coach Billy Cunningham during the fracas and unleash a torrent of unflattering verbal abuse. He thought the 76ers were trying to control the physical tempo of the game at his team's expense, and he was damned if he was going to let that happen in his own building. "That was a classic thing, what Red did," said Cunningham, who came away from the evening's dustups with a torn sports jacket and frayed nerves. "As much as I love the man, that was unbelievable. Only one person could do that and get away with it. He's the one and only, and I love him. I'm going to keep the tape of this game. It was a classic." The sellout home crowd took no offense at Auerbach's behavior as they shook the ancient Garden rafters with roars of approval. "Funny, you could notice how everyone went 'woooooo' when [Auerbach] went out there, and then started to cheer him on," Kevin McHale said. "Everyone was thinking 'this thing's going to be settled now.'"[30]

Arnold Jacob Auerbach took no quarter from anyone. The late St. Louis Hawks owner Ben Kerner discovered this before Game 3 in the 1957 NBA Finals when he got into a heated exchange with Auerbach over the height of the basket the Celtics were warming up on in his home arena. Auerbach insisted that it was substantially below the league standard of 10 feet despite a subsequent measurement by game officials proving him wrong. Kerner accused Auerbach of being "a bush-leaguer," and the fiery Boston coach responded with a right-hand hook to Kerner's mouth. "Aw, all I called him was a busher," Kerner said afterward. "He's a big sorehead. That stuff he was pulling was bush. With all the talent he has he still has to pull tricks like that." Auerbach remained unrepentant. "I wasn't going to take it," he said.[31] He never ever did.

"If punches are to be thrown," Auerbach always told his players, "I don't want anybody on this team to punch second."[32] To do otherwise, he believed, gave the opposition an advantage, thus reducing your chances at winning. And winning had always been his raison d'être. As Irv Goodman of *Sport* magazine observed, "Many men love victory. But Auerbach loves it and respects it, and, toughest of all, understands it. He comprehends better than most men that winning is its own reward. The cheers, the silver cup, the gold coins, the bowed head and upraised hand—these come after the fact. The fact itself, the only fact is winning."[33]

Bill Russell sensed this about Auerbach the instant he started playing for him. "He ached when we didn't win; his whole body would be thrown out of whack when we lost," Russell wrote. "He didn't care about any player's statistics or reputation in the newspapers; all he thought about was the final score and who had helped put it on the board. He was our gyroscope . . . and it was difficult for any of us to deviate from the course he set for us."[34] Although this unrelenting commitment to winning irked opposing teams and their fan bases, particularly when the Celtics began stockpiling championships in the 1960s, Auerbach did not especially mind. What were a few boos and catcalls, anyway? It was merely the price you paid for succeeding in one of the most highly competitive industries on the planet. "You see, when you're winning, and you've been around as long as I was, more than any other coach, they're always looking for angles to get to you," he said. "Anything to put you down, say something derogatory about you. It's a form of jealousy, so I dismissed it."[35]

Of course, Auerbach virtually ensured himself of pariah status outside of New England when he routinely lit up a celebratory cigar in the closing moments of Celtics victories. "He really liked to embarrass an opponent that way," noted New York Knicks small forward and future Democratic presidential candidate Bill Bradley.[36]

OUT OF THE BLOCKS

In his defense, Auerbach insisted that he had never intended the gesture to humiliate others; rather, it started as an act of spite directed against the ruling NBA establishment. "Years ago when they were picking on me for a hundred different things [as coach]," he said, "I tried to think of something to aggravate them."[37] Then it came to him one day when he received a curt note from the league office asking him to refrain from his then occasional habit of smoking cigars on the bench. He flatly refused, and when a now defunct Scranton, Pennsylvania-based cigar company named *Blackstone* asked him to endorse their product, there was no turning back. "Some of the coaches got aggravated," Auerbach told *Sports Illustrated* in a 1965 interview. "They thought I was lording it over them. The cigar is a sign of relaxation. The cigarette is a sign of tension. I explained to them that it was an endorsement, that I get money and all the cigars I can smoke. That calmed them down. Why stop a guy from making a buck? However, the fans think this is a major thing."[38] Celtics players did as well, believing that the practice needlessly offended opponents and made them play harder, especially on the road where the environment was decidedly hostile to begin with. Not that that made a difference. "The thing was [Auerbach] never got burned—not once did we blow a game after he fired up a cigar," noted Bob Cousy.[39]

As much as Cousy and his teammates were leery of Auerbach's cigar smoking, they were positively terrified of his lack of skill behind a steering wheel. "He had a blue convertible Chevy and he drove it like a madman, 80 miles an hour, through the White Mountains to get to these exhibition games he had set up in little towns" remembered Ed Macauley, who once half-seriously demanded a trade if he had to be Auerbach's passenger.[40] Cousy did the Hall of Fame center one better by actually having it written *into* his contract that "he didn't have to ride with [his coach] in an automobile."[41] "I don't think there's ever been a clause quite like it in NBA history," maintained team broadcaster Curt Gowdy in his 1993 memoir *Seasons to Remember*. Yet it must have made perfect sense to Cousy, who once claimed Auerbach "wrecked more cars than Evel Knievel."[42] Jim Loscutoff contended that this unfortunate tendency was due, in part, to Auerbach's own hypercompetitive nature. "When he drove us to exhibition games," Loscutoff said, "we played a game called Zit. If you saw a dog, it was one point. If you saw a dog taking a leak, it was five points. A dog taking a dump was 10 points. If you saw two dogs screwing, you won. Red would weave all over the road, nearly causing accidents as he looked for dogs."[43]

A key element to Auerbach's success was a PhD level of understanding in human behavior. Unlike other NBA contemporaries, he forwent the standard practice of treating his ballplayers all the same. They were too quirky and individualistic for that. He knew, for example, it would be counterproductive to harshly criticize a Bill Russell or a Cousy due to their fierce personal pride. On the other hand, it was perfectly acceptable to ride a Tom Heinsohn because the fun-loving, laidback shooting forward often needed a kick in the pants. "Basically, Red treats people as they perceive themselves," Russell once explained. "What he did best was to create a forum, but one where individuals wouldn't be confined by the system. And he understood the chemistry of the team. People tend to think of teamwork as some mysterious force. It isn't. It can, really, be manufactured, and he knew how to do that, to serve each player's needs. And people always say you need to know *how* to win. But that's not enough if you want to keep winning. You also have to know *why* you win. Red always knew that as well."[44] Although Auerbach ran out of fingers on his hands to wear all the championship rings he earned with the Celtics, he made a conscious effort not to get carried away with his own importance. Auerbach said, "You're dealing with a game where everybody wants to be heard, to go down in history. A man thinks he's infallible, he's ridiculous."[45]

Such humility and restraint did not apply when Auerbach interacted with the men in striped jerseys. Referees were deemed the enemy and therefore had to be brought to heel through constant goading and physical harassment. A frequent target for this abuse was the highly respected NBA referee Joe Gushue from Philadelphia. "Every night he put me to the test," he confessed to sportswriter Terry Pluto. In one contest Auerbach went too far, however, and earned a three-game suspension for pushing Gushue. "Red's excuse was that I tried to make a name for myself by throwing him out of a game, and he wasn't going to be intimidated . . . so he shoved me. But the truth was that that I didn't even eject him until he wandered out on the court, went chest-to-chest with me and spit all over me with that foul mouth of his."[46] Fellow ref Sid Borgia, a hard-nosed, hot-tempered West Virginian whose career spanned from 1946 to 1966, also experienced his share of run-ins with Auerbach. "Red would do every trick in the book to upset the officials, to harass them, to intimidate them," he recalled. "Whenever I'd try to explain my point of view to him, it always ended up with him telling me, 'You're full of shit.' And because he was so damn loud, everybody in the joint heard it, so that's when I'd call the technical."[47]

Auerbach's coaching model was no basketball figure but rather Hall of Fame baseball manager Joe McCarthy, who piloted the New York Yankees during their dynastic run in the late 1930s and 1940s. Although he had never met McCarthy, the Yankee skipper left an indelible impression on Auerbach, thanks in part to conversations he had with old friend and former All-Star shortstop Phil Rizzuto, a key contributor on those great Yankee teams. "[Rizzuto] told me McCarthy was vitally concerned with the image of the Yankees," Auerbach said. "He said Joe believed the way a team conducted itself off the field had a great deal to do with the play it performed on the field." The idea made perfect sense to Auerbach. "A guy like Joe DiMaggio actually looked and acted like a champion. If you could get a whole team to look and act the way DiMaggio did, you'd have one helluva ballclub on your hands." He made up his mind then and there that he wanted his ballclubs "to look and act like champions, too." "When you talk about the Celtics tradition," Auerbach later said, "it's more than just winning. We didn't just play the best. We also wanted to look the best, dress the best, act the best. It was a certain championship feeling."[48]

Auerbach developed his rage to succeed while coming of age in the rough Williamsburg section of Brooklyn during the Great Depression. Money was tight in the Auerbach household, but young Arnold and his two siblings never did without as their Russian Jewish émigré father worked around the clock at a local dry cleaning shop that he co-owned with his brother to make ends meet. Auerbach would spend long, grueling hours there after school helping to keep the business afloat. "Ten at night until eight in the morning," he reminisced. "I'd get myself a pastrami sandwich and a cream soda and go to work. I did one hundred suits a night."[49] When he wasn't working the steam press, Auerbach was using his fists to ward off neighborhood bullies who often targeted him because of his Jewish heritage. "I learned early to stand up for myself and for what I believed in," he later wrote. Basketball entered the picture when he took up the game at an outdoor gym on the roof of Public School 122. "Unless it snowed or rained, we played," he said. Auerbach became a good enough player to make the All-Brooklyn second team as a guard in high school and secure a basketball scholarship to George Washington University in Washington, D.C. This turned out to be a lucky break as he got to play under the tutelage of pioneering coach Bill Reinhart, whom many credit with being among the first to employ a fast-break offense. Most essentially, Reinhart demonstrated to the impressionable youth how to "handle" ballplayers. "You see, he *didn't* handle them," Auerbach said. "Players are people, not horses. You don't handle them, you teach them . . . you listen to them. The best players are smart people and a good coach will learn from them."[50] This valuable lesson was never lost on Auerbach when he became an NBA champion behind the bench and in the front office.

As the Celtics wrapped up their preseason in late October with a 6–2 exhibition record, the clubhouse mood was genuinely upbeat and optimistic. Gone were the long faces from the previous season when Bill Fitch's autocratic ways had worn thin on most of the veterans. "There's a lot less tension and that's the appropriate word," said Quinn Buckner, a former frequent target of Fitch's tirades. "Guys are more prone to work because they feel freer. There are no apprehensions about what you're trying to do. Everyone's trying to play basketball. Nobody's criticizing."[51] Larry Bird noted the marked difference in atmosphere as well. "Everybody's relaxed," he said. "We know the job we have to do, but we know we won't be embarrassed by the coach during the game."[52] K. C. Jones made sure of that by adopting a looser, less antagonistic approach, setting the tone in the club's first practice when he tossed the ball onto the court and described the kind of drills he wanted performed in a calm professional manner. "That was it," he wrote in his 1986 autobiography *Rebound* with Jack Warner. "If I'd given a speech the players would have thought that it wasn't me. We went right to work."⁵³ And it became apparent to Jones right away that the team needed no dramatic overhaul, just a little fine-tuning. As Jones told Mike Carey of the *Boston Herald*, "The players, since four years ago when we started doing well, have been phenomenal together. That's a 10-point edge in every game. It eliminates intra-squad problems. The togetherness was still there last season although there were a couple of things which shouldn't have occurred."⁵⁴

One of those things involved Fitch's inability to clearly define roles for players whose last names were not Bird, Parish, or McHale. Scott Wedman was a case in point. Obtained in a January trade with the Cleveland Cavaliers for washed-up first-round draft pick Darren Tillis and cash, the two-time All-Star small forward was expected to provide some much-needed outside shooting off the bench. But Fitch seldom used him in that or any other capacity, sowing feelings of deep frustration in the normally easygoing Kansan, who posted career-low numbers in scoring average and field goal percentage. "He didn't get a chance to play," Jones said. "Any time a good player sits and only gets a minute or two, his game suffers." To prevent a reprise, the 54-year-old head coach went out of his way to assure Wedman that he would be getting more touches. "He gives us another weapon," Jones said. "When I see him go up for a shot, I get a good feeling. It's like you know the ball is going in."⁵⁵ The vote of confidence was duly appreciated. "This year everyone will know their roles from the start of the season," a relieved Wedman told a reporter. "You won't see players swapped around every three or four games. That will take a lot of pressure off. . . . It will be a set situation from the start."⁵⁶

Also unlike his predecessor, Jones refused to rely strictly on his own counsel. For in Red Auerbach he had an invaluable font of basketball wisdom from which to draw. "Everyone needs someone to bounce ideas off, someone whose opinion he trusts, and for me that someone has always been Red," Jones said during the official Boston press conference announcing his hiring. "We're talking about one of the brightest minds I've ever come across. You just sit with him for a while, and before you know it he's tossing out theories and philosophies on basketball as if they're nothing at all—yet if someone else came up with just one of those ideas, he'd think he had stumbled onto something big. What better guy in the world could I hope to get feedback from?" Auerbach offered no objections, having developed a close personal bond with Jones since he had drafted and developed him as an undersized defensive guard out of the University of San Francisco in the late 1950s. In fact, the old coaching legend positively relished the idea. "It's like a shot in the arm for me," said Auerbach, whose offers of advice had been routinely met with icy stares from Fitch. "People are always talking about the past, and about the way things used to be around here. I can appreciate how that might bother someone who wasn't part of it. But, see, that's where K. C. and I won't have any problems at all, because those aren't my [championship] flags up there anymore. They're our flags now."[57]

Fame, riches, and accolades did not appear to be in K. C. Jones's future when he entered life in rural central Texas during the spring of 1932. Jim Crow was the law of the land, and if you were of African American descent, that meant living under an oppressive apartheid regime that mandated "separate but equal" public institutions ranging from hospitals to water fountains. If basic human rights were few, economic opportunities were even fewer, especially for Jones's hardworking mother and father, Eula and K. C., for whom he was named. "They struggled to feed us, to put clothes on us and to keep a dry roof over our heads," Jones wrote. "We wandered across the heart of Texas through the depression years as my Mom and Dad looked for work." Eventually the family wound up in the relatively prosperous community of McGregor, located 16 miles southwest of Waco and best known for its artesian waterworks. But the same ingrained societal structures of racism and inequality that had held back so many post-Reconstruction blacks in the South remained in place, leading a nine-year-old Jones to conclude that white folks made all the rules. "We didn't see ourselves as second class citizens," he recalled. "We didn't see ourselves as citizens. We didn't vote or ever think about the political world; it was beyond us. Washington, the State House or City Hall, we hardly knew they existed. That was the white man's place where he ran things." Jones loathed the stifling atmosphere and came to appreciate what his father meant when he said, "If you're black, step back."[58]

Even public school offered no respite. His fifth-grade teacher accused him of cheating one day in front of his classmates after he solved a long division problem. She "must have been amazed that I came up with the right answer," he conjectured. "I hadn't cheated but she sure cheated me out of some good, positive feelings about myself."[59]

Jones and his five younger siblings eventually quit Texas at the start of the Second World War when his mother suddenly decided it was best for the family to pull up stakes and head west to San Francisco, where the racial climate was more inclusive and welcoming. One notable absentee, however, was the elder K. C., who had earlier separated from Eula. "There wasn't any great explosion," Jones wrote. "He was just gone. It was like somebody holding your hand and suddenly letting go and you can never reach that hand again. We were on our own and I was now the man in the family. It didn't seem fair to me, but our lives had nothing much that was fair."[60]

Be that as it may, Jones thrived in the "City by the Bay," savoring the community's rich cultural diversity and becoming a football and basketball star in high school. Indeed, his hoop prowess was such that he attracted the attention of the University of San Francisco Dons coach Phil Woolpert, a progressive-minded army veteran with movie star handsome looks who offered Jones a full athletic scholarship to attend the Jesuit-run school. Woolpert differed from most of his contemporaries in that he actively sought African American players to fill his team roster. "Phil was so far ahead of other coaches . . . it was scary," noted Pete Newell, Woolpert's predecessor at USF. "There were a lot of rednecks back then."[61] The supportive Woolpert would go on to play a key role in Jones's life as well as the life of his other local standout recruit, Bill Russell. "Russ and I never would have made it if not for him," Jones said. "We both would have wound up rejected, which happens to a lot of kids who come from environments where there aren't opportunities to develop their minds. Maybe the parents never got through school themselves, so they don't know how to help, except to ask, 'Hey, how's school going?' Or maybe they're just too busy trying to put food onto the table. Meanwhile, there are gangs, pot smokers, friends trying to get you to parties—all kinds of things that work against bringing out the best of what's inside you. Once in a while a kid from that kind of environment gets lucky. I got lucky. Russ got lucky."[62]

Luck had nothing to do with USF reeling off 56 straight victories and back-to-back NCAA championships in 1955 and 1956. Although Russell deservedly received the lion's share of the credit by averaging 20 points and 20 rebounds a game, Jones's contributions at point guard were not insubstantial. He ran the club's up-tempo offense with skill and confidence while also providing lock-down defense on the other end against top-flight opponents like Tom Gola of the La Salle University Explorers. Gola, a three-time All-American forward averaging more than 20 points, was an especially difficult assignment as he held a sizable height advantage over Jones. Still, when Woolpert informed Jones the night before the 1955 title game against the Explorers that he would be covering Gola, he did not flinch. His mind went into immediate over-drive, devising a clever strategy to stop the celebrated Philadelphia cop's son. Recalled Jones, "I found that I could keep Gola from driving around me because I was quicker, and I would harass him when he put the ball on the floor. That meant he would have to shoot long range or try to drive and pass the ball off. I knew guarding him would be difficult, but I also knew that if he posted up or got by me, Russell would be there. And he did get by me a couple of times. But you're never going to stop a great player one-on-one. The important thing is, I was not intimidated."[63] It showed. Gola was held to 16 points while Jones hoisted up a game-leading 24 to put USF into the victory circle.

The Dons' success, noteworthy because Jones, Russell, and fellow African American Gene Brown comprised three-fifths of the starting lineup at a time when blacks were rarely given opportunities to play at the big-time collegiate level, did not shield the club from racial attacks. One upset USF alumnus went so far as to openly complain in a letter to Woolpert about the number of blacks on the roster and how they were "scarcely representative of the school."[64] The ugliness did not end there. During a team practice held in Oklahoma City before a tournament, locals showered all the players of color with coins thrown from the stands. This did not sit well with Jones or his teammates. "The fact the 'fans' there considered us some kind of circus attraction created anger and frustration is us," Jones wrote. "Their attitude caused us to play even tougher basketball. We hustled more than ever in that tournament. It triggered feelings in us that made us more intense and even grouchier in our games."[65] USF easily won the tournament, but not before Jones experienced one of the most satisfying moments of his hoop career. Late in the championship game against the University of Oklahoma, a Sooner player unexpectedly turned to him and said in a tone of deep respect that the Dons were "really terrific."[66]

Although drafted by the Celtics after graduation, Jones opted not to enter the NBA right away. To the surprise of many, he decided to join the U.S. Army instead, figuring that Uncle Sam would eventually call his number anyway as this was decades before the concept of the all-volunteer military force came into effect. "I might as well get it over with," he thought.[67] Serving primarily as a clerk typist at Fort Leonard Wood in Missouri, Jones still found ample time for athletics, starring on the post's basketball and football teams. In fact, his play on the gridiron was good enough to earn him a tryout at the Los Angeles Rams summer training camp after he completed his two-year hitch in 1958. Starting in the team's first three exhibition games as a defensive back, Jones performed well under the discerning eye of Rams coach Sid Gillman, a future Pro Football Hall of Famer. "If I sound like I'm bragging it's because I am when I tell you nobody completed any passes around me," Jones later claimed.[68] But when he suffered a painful muscle tear in his thigh during the third contest, Jones began having doubts. Was the NFL with all its bone-crushing physicality really for him? His mind turned to the idea of playing basketball again with his old roommate Russell, who had joined the Celtics the previous year and carried them to an NBA title. The prospect appeared too tempting to resist. "So I quit," he said.[69] His departure did not please Gillman, who believed Jones had the potential of being an All-Pro. "That's how impressed I was with K. C.," he later said. "My loss was Auerbach's gain."[70]

Jones never regretted the decision, even though it took several seasons for the sleek 6–1, 200-pound guard to become a starter in the Celtics' backcourt. That's because Auerbach preferred to bring him and talented shooting guard Sam Jones (no relation) along slowly behind the more seasoned Hall of Fame talents of Bob Cousy and Bill Sharman, who received the bulk of the minutes. "K. C. and I understood the situation," Sam Jones said. "Those guys played ahead of us and those guys won championships together. When you're winning you're willing to sacrifice. We knew we could play."[71] By 1964, Cousy and Sharman were gone, and the "Jones Boys" became permanent fixtures in the starting lineup. Whereas Sam dazzled with his offense, K. C.'s game was subtler, harder to appreciate without a trained basketball eye. Remembered team broadcaster Johnny Most, "You wouldn't even notice it when K. C. went into a [contest], but he'd be guarding the toughest scorers in the league night after night, and he consistently held them to ten or so points below their averages."[72] Lenny Wilkens counted himself among the many victims. "K. C. stuck to you like glue," the All-Star St. Louis Hawks guard said. "He was with you, right on you, every step. He'd bump you, hold you, get in your way. And with Boston, all he had to do was think about defense because they had so many other guys to score."[73]

Perhaps the greatest compliment came from Boston sports journalist Bud Collins, who ran out of the standard superlatives to describe the outstanding defensive job Jones had performed on Oscar Robertson of the Cincinnati Royals one evening. "Oscar couldn't have washed K. C. out of his hair if he had stayed in the shower all night," he wrote.[74]

Modest by nature, Jones rarely tooted his own horn, preferring instead to let other teammates bask in the public spotlight. But there were exceptions, such as the time he reduced Jerry West's torrential scoring output to a mere trickle in a playoff game against the Lakers. Recalled Jones, "Afterward, the press crowded around my locker—something I wasn't used to—and it seemed like every newspaper writer in the country was there. They were asking, 'what did you do to him? How did you stop him?' So I held court. I lost my head and told them *everything*. 'I did this and that, and that and this, and so forth and so on.' Man, I really poured it on." Such candor did not come without a price. "Mr. Clutch" scored 43 the next game, leaving Jones holding the proverbial bag. "I had forgotten," he said, "that besides knowing what to do with the basketball, Jerry West also knew how to read. It taught me a very big lesson: Be ever so humble when you're covering a superstar."[75]

After winning six titles with the Celtics, Jones retired from playing at the end of the 1966–67 season to begin a new career in coaching. His first stop was at Brandeis University, a short commuter train ride from Boston Garden in suburban Waltham, Massachusetts. There he served as a winning men's head coach for three seasons before moving on to Harvard University as an assistant for one year. His big break came in 1971 when old Celtics teammate Bill Sharman became head coach of the Los Angeles Lakers and recruited Jones to serve as an assistant. "We had spent years killing one another in practice," he wrote. "[Sharman] was competitive and determined. I knew what a quiet, steady man he was and I felt good working for him. I had great respect for him."[76] What he did not feel so good about was that he was now working for a team that had been a bitter archrival during his playing days. It would take some adjusting, especially since the LA roster was dotted with superstars like Jerry West and Wilt Chamberlain. "I was nervous about dealing with these stars," he later confessed. "I knew the Lakers were not a humble group but IBM isn't humble either. Why should they be?"[77] Why indeed. The Lakers waltzed to the 1972 NBA championship, and Jones had another championship ring to add to his growing collection.

He was not so fortunate when he became head coach of the Washington Bullets in 1973 and piloted them to the NBA Finals against the Golden State Warriors two years later. In a stunning upset, the Warriors upended the heavily favored Bullets in a four-game sweep while Jones drew heavy criticism from the media and fans for an incident that occurred during a timeout in Game 3. Network television cameras showed Washington assistant Bernie Bickerstaff diagramming a play for the team while Jones appeared kneeling on the floor in a weirdly detached, sphinxlike silence. The optics suggested that Bickerstaff was in charge and not Jones. "I was there. I know what happened," Bullets star center Wes Unseld later said. "K. C. controlled the huddle, controlled the timeouts, told us what he wanted done. He didn't have to pull out a board and draw things for the TV crew. I never understood why that got so much play or what was so important about that one incident, that perception."[78] Nevertheless, the image stuck, and when the Bullets failed to advance to the Finals the following season, Jones was fired. "That one incident has followed me everywhere," Jones complained afterward. "That's all people seem to remember about me, but I guess that's the business."[79]

Business, as in taking care of it, was foremost on Jones's mind as the Celtics waited for the regular season to begin. "If the team stayed healthy they should win it all," he thought.[80] The confidence was understandable. Just two seasons removed from their last championship, the Celtics were loaded. Not only were the Big Three of Bird, Parish, and McHale returning, but the backcourt had been greatly improved with the addition of Dennis Johnson. Towering 6–11, 250-pound first-round draft pick Greg Kite out of Brigham Young University provided needed depth at center with Robey's departure. Scott Wedman gave every indication in the preseason that he had regained his scoring touch. And lest anyone had forgotten, former 1981 NBA Finals MVP Cedric Maxwell was back at small forward with his game-changing defense and clutch offensive rebounding. "We have the internal leadership to help us go a long way," Maxwell told a reporter. "The veterans have a little more say-so. They can police themselves. There are no real questions other than getting down and playing."[81]

Even so, the Celtics needed no reminding that it would probably not be a cakewalk to banner 15. In the Eastern Conference, the defending champion Philadelphia 76ers topped the list of contenders with reigning league MVP Moses Malone (24.5 points, 15.3 rebounds, and 2.1 blocked shots a game) resuming his customary dominant perch at center; and erstwhile scoring machine Julius Erving showing few signs of performance drop-off at 33. They could also rely on the explosive offense of 6–3 shooting guard Andrew Toney off the bench and the flypaper defense of forward Bobby Jones. Dubbed the "Boston Strangler" by awed Beantown sportswriters for his many big game performances against the Celtics, Toney had the uncanny ability to strike fear into the hearts and minds of Boston players. "You say that name to me, and it messes up my day," M. L. Carr once confessed. "He was the best when it came to undressing a player."[82] A product of Dean Smith's legendary University of North Carolina Tar Heels program, Jones had started his pro career with the Denver Rockets of the ABA before moving on to Philadelphia, where he became a yearly lock for NBA All-Defense First Team honors. He won the league's first Sixth Man of the Year Award in 1982–83. "We're approaching [the year] as if we hadn't accomplished anything yet," 76ers coach Billy Cunningham said.[83]

The Milwaukee Bucks, coming off a 51-win season and a deep play-off run, looked again to be in the thick of things. The explosive scoring tandem of guard Sidney Moncrief, 26, and forward Marques Johnson, 27, constituted the heart of the offense while the aging but still effective Bob Lanier could be counted on to provide quality minutes in the paint. "Our time is now," Moncrief said. "Our guys aren't getting any younger. It's real important that we stay healthy. We can't think towards next year. We have to win now."[84] In New York, more big things were expected from star acrobatic Knicks forward Bernard King, who had been a reliable lock for more than 21 points per game the previous season. "He's like a bird," New York coach Hubie Brown said. "He's swooping toward the basket and you think he's descending. Then all of a sudden, at the last instant, he elevates and you'll see an incredible move."[85] The big question was whether the supporting cast of center Bill Cartwright, forward Len "Truck" Robinson, and the fleet backcourt of Rory Sparrow and Ray Williams were good enough to lift the club to elite status. Speaking of lifts, the New Jersey Nets were banking on one from colorful veteran dunking sensation Darryl Dawkins. "Chocolate Thunder" had arrived in the Garden State during the 1982 offseason after Philadelphia, the team that had selected him as the fifth overall pick in the 1975 NBA Draft, opted to upgrade their center position with the acquisition of Moses Malone. Dawkins put up pedestrian numbers, but Nets coach Stan Albeck was voicing optimism that 1983–84 would be different. "He's going to be a force for us," he promised.[86] The Washington Bullets were a club that no one wanted to play due to their imposing, in-your-face physicality. For sure, the frontcourt of "Bruise Brothers" Rick Mahorn and Jeff Ruland considered it their sacred duty to make opponents pay for every possession with a well-timed elbow to the head or a none-too-subtle shove to the floor. They were never to be taken lightly. As the *Sporting News* said, "No one . . . questions the bulk, the tenacity or the intentions of the Bullets' big men."[87]

As for the rest of the league, the Los Angeles Lakers were head and shoulders above their competition in the Western Conference despite having traded away popular All-Star point guard Norm Nixon to the San Diego Clippers in the preseason in exchange for center Swen Nater and the drafting rights to athletic guard Byron Scott, who had averaged 21.6 points per game at Arizona State. "People tend to take you for granted when they see you a lot," an embittered Nixon said afterward. "It'll hurt [the Lakers] chemistry-wise. It may not be obvious until the playoffs, but it'll hurt them."[88] The latter remained to be seen as the team still started and ended with incomparable playmaking gifts of Magic Johnson and the prolific post offense of Kareem Abdul-Jabbar. That lethal combo had spurred the Lakers to the NBA Finals in three of the previous four seasons, and it appeared that another appearance was a certainty, especially with Magic now the team's primary ball handler. Johnson and Nixon "weren't good at sharing," recalled longtime Los Angeles sportswriter and talk radio show host Doug Krikorian. "Norm liked to bring the ball up. I remember Magic would reluctantly, reluctantly give him the ball and let him bring the ball up, which was ridiculous."[89]

The Celtics opened their regular season on the road against a scrappy young Detroit Pistons squad on October 28 and submitted a performance that brought back ugly memories of their early playoff exit from the previous spring with a disappointing 127–121 loss. "We played tonight the way we ended last season," said Robert Parish, who earned the evening's goat horns with a dismal six points and four rebounds.[90] Meanwhile, his Detroit counterpart—brawny All-Star fourth year center Bill Laimbeer—scored 26 points with 13 boards and a pair of timely blocks on Bird and Maxwell down the stretch. "Parish just never got in gear," Laimbeer said. "He got into early foul trouble and really didn't look like himself after that."[91] *Boston Globe* scribe Dan Shaughnessy was noticeably more skeptical, writing that the Celtics big man "left everyone wondering if perhaps he is still holding out and hasn't told anyone."[92] Nevertheless, there was plenty of blame to go around. Boston's team defense went MIA for most of the game, allowing flashy 22-year-old Detroit point guard Isaiah Thomas (16 points and 5 assists) to spoil a late fourth-quarter Celtics comeback by draining an 18-foot jumper followed by a pair of clutch free throws with 47 seconds left. "Believe me, I wasn't trying to save anything," the baby-faced Indiana University product said. "At the end of the game, I want to take over because the decisions I make can win or lose the game."[93] Such confident assertiveness did not escape the notice of K. C. Jones, a man who knew a thing or two about backcourt play. "He's awesome," assessed Jones. "He brings the ball up like Magic. He's a creative passer and a great outside shooter."[94] On the losing side, Kevin McHale scored a team-high 25 points, and Bird chipped in with 23.

All things considered, it was a dispiriting setback given the surfeit of high expectations and goodwill that had been built up during training camp. But the Celtics rebounded the following night with a convincing 108–89 win over the Cleveland Cavaliers at Richfield Coliseum in Richfield, Ohio. The game was never in doubt as the Celts sprinted to a 12–0 lead out of the locker room and never looked back. McHale once again proved that his fat new contract was money well spent as he paced his teammates with 22 points. Five other Celtics also scored in double digits, and Bird grabbed 13 rebounds to lead both teams. "Winning this game is a relief," said Gerald Henderson, who contributed with 18 points. "Last night was not the way we wanted to start this season. The first half tonight—that's the way we wanted to get started."[95]

As satisfying as the victory was, the Celtics had little time to savor it. Milwaukee was the next opponent for the club's November 3 home opener, and more than a few of the men in green were eager to avenge the humiliation the Bucks had inflicted upon them in the Eastern Conference semifinals six months earlier. "They embarrassed us and the only way to get back at 'em is to go out and beat 'em,'" Bird said.[96] Boston Garden promised to be rocking.

Built in 1928 for the then exorbitant sum of $4 million by boxing promoter George Lewis "Tex" Rickard, a colorful former gold miner and professional gambler who drew comparisons to P. T. Barnum, the once grand double-balconied arena had become a decrepit, vermin-infested edifice. Perched atop North Station, a tangled cluster of railway lines connecting the city to its western and northern suburbs, the building seemed to spring from the dog-eared pages of a Damon Runyon book.

"It's echoing corridors smell of cigar smoke and stale beer," best-selling sports author Pat Jordan once wrote. "It is the kind of [place] where people instinctively reach to their back pockets when jostled in a crowd. The Garden's shadowy runways are patrolled by sour-faced ushers in stiff red uniforms who seem to get more pleasure from pushing people out of the aisles than leading them to their seats."[97] Kevin McHale vividly remembered an encounter he had with an oversized rat so big that he felt he could have had it shot and stuffed. "I was walking across the court, and I saw this thing at the stairs that went to the exit," he told *Sports Illustrated*. "He was standing on his hind legs. I said, 'What's a rabbit doing in here?' That's how large he was. I thought he was a rabbit."[98] Rats were not the only animals taking up residence there. When the building was being torn down to make way for a new arena in 1998, a demolition crew discovered the long-dead remains of a monkey believed to have escaped from a circus years earlier. "The Garden was built by roof trestles because there were no roof beams in the middle," said one of the workers. "We were exposing certain areas of the roof when we would cut the trestles to take it down, and when we were peeling back the roof, that's when we found the monkey wedged in between one of the trestles and the roof of the Garden."[99] Interestingly enough, the unfortunate simian commanded a bird's-eye view of center court before he expired, meaning he could have conceivably drawn his last breath watching the Big Three play. "The Celtics might have to change their [leprechaun] mascot," joked a former Garden executive. "This obviously was a true fan."[100]

True fans like John Powers, a Cambridge native who went on to cover the team as a sportswriter for the *Globe*, fondly remembered the Garden when he was growing up in the late 1950s and 1960s as a "sporting Louvre." "You could see Auerbach talking in the huddle, circled by attentive faces," he wrote. "You could see the sweat pouring off Bill Russell as he came to the bench. And when the lead had reached 20 points or so, you could watch Auerbach dip into his jacket pocket—a loud plaid tonight—and extract the cigar."[101] The gleaming white wooden parquet floor that was laid out in checkerboard fashion atop the ice surface the National Hockey League's Boston Bruins skated on in the winter months added a further distinctive element. The floor had earned notoriety around the

NBA for its alleged "dead spots"–sections of the court where the ball did not achieve a true bounce due to the cracks from the ice underneath. Bob Cousy categorically dismissed the idea as absurd. "Think about it, the dead spots," he harrumphed. "You're telling me that in a game as fast as basketball I could have the presence of mind to push someone over to the fifth board from the right because that's supposed to be a dead spot? Maybe in a slower game like baseball you could use that kind of local knowledge, but basketball? Come on."[102] Whether true or not, the belief that such things existed helped give the Celtics a clear home-court advantage. "I mean teams were intimidated to play us there," K. C. Jones said. "The floor added to it."[103]

Just walking to the Garden down from the garbage-strewn steps of the rusty elevated subway along Causeway Street elicited a special thrill with the sight of strange flat-nosed men with "ruined voices and big rings" darting in and out of the shot-and-beer taverns, cheap pizza restaurants, and run-down porno theaters populating the area. "You belonged to another era, one that seemed perpetually stuck at nine o'clock on some bygone Friday night," Powers wrote.[104]

The warm, nostalgic feeling was not shared by the players. Havlicek had been shocked at his first glimpse of the place. Arriving in Beantown on a late-night train from the Midwest in the spring of 1962, he could not get over how dank and depressing everything looked. "What have I got myself into?" he asked himself. His spirits did not improve the following day when he received a personal tour of the Celtics locker room. "I was devastated," he said. "It was this tiny little room, tucked underneath a stairway. There were no lockers, just nails hammered into these furring strips around the room. The steps cascaded down, so one end of the room had a normal 15-foot ceiling, but the end was as low as six feet. The shorter guys dressed at that end. The nails for the clothes, it seemed, were based on seniority. If you were a rookie, you were a one-nail guy. I had just finished my four years at Ohio State, which had the best facilities, and to come to this . . ." The nails had been replaced with regular lockers by 1984, but conditions remained relatively austere. "There were only two stalls in the bathroom in our locker room," McHale said. "No matter how early I got there, someone else always would have been there before me." Eventually the enterprising big man found a way out of his quandary. "I got a ball boy to let me in the officials' locker room before they got there. I did that every night. It was perfect. Quiet. I could read the paper. It was my little secret. Somehow I thought it was justice. I was making a statement."[105]

A far bigger statement was made by McHale and his teammates on opening night as they crushed the Bucks, 119–105, before an appreciative sold-out Garden audience. "No, the Celtics didn't float like butterflies, but they stung like bees; drones in fact," wrote Jack O'Leary on the back page of the tabloid *Boston Herald*.[106] Never trailing the entire game and outscoring Milwaukee every quarter, the Celtics dominated in a fashion that brought to mind Popeye pummeling Bluto after ingesting a can of spinach. "We had to establish that this is our home ground and you have to fight a little harder to ensure teams don't walk in here and think they can beat the Celtics on their home court," K. C. Jones said.[107] In the opening quarter alone, Boston shot a blistering 80 percent, connecting on 12 of its first 15 attempts. Larry Bird paced the team in scoring with 27 points, and Robert Parish swept the boards with 16 rebounds. "Better late than never, I guess," said Quinn Buckner, who came off the bench with 16 points, 5 assists, and 3 steals.[108] Indeed, the contest was all about vindication. "Last year didn't work out like we thought it would," Buckner admitted. "It was tough for all of us after the great promise we had. And I don't think any of us want that kind of year to happen to us again. So I think you'll see us play much more determined this year."[109] Heralded new backcourtmate Dennis Johnson also made his presence felt with 19 points after his outside jumper failed to drop in the first half. "I realized that I wasn't shooting that well and took the initiative to do something, so I went inside," Johnson said.[110] Nor did he back down on defense, making sinewy All-Star Milwaukee guard Sidney Moncrief (28 points) scrap and claw for every bucket.

"This game meant something as far as winning goes," Cedric Maxwell said, "but it doesn't make up for the end of last season."[111] Nonetheless, the victory represented an encouraging sign of better things to come.

CHAPTER FOUR

Magic

As blustery cold autumn weather settled upon New England like an unwelcome houseguest, the Celtics kept their fans warm and comfy by extending their winning streak to nine games—a mark no other NBA team would be able to duplicate that season. The high point of this successful run came during a 126–118 slap down of the Isaiah Thomas-led Detroit Pistons at Boston Garden on Veteran's Day, November 11. These were the same Pistons who had delivered a slice of humble pie to the Celtics two weeks earlier at the Detroit Silverdome to launch the 1983–84 campaign. Now it became payback time for K. C. Jones's merry band of hoopsters as a fired-up Larry Bird exploded for a game-high 39 points to hold off a second-half Detroit rally and secure the victory. "They played like they want to win a world championship," Pistons coach Chuck Daly grudgingly conceded. "Bird had a classic game and they just ran it down our throats."[1] Bird, who also had eight rebounds, five assists, and four blocks, was active on both ends of the court as Jones, in an unusual move, used him for significant minutes at guard. "When you get into trouble, you want to go with your power, especially down the stretch," Jones explained. "That's why we went with Larry in the backcourt and kept trying to get the ball down low."[2]

Lost in all the accolades heaped on Bird was the exemplary play of Robert Parish. After laying an embarrassing egg in the first Detroit game, the Chief—a nickname Cedric Maxwell bestowed upon him for his resemblance to the preternaturally silent Chief Bromden in the Oscar-winning 1975 film *One Flew Over the Cuckoo's Nest*—had come back and submitted his most dominant performance of the young season, netting 28 points while pulling down 12 boards. Of course, the jump-shooting 7-foot, 230-pound center with the impassive countenance of an undertaker on duty was used to being the overlooked member of Boston's celebrated Big Three. In fact, he preferred it that way. As Parish once said, "The key to my effectiveness with the Celtics is that I'm willing to play a complimentary role. All I care about is winning."[3] There was certainly no shortage of the latter when he donned the green uniform.

Robert Lee Parish had never given basketball much thought or priority when he was coming of age in Shreveport, Louisiana, during the 1960s. It's easy to understand why. The civil rights movement led by Nobel Peace Prize–winner Dr. Martin Luther King Jr. was in full swing, and Parish had a front row seat to many of the monumental changes it wrought, including the federally protected right to vote for formerly disenfranchised blacks in the Deep South. Stuffing a ball through a round metal cylinder frankly did not seem all that important by comparison, especially with open-minded parents like Robert Sr. and Ada Parish, who taught their eldest child and his three younger siblings the importance of social justice and respecting the differences in others. "Treat people like they treat you and don't have any preconceived ideas," Parish said. "That is something that I tried to carry with me and I passed it on to my children." This progressive approach was all the more remarkable, Parish added, given the kind of extreme segregationist environment his lower-middle-class parents had been reared in, where it was not uncommon to see African Americans dangling from tree limbs for the perceived crime of looking at a white person the wrong way. "They came up through some difficult times, in terms of race relations," he said. "Oh, you're talking about the Thirties, Forties and Fifties alone."[4]

Apart from his mother and father, the other major adult authority figure to exert a powerful influence on young Robert was Coleman Kidd, the coach of his junior high school basketball team. Impressed more by his sheer size—Parish stood a towering 6–5 in the seventh grade—than by his athletic ability, Kidd took it upon himself to recruit the future NBA Hall of Famer and develop his game. The only problem was that Parish did not appear to have any game whatsoever to speak of, as the simple act of dribbling a basketball might as well have been asking him to drink water from a fire hose. For sure, the awkward teenager exhibited rock hands, poor hand-eye coordination, and absolutely no clue as to what to do around the basket. Perhaps appropriately, he was assigned a 00 jersey for being the last player selected for the team, a number he would come to embrace and wear until the day he retired from basketball.

"It took me a year before I made a layup," he confessed. "It was a great moment. I was in the eighth grade. I remember feeling very good about myself."[5] Parish would have more to smile about when he moved on to the locally integrated Woodlawn High School. Thanks to Kidd's earlier tireless efforts ("If it weren't for him, I would have been just another tall kid walking around the streets of Shreveport," Parish later said), the young center had blossomed into a dominant force on the floor, averaging more than 30 points a contest to propel Woodlawn to a state championship his senior year.[6]

Even then, the stoic 1972 Louisiana Player of the Year was reluctant to draw too much attention to himself at the expense of his teammates. Indeed, Parish's shunning of the spotlight was on full display during a blowout win earlier in the season over rival Lake Charles, when he was four points shy of establishing a new individual school scoring record. Having already been pulled from the game by Woodlawn coach Ken Ivy to avoid running up the score, Ivy decided to put Parish back in. "I told Robert to go out there, get the record, and then get off the floor," he said. "I didn't want to keep him out there. The other coach was a good friend of mine. Well, sure enough, we put Robert back in after a time-out and what does he do? He throws the ball back out after getting it inside. So I call another time-out and tell him, 'Robert get the four points, will you?' He scored a couple of quick ones and that was that."[7]

Inundated with hundreds of scholarship offers from nearly all of the top-ranked hoop programs in the country, Parish surprised everyone by staying in Shreveport and attending Centenary College, a tiny liberal arts school affiliated with the Southern Methodist Church. According to pro basketball writer Peter May, who covered Parish throughout his Celtics career, this mystifying decision for an elite player was akin to the former Lew Alcindor forgoing UCLA in the late 1960s and opting to play his college ball for Hunter College in New York. "There is nothing that even comes close," May writes.[8] Still, Parish had his reasons. Most important of all, his parents were sold "hook, line, and sinker" on the educational benefits such a highly regarded academic institution could provide their eldest child.[9]

Truth be told, though, Parish's preference was to go to Indiana University and play for irascible Hall of Fame coach Bobby Knight. "I liked his toughness, [his] no-nonsense approach," Parish said. But over the course of the recruiting process, Knight somehow managed to alienate Robert Sr. with his snappish, bullying behavior. That settled matters. No son of his would be exposed to such a toxic individual. "My father didn't take no shit—except from my mother," Parish explained.[10] Alas, Parish might have been better off if he had gone to Indiana, for the NCAA ended up sanctioning Centenary for serious athletic scholarship violations, which resulted in the school being suspended from all postseason tournament play and television appearances. The ban lasted beyond the balance of Parish's varsity collegiate career, thereby earning him the dubious distinction of being, in the words of Bob Ryan, "The Best Player Nobody (outside of the Bayous, anyway) Ever Saw."[11] Parish had been given the option of transferring out but decided against it primarily because he had become the father of two small children born out of wedlock and wanted to remain close to them in Shreveport. He also felt an outsize sense of loyalty to his teammates. "There were six or seven of us," he said. "We met and talked about it, and as a group we decided to stay on at Centenary College."[12]

Despite performing in relative obscurity, Parish enjoyed his time at Centenary, earning a diploma in four years while continuing to excel on the basketball court, amassing 2,334 points and 1,820 rebounds for averages of 21.6 and 16.9, respectively, in 108 games. His stellar play, which *Sports Illustrated*'s Sam Moses claimed made him "one of the three best centers in the country," aroused interest from the ABA's Utah Stars, who had been keeping close tabs on Parish since his high school days.[13] They offered him a then-impressive six figures to sign with the club, and Parish was sorely tempted to accept before he graduated. But he ultimately turned the Stars down, mostly due to pressure from his mother and father. "My parents would have broken my back if I had left," he said. "Getting that degree was more important to them than the money. And we definitely could have used the money." Yet it was a close call, and not just because he could have fattened his bank account. "I wasn't getting any better, I didn't think," Parish said. "I felt like I grew my freshman and sophomore years, but the last two years I felt I stayed at the same level."[14] He believed that this lack of progress was largely the result of the quality of coaching he was receiving. Specifically, Centenary head coach Larry Little and his staff left much to be desired when it came to instructing big men on the finer points of playing inside the paint and preparing them for a higher level of competition. "My coaches . . . were fine, fine coaches, but I think Bob Knight was a better coach," Parish said. "So, in that context, I would have been a better player [with Indiana or another big-time basketball school]."[15]

Drafted by the Golden State Warriors as the eighth overall pick in the 1976 NBA Draft, Parish had difficulty getting used to the demanding physicality of the pro game. "It took me a while to adjust to going into traffic and someone touching me," he said. "They used to fuck me up. I'd go for a shot, someone would put their hand on my hip, [or someone] got their hand in the middle of my chest or they'd bump up against me and the referee would say nothing. That was a real, real tough adjustment for me. . . . I wasn't accustomed to that."[16]

In hindsight, Parish realizes he could have ended up as another James Edwards—a contemporary journeyman center "with a jump shot and nothing else." Fortunately, he avoided that fate by coming under the wing of Warriors assistant coach Joe Roberts, a former college teammate of John Havlicek's at Ohio State in the early 1960s who had played four years in the NBA. "He's the one who told me I shouldn't be a one-dimensional offensive player, just relying on the jump shot. He said that as I got older and couldn't jump as high or run as fast, I'd need variety to my game. Joe taught me little moves and tricks and how to keep my man off balance."[17]

Outside of Roberts and bearded veteran big man Clifford Ray, who reminded the 23-year-old that teams could not hope to win without someone like him up front who "rebounds and plays defense and brings people together," Parish received little encouragement or support from his other Warrior teammates.[18] Rick Barry was the worst. The pioneering passing forward—an 11-time ABA and NBA All-Star with a reputation among his peers for being "the most arrogant guy ever"—could barely be bothered to acknowledge Parish's existence.[19] "Rick was old school," Parish explained. "He didn't have anything to say, nothing to do with rookies. You got to earn your sweat, so to speak."[20] But then, who could blame him? Parish played limited minutes and posted fairly pedestrian numbers. Although he increased his time on the floor and showed steady improvement over time, he was viewed as a disappointment by most ardent Golden State followers who blamed him for the team's poor showing in the standings and mistook his trademark "loping gait for indolence and his poker face for indifference." Boos became commonplace. "I looked like I didn't care if we won or lost," Parish told an interviewer late in his career. "Like I had no fire."[21]

Parish's fortunes abruptly changed in 1980 when Red Auerbach swung the epic deal that brought him to Boston along with Kevin McHale. "It came out of the blue for me," Parish said.[22] Once he recovered from the initial shock, however, he literally jumped for joy. For he was joining a club that had won 61 games the season before with a young roster loaded with proven talent. "I had just gone from the penitentiary to the penthouse," he said.[23]

But that feeling of exaltation wore off when he had to report to his first Celtics preseason camp and acclimate himself to the physically grueling, disciplined way the Celtics did things under ironfisted coach Bill Fitch. "I just wasn't used to the continual running," Parish said. "It never stopped. I know now you've got to be in regular season shape when you first come in. And I think they were hard on me because they didn't know what to expect. They didn't know if I had a competitive edge or was tough enough mentally to play here."[24] Parish soon put to rest such concerns when he became one of the principal reasons why the Celtics were able to win the 1981 NBA title after starting center Dave Cowens unexpectedly announced his retirement before a preseason exhibition game. "Everybody was surprised," Parish recounted. "He just walked off the bus and told the coaches, 'I am retired.'"[25]

The Louisianan responded with what up to then was the best season of his career, averaging 18.9 points and 2.61 blocked shots while making his first All-Star team. "They let him play," Milwaukee coach Don Nelson later said. "They didn't complain about his effort, or say that he could give them more. They looked at him and said, 'Look at the numbers the guy puts up. Let's not try to ask for more, like they did at Golden State. Let's not accuse him of having to give more or being nonchalant or whatever his history had been because of his personality.'"[26] Freed from unrealistic expectations, Parish was able to embrace what he had always been on the basketball court: an unselfish team player. Celtics guard Tiny Archibald put it best when he shrewdly noted to columnist Joe Fitzgerald that Parish could go out and score 40 or 50 points on most nights, but steadfastly declined to do so. "Watch him," Archibald said. "You'll see he sacrifices a lot of his shots, sometimes because a teammate has a better chance, and sometimes because he just wants to help somebody else's confidence."[27]

Parish did not miss a beat in the seasons to follow either, prompting Red Auerbach to muse that the center had far exceeded his original expectations. "Unlike the other guys," Auerbach said, "Robert is fundamentally better now. He's changed his game and I don't thimk there's anyone I've ever traded for who did that. He's playing under control, his defense is impressive. And he's still doing the things he did well before, like shot blocking."[28] Auerbach was not alone in this observation. "The Robert Parish on display every night is flat-out fun to watch play basketball," Bob Ryan wrote in the pages of the *Boston Globe*. "He is a constant threat to sprint downcourt for a sneak away layup or dunk. He intersperses his basic jump shot with sweeping hooks and graceful drives that would have been the envy of any 6-footer decades ago. . . . He blocks shots with ferocity, and he has become so attuned to the fast break while playing for the run-conscious Celtics that he occasionally even flings lefthanded outlets to streaking mates. Even the way he sometimes receives a high post pass, arms and knees flailing in a 'get-the-hell-out-of-my-way' symbol of defiance, is a kick."[29]

No longer a kick was playing for Bill Fitch. Like most of the veterans on the squad, Parish had soured on the coach's heavy-handed style and constant criticism by the end of the 1982–83 season. "We needed a change because we no longer needed a drill sergeant [with] that take-no-prisoners attitude," Parish said. "Coach Fitch, give him credit for this, he made us a bunch of tough motherfuckers. I guess that's what we needed [at the beginning] and that's one of the main reasons why we were champions my first year with the Celtics."[30] But K. C. Jones offered a kinder, gentler approach that was sincerely appreciated. "He was like Red in terms of relating to his players," Parish said. "I admired his ability to make the guys on the end of the bench feel like their roles were just as important as guys in the core rotation. I think that was one of the reasons why we were so successful. In the NBA, it's so important to understand the personalities of the players and how to get the best out of them. It takes a special talent to do that and K. C. had that ability."[31] Jones also knew a thing or two about maximizing Parish's strengths in the pivot, particularly on the offensive end. As Parish revealed to Mike Carey of the *Boston Herald*, "Under K. C., I'm playing a lot closer to the hoop. That makes my jumper, which is my bread and butter shot, a lot more accurate. It also gives me a chance to drive more than in the past. All this is by design. The end result is that the guy who's guarding me isn't able to use any one trick to keep me from scoring."[32]

The Celtics fell into a bit of a rut after their early season success, losing four consecutive games in late November. The rough patch began in Utah where they were upended by the Jazz, 122–109. The Celtics were playing their third road game in four nights, and the fatigue showed as they could not keep up with a good young Jazz team led by wingmen John Drew and Adrian Dantley, who torched them for a combined 51 points. Sophomore 7–4 center Mark Eaton (17 points, 12 rebounds)—a former Arizona Automotive Institute graduate with a passion for water polo— also had a strong night, blocking shots by Larry Bird and Kevin McHale in a key stretch in the fourth quarter to derail a Celtics rally. "He's the reason they won," K. C. Jones said. "All of 'em played great but Eaton's the one that did it to us."[33] The Celtics stumbled further with home and away setbacks against the Knicks and a one-point road loss to Philly. The latter was the most painful. After overcoming a 14-point deficit to grab the lead late in the fourth quarter, the Celtics' offense inexplicably ground to a halt. "When we first went ahead by one, we went down [court] on three straight possessions without getting a good shot," Jones said. "In Philadelphia, you can't go that long without paying for it."[34] The bill collector in this case was old Celtics nemesis Andrew Toney, aka the Boston Strangler, who made two clutch shots, including a nifty off-balance runner in the closing moments, to help his club retake the lead and secure a 92–91 victory. "How many times have you seen it in our rivalry with Boston?" Julius Erving asked reporters afterwards. Toney "loves the challenge. With most guys, that [runner] wouldn't be high percentage."[35]

The Celtics ended their minislump just in time for the holidays. The team reeled off 15 wins in 18 games between Thanksgiving and New Year's Eve to storm over Philadelphia to the top of the Atlantic Division in the Eastern Conference with an NBA-best 24–8 record. They were even better after all the festivities were over, dropping only one game—a lopsided defeat to the Milwaukee Bucks on the 15th—for the entire month of January. To call them a juggernaut somehow did the club a grave disservice. "This is the best I've seen [the Celtics] play in six years," praised New York Knicks assistant coach Rick Pitino, who had toiled several seasons as head coach of the Boston University Terriers before joining the Knicks. "Emotionally they have more going for them this year, and Bird has taken it upon himself to challenge everybody to get the most out of their abilities."[36] For certain, the 27-year-old trash-talking Boston forward was operating on a higher basketball plane that season, on target to pocketing his first NBA MVP award to go with a slash line of 24.2 points, 10.1 rebounds, 6.8 assists, and 1.6 steals. In addition, Bird had 7 triple-doubles and 45 double-doubles while sinking 88.8 percent of his free throws. His greatest offensive performance came on December 2 when he burned the Portland Trail Blazers for 41 points, 14 rebounds, and 7 assists in a 115–106 Boston win. Typically, Bird sought to downplay his heroics afterward. "They were running plays for me," he said, "and I knew I had Robert [Parish] picking for me. I knew if I didn't have the open shot, I could drop it down to him. Things started going my way, and I kept shooting."[37] Blazers coach Jack Ramsey was not buying any of it. "When you've got a Larry Bird," Ramsey asserted, "you make sure everything revolves around him. He'll make everyone else better. If the job is going to get done, odds are he'll find the ways to do it. He was almost the team tonight."[38] Bird's teammates could not disagree. In fact, Cedric Maxwell had noted the difference in his famous teammate from the season's opening bell. "When he came to camp, he was in the best shape he'd ever been," Maxwell recalled. "He was thinner and a step quicker. By the time we'd come out to practice, Bird would already be running the concourse of Boston Garden. Seeing that, we knew he'd dedicated himself."[39]

Dedication also explained how Johnny Most was able to return to the radio booth in late February. The popular longtime team announcer—broadcasting home games from his familiar perch "high above courtside" in the Boston Garden balcony overlooking the Celtics bench—had suffered a debilitating stroke the previous winter, which had temporarily robbed him of his trademark raspy voice. "Naturally, I was in a state of panic," Most wrote in his posthumously published 2003 memoir with his son Jamie and Mike Carey, "yet my thought process hadn't been affected by the stroke. I could understand everything that was happening. I could grasp every sentence that was said to me or about me. But I had absolutely no way to respond."[40] Following a lengthy and arduous rehabilitation process, in which a nonplussed Red Auerbach had *ordered* him to get better, Most was ready to resume his regular play-by-play duties.[41] But his mind became plagued by a stream of constant self-doubt, not made any easier by the fact that he was now coping with a permanently paralyzed right hand. "Before the stroke," he recounted, "I thought of myself as a hulk, a guy who was virtually indestructible. After the stroke, I saw myself as just a shell of what I had been."[42] Yet these dark thoughts quickly dissipated when he found himself comfortable again behind the mike "growling at referees, shouting at opponents for dirty, dangerous, sneaky and vicious fouls, and lauding the efforts of the heroes in green and white uniforms."[43] For sure, nothing could ever keep the irrepressible Most down for long.

Raised as the only child to a struggling dentist and a Russian immigrant homemaker during the Great Depression, Most became obsessed with sports at a young age, often fantasizing about being a baseball announcer before turning in at night at his modest family home in the Bronx section of New York City. "I'd pull the blankets over my head and pretend I was broadcasting a Dodgers–Yankees World Series game from the press box of old Ebbets Field," he recalled.[44] An empty drinking glass or a hollowed-out flashlight served as a stand-in for a microphone when Most did the play-by-play. "Yes," he noted, "even in my imaginary under-the-covers games, I devised my own nicknames for both the good and bad guys. My 'productions' had to be thrilling, nail-biting and 'edgy.'"[45] With the outbreak of World War II in 1941, Most was drafted into the army, serving first in a mobile artillery unit and later as a waist gunner and radio operator on a B-24 bomber in the air corps. Participating in 28 combat missions above the skies of Europe, he was awarded a Purple Heart, a Distinguished Flying Cross, and a host of other decorations. Like many members of "The Greatest Generation," however, he chose to speak little of his exemplary service in later years. "Medals never ease the memories of the horrors of war," he explained.[46]

Following his discharge, Most pursued a career in radio and juggled an assortment of broadcasting jobs, including a stint playing a hoodlum on the popular *Dick Tracy* detective series in the late 1940s. Longing for meatier dramatic roles, Most grew frustrated when he was routinely passed over by unimpressed program directors. "Who knows, maybe I could have been Telly Savalas," he once wistfully speculated to the *Boston Herald-American*.[47] Most had better luck when he focused exclusively on sportscasting. Pairing with the legendary play-by-play man Marty Glickman, he broadcast New York Knicks games from Madison Square Garden and was taught some invaluable lessons on how to present basketball games on the radio. "Marty Glickman influenced my rapid-fire description of ball-handling, playmaking, shooting," Most said. "The medium is sound, not sight; fans can't see it, but they can sense as well as hear the game, if the announcer speeds with the pace of the court action."[48]

The Celtics entered the picture in 1953 when Most joined 59 other hopefuls in auditioning for the team's vacant lead announcer job. "There were six applicants left, and it just happened the Celtics were undertaking a six-game exhibition trip," Most said. "Each of us was assigned to do one of the games. I was to do the sixth game. The big break was that the Celtics were playing the Knicks when my turn came, and my familiarity with the Knicks didn't hurt me." Indeed, then Celtics owner Walter Brown became so impressed with what he had heard that he immediately phoned Red Auerbach to declare there was no need for any further auditions. "I had won the Celtics job," Most said triumphantly.[49]

Neither Brown nor Auerbach ever found cause to question the wisdom of the decision as Boston fans could not get enough of Most's staccato, machine gun–like delivery or exuberant putdowns of opposing players that routinely involved assigning them unflattering nicknames such as the "Baby-Faced Assassin," "Mr. Nasty," "Little Lord Fauntleroy" and "Big Coward." It was all in a day's work for Most, a brazen homer who made no pretensions about being impartial. "I'm a one-way street, no question about it," he told *Sports Illustrated* in a 1985 interview.[50] Although everyone within the Celtics orbit genuinely prized this salty over-the-top, biased approach ["Johnny probably exemplified the word loyal," Kevin McHale said], outsiders were less enamored.[51] As acclaimed basketball reporter and author Jack McCallum wrote, "Most represented, by any objective standards, the clearest examples of Celtics arrogance gone berserk, a man absolutely unable to separate fact from fiction whenever his beloved Green was involved."[52] All the same, Most had moments that belied such damning critiques. In the deciding contest of the 1965 Eastern Finals between the Celtics and the Philadelphia 76ers, he delivered what is arguably the most memorable call in NBA history when John Havlicek intercepted an inbounds pass from Philadelphia's Hal Greer to an open teammate in the closing seconds to preserve a 110–109 Boston victory. "Havlicek stole the ball!" Most elatedly screamed into his microphone. "Johnny must have had some good coffee that day because he was really excited," Havlicek said. "He was the one who made that play different." Most concurred. "It was something to be remembered for, something to hang my hat on," he said.[53]

Most was also responsible for some other less-dignified acts that earned him a different sort of lasting fame. During a 1959 playoff game against the Syracuse Nationals, he became so emotionally charged up that he temporarily lost his set of false teeth in midsentence. As Most explained, "The Celtics were roaring from behind and I really was into it. That morning a clip of my partial plate had broken and my teeth were wobbling all over place during the broadcast. Finally, after some big play, the teeth just flew out of my mouth. I caught the damn things in mid-air and turned to Al Gernert, who was helping me with the broadcast and asked him: 'How do you like those hands?'"[54] Decades later, Most's radio partner Glenn Ordway remembered an equally humorous, if potentially more dangerous incident. "I was doing color, and sitting next to him, and I smelled something burning," Ordway elaborated. "I said, 'Johnny, do you smell smoke?' He said, 'My pants are on fire.' He was always smoking, and he'd had a stroke . . . so it was hard for him to do some things, and his cigarette had dropped onto his polyester pants, and they'd caught on fire. He always wore that polyester. The fire was right on his crotch, and he poured coffee on it and I helped beat the flame out. It was funny, really. We came back on the air, and neither of us could stop laughing for maybe 45 seconds. We couldn't talk." Things only went steadily downhill from there. Ordway: "The first promo I had to read turned out to be, 'Our guest today at halftime will receive a gift certificate from Eastern Coat of Watertown.' Johnny said, 'Not today he won't. I need new pants.' We started howling again."[55]

The Celtics were in need of some comic relief themselves after the Western Conference–leading Los Angeles Lakers rolled into town on Wednesday, February 8, for what many Boston hoops enthusiasts viewed as a sneak preview to the NBA Finals. If so, it was not a very propitious omen. For the Lakers, coming off an impressive seven-game winning streak, handed the Celtics a deflating 111–109 loss to maintain a firm grip on the second-best record in the league with 32 victories against 16 losses. "We wanted to make a statement tonight," LA sophomore forward James Worthy said.[56] The Lakers certainly succeeded in checking that box, displaying an explosive offense with Kareem Abdul-Jabbar accounting for the most damage. Displaying the energy, commitment, and passion of a player a decade younger, the 36-year-old center connected on 12 of 19 shots for 27 points to set a new NBA mark for career field goals with 12,685. Celtics fans, not exactly known for their graciousness, especially toward dominant 7-footers hailing from the West Coast, responded to the milestone achievement with an unusually warm standing ovation. "This game means so much to us," an unusually emotional Abdul-Jabbar revealed in his postgame remarks. "[It] shows we can beat great basketball teams."[57]

Of equal import, the victory represented only the sixth time in NBA regular season play up to that point that Larry Bird and Magic Johnson—Abdul-Jabbar's mega-talented teammate with a 1,000-watt smile—had competed on the same floor since breaking into the league together during the 1979–80 season. For the record, neither superstar's team could claim any decisive competitive edge as their encounters over the years had resulted in a dead-even split in games. Regardless, it was still Bird versus Magic—a quintessential basketball rivalry that had captured the imagination of the American sporting public in a way not witnessed since the fabled Russell–Chamberlain battles of the 1960s. Or as Johnson liked to tell people, "Me and Larry's just *different* from everybody else."[58] Indeed, they were. But what made their competition extra compelling was the racial element involved. Bird was white, and Johnson was black, at a time when the country was still dealing with the powerful aftershocks of the civil rights movement from the 1960s that had given darker-skinned Americans the ability to exercise their full constitutional and legal rights as citizens for the first time.

Many whites, especially those from rural and urban working-class backgrounds, resented the change, feeling that black progress had unfairly been achieved at their expense. This group tended to root for Bird while broader communities of color gravitated toward Magic. Though Bird and Johnson were not naive to the larger political and cultural forces at play, they did their best to defuse the sticky situation through their own innate colorblindness and mutual respect for one another functioning in tandem with the sheer brilliance of their performances on the court. For sure, individual talent and skill were the only things that mattered to them. Consequently, their actions demonstrated to a divided nation without necessarily meaning to that integration, equality, and diversity could not only work but thrive if given the chance. As Robert Parish once insightfully noted, "You have to ponder not only what Magic and Larry did for basketball and the NBA, but what they did for race relations."[59]

The unlikely pair had first crossed paths in the summer of 1978 as part of a squad of traveling American college all-stars going head-to-head against visiting international competition. Coached by Kentucky's Joe B. Hall, who exhibited an undisguised favoritism toward his own Wildcat players on the roster, the U.S. team consigned Bird and Johnson to bench roles, much to their mutual dissatisfaction. "One thing we had agreed on right away was that we both should have been playing," Bird wrote. "In practice, we had played together on a second unit that was besting the first team. I loved playing with Magic." Hall, however, did not count himself a fan of their highly creative, freelancing style of play to the point where he angrily called them out in practice one day. "How can we work on this stuff if you guys are throwing these crazy passes and taking these stupid shots?" he thundered. Bird and Johnson were hardly cowed. "Coach," they responded, "those shots are going *in*."[60]

The so-called crazy passes and stupid shots were on full display the following spring at the Special Events Center in Salt Lake City during the NCAA Tournament title game featuring Bird's undefeated Indiana State Sycamores squaring off against Johnson's underdog Michigan State Spartans. Attracting a record national television audience, the 75–64 Spartans win saw Johnson have his way with the plodding Indiana State defenders attempting to guard him, scoring 29 points and setting up his teammates for easy buckets with the ease of the late Jimi Hendrix pulling off a guitar riff. "If we keep playing like this," Magic joked to Spartan forward and future Detroit Pistons first round draft pick Greg Kelser (28 points), "it's going to be worth a couple million dollars for us in the pros."[61] As for Bird, the evening turned out to be far less fun as the 1979 College Player of the Year had trouble with the swarming Michigan State double-teams targeting him and ended up missing 14 of his 21 shots from the field. "We thought we had proved that we could beat every kind of defense, but we had never seen anything like that zone of theirs," Bird lamented. "I couldn't do anything at all against it. I couldn't get the ball and make moves anywhere on the floor. They did a really good job on me."[62] In the flush of victory after the nets were cut down, Magic could not resist stealing a look of sympathy at his bowed rival in the throes of agonizing defeat. "I'll never forget what I saw," he recalled. "While half the arena was screaming with joy, Larry Bird was sitting there with his face buried in a towel. He was obviously crying, and my heart went out to him. As happy as I was, I knew that if things had gone just a little differently, I would have been the one sitting there, with his face in a towel. I take losses the same way." Turning his attention back to the celebration, Johnson was suddenly struck by a premonition: "I knew in my gut that this wasn't the end of the story. Somewhere, somehow, Larry Bird and I would be seeing each other again."[63]

Earvin Johnson Jr. was born on August 14, 1959, as the middle child of a large blue-collar family scuffling to get by in Lansing, Michigan. From an early age, his down-to-earth parents—a General Motors auto assembly line worker and a school cafeteria supervisor—had drummed into Johnson and his nine siblings the value of hard work and discipline. "They expected all of us to help out around the house," Johnson wrote. "Like my brothers and sisters, I washed the dishes, took out the trash, vacuumed, cooked, and took care [of younger family members]."[64] Handouts of any kind were considered verboten, leaving Johnson to scramble about finding ways to earn spending money. Undaunted, he started his own neighborhood business at 10, raking leaves, cleaning yards, and shoveling snow.[65] "I was taught to get what I wanted," he revealed in a 1985 *USA Today Weekend* cover story. "That's probably why I appreciate the real hard-working players like Larry Bird and Moses Malone."[66]

On the subject of basketball, Johnson fell in love with the sport almost instantaneously. "When he was just a little boy, he'd get up on Sunday mornings and go up to the basketball court while we were still asleep," his mother said. "When he'd get back I'd say, 'Earvin, where you been?' and he'd say, 'I been up to the basketball court, Mama, playin' ball.' I'd be stern and say, 'don't you ever leave home without lettin' us know.' And from then on, for years, he'd wake me up just about daybreak every Sunday morning and say, 'Bye, Mama, I'm goin' up to the court.'"[67] Although Earvin Johnson Sr. was usually exhausted after laboring all week on the graveyard shift at the GM plant, he still found the time to share his own passion for the game when NBA contests were nationally televised on Sunday afternoons. "My father would point out things to me like Oscar [Robertson] taking a smaller guard underneath, or showing me how they ran a pick and roll," Magic said. "So when I started playing organized ball, if the coach asked if anyone knew how to run a three-man weave or shoot a left-handed layup, I was always the first one up."[68]

By the time he entered the eighth grade, Johnson had sprouted to 6–3 with a thin, sinewy build to go with an already highly developed sense of what it took to win. "I'd get down to the playground and usually be picked for a team right away," he explained. "But I'd always ask the guy who else he had. And if he said he had a couple of big scorers, I'd turn him down and wait for a guy who picked me but still didn't have any others. Then I'd tell him to get so-and-so, who was a good rebounder and so-and-so who was a good defensive player. That would make a good mix and I'd knew we'd have a team." His reasoning flowed from simple common sense and a surprisingly sophisticated understanding of human nature at this early stage in his life. "If you had all the big scorers and one-on-one players," he maintained, "then the game breaks down. Before you know it, everyone is mad because one guy is showing off for a girl or another is trying to prove he's the best shooter from 25-feet out. But the team that played together always won, and my team won all the time."[69]

Johnson continued to win when he matriculated into high school, even though he initially took issue with the center of learning he ended up attending. That's because he had not foreseen federally mandated efforts to desegregate public schools nationwide in the 1970s through the controversial practice of busing students from all-white and black neighborhoods to achieve racial balance. For Magic, the situation meant having to forgo entering Sexton High, his preferred choice only five blocks away from his home, to the more distant and predominantly white Everett High across town. "I was furious," Johnson remembered. "No black kid wanted to attend an all-white school." Equally important from his perspective was the uncomfortable fact that Everett was the opposite of Sexton athletically. "Maybe if Everett had had a great basketball team I could have lived with it. Or even a half-decent team. But the Vikings were terrible. They couldn't run, couldn't shoot, and worst of all, they couldn't win."[70]

Johnson would reverse that losing trend by leading Everett to a state title in his senior year, but not before making an important adjustment after starting the season averaging more than 40 points. Everett High coach George Fox provided the impetus. "You are putting on such a show, Earvin, that the other players are just standing around, watching you," Fox told his all-Michigan hoop prodigy. "If you want to win a state championship, you have to lower your average to only 25 to 30 points and get everybody else involved."[71] Something automatically clicked in Johnson's mind. "I listened, and I changed my game," he wrote. Lowering the number of shots he attempted and increasing his passing totals, he now "took over a game only when it was absolutely necessary."[72]

Johnson's slightly less gaudy numbers did not diminish his attractiveness to college recruiters. For certain, he was a primary target for most major national programs, including Bobby Knight's Indiana Hoosiers. Knight was so intrigued by the prospect of Johnson anchoring the Hoosier backcourt that the bombastic, chair-throwing coach made a personal trip to Lansing to secure the guard's signature on a letter of intent. "I'll tell you one thing," Knight snarled at him. "If you come to Indiana, we are not going to give you anything. You are going to have to earn it."[73] Unimpressed by the sales pitch, Johnson decided to stick closer to home by going to Michigan State in East Lansing. The move did not endear him to boosters of in-state rival Michigan, who had all but assumed that Johnson was a lock to attend the higher profile Ann Arbor school. They assumed wrong. "Michigan thought it had a lot more to offer than Michigan State and in some ways it did," Johnson said. "But I decided to pick the underdog school, since I've always enjoyed being the underdog. Every team I have played on wasn't supposed to win, but we did."[74] Also steering him into Spartan arms were the assurances of new Michigan State coach Jud Heathcote, a hotheaded recent hire from the University of Montana, who told Johnson that he would start at point guard, his preferred position. Other programs had been unwilling to make the commitment because they saw Johnson as a better fit in the frontcourt due to his superior rebounding skills. "I may be a hayseed from Montana," Heathcote said, "but I've seen you play enough. You will have the ball on the fast break. You will set the offense."[75]

Arriving on the East Lansing campus in the fall of 1977, a confident Earvin Johnson—or Magic, as he was now better known due to a popular nickname a local sportswriter had given him from his high-school days—was struck by the superior quality of competition he faced. The Spartans played in the Big Ten Conference, which served as a veritable talent pipeline to the pros with such future NBA stars as Kevin McHale, Herb Williams, and Mychal Thompson cutting their teeth there. "Every team we played had two or three terrific athletes," Johnson recalled. "And just about every guy on every team had been a star of his entire high school."[76] The pride of Everett High had no problem proving that he was up to the task, averaging high double figures in scoring, rebounding, and assists as a freshman to propel the Spartans to a Big Ten championship.

But relations with the volatile Heathcote, who liked things done a certain way, were not always so smooth. Johnson often came into conflict with his coach over how the Spartans should run their offense. "They would go back and forth all the time," teammate Jay Vincent later confirmed to author Seth Davis in *When March Went Mad*, his definitive chronicle of Johnson's Michigan State years. "One time during a game, Magic threw the ball away a couple of times. So Coach is yelling at him while Magic is dribbling the ball, and Magic stops dribbling and yells at Jud. This wasn't during a time-out, it wasn't a break, it was during the *game*. Magic just stopped, they yelled at each other, then Magic kept playing."[77] The tensions resumed the following season, but Heathcote was eventually able to reach an amicable accord with his young star as Michigan State marched its way to a NCAA championship, the first in school history. "Jud could be stubborn," Johnson acknowledged, "but what made him a great leader was that he knew how to listen."[78]

Having conquered the world of college hoops, Johnson determined that there were no more challenges left at that level and made himself available for the 1979 NBA Draft. The big question then became in which big-city market he would end up playing. Holding the top pick, there was some doubt whether the Los Angeles Lakers would choose Johnson over the equally well-regarded guard Sidney Moncrief from Arkansas. Jerry West, who had just stepped down as Lakers head coach to take on a behind-the-scenes club advisory role, recommended Moncrief to team owner Jack Kent Cooke. "They worried that I was a flash in the pan, a college showpiece with no outside shot who wouldn't survive in the pros," Johnson later wrote in his autobiography.[79] But Cooke—in the midst of selling the Lakers to real estate developer and huge Johnson fan Jerry Buss—was told bluntly by Buss that the deal was off if the team did not take the charismatic, box office–friendly Michigan State under-classman. "It's Magic, or find yourself another buyer," he said.[80]

Cooke did as instructed, and a glorious new chapter in NBA history began. Other Lakers did not see it that way at first, however. The league had a long history of heralded No. 1 picks not panning out; and besides, Johnson's high-octane, ebullient nature rubbed many jaded veterans the wrong way. "I don't think anyone was mad at Earvin personally," fellow rookie Ollie Mack offered, "but he represented change and veterans generally don't love the idea of doing things differently."[81] Spencer Haywood was an exception. A former Olympic gold medalist and four-time NBA All-Star, the personally troubled power forward, who ended up washing out of the sport due to a cocaine addiction, immediately grasped how special a talent Magic was. "I couldn't believe it," Haywood reflected. "You would hear people from Michigan talking about how good he was, but in training camp in Palm Springs, I was like, 'Wow.' But I loved his enthusiasm. I used to love that shit."[82]

As for Johnson, he was just glad having reached the big time. "I never thought all this would happen to me," he said. "All-City was what I was shooting for, 'cause then you got your name in the newspaper. People told me I'd do good, but I never saw it. And the strangest thing is, now that I'm here, in the NBA and all, it just feels natural, like this is where I always belonged."[83]

Johnson showed that he belonged in his very first regular-season game wearing the iconic purple and gold. Playing on the road against the then woeful San Diego Clippers before a national television audience, Johnson scored 26 points in an exciting Lakers win that was settled at the buzzer on a no-doubt-about-it skyhook by Kareem Abdul-Jabbar. Overjoyed with the outcome, Johnson jumped into the arms of the notoriously reserved Abdul-Jabbar and gave him a big bear hug. Abdul-Jabbar did not reciprocate the gesture, instead giving the rookie an incredulous look. "I was a little embarrassed—such a public display, so little cools—but he was so happy that it dawned to me," the goggled Hall of Fame center wrote in his first autobiography *Giant Steps*. "I'd had a lot of fun making that last shot! If Earvin had any effect on me, it was because he helped the team win and reminded me just how good that made me feel."[84] All the same, Abdul-Jabbar reminded Johnson in the locker room afterward that there were 81 more regular season games to go and that he needed to "[c]alm down." Such advice was akin to instructing the Beatles to cut their hair at the height of their fame. It was never going to happen. "I'd always played with passion, and eventually my teammates would get used to it," Johnson thought at the time.[85] Indeed, the palpable excitement he brought to the arena every night was felt by opponents as well. "He really is magic," Clippers guard Brian Taylor gushed. "He's got great charisma. It's fun just to watch someone who can get the ball to his teammates when they're open. There are few other players in the league who can do that, but what makes Magic special is the way he brings his own personality into it."[86]

Bolstered by the addition of Johnson, who averaged 18 points and 7.7 rebounds to secure a spot on the NBA's All-Rookie first team, the Lakers won 60 games in the regular season and lost only twice in early rounds of the playoffs to earn a date with Julius Erving's Philadelphia 76ers in the Finals. Despite building a 3–2 lead in games, the Lakers championship hopes suffered a severe setback when Abdul-Jabbar badly injured his left ankle late in the third quarter of the fifth contest, rendering him unable to walk after the game and therefore play for the remainder of the series. The news was so unexpected that the 76ers and their fans dismissed it as clever gamesmanship designed to lull the team into a false state of complacency. "Everyone in the city of Philadelphia believed we were faking the severity of Kareem's injury," Lakers head coach Paul Westhead said. "Believe me, I wish we were."[87] Staring at a now large void at center for the rapidly approaching Game Six, Westhead decided to go the unorthodox route and tap Johnson to fill Abdul-Jabbar's size 16 shoes. Westhead's reasoning was that his speedy 6–9 guard's presence in the pivot would stretch the floor and force the 76ers to play a full-court game over a half-court one, which negated the latter's advantage up front with the athletic but plodding Darryl Dawkins jumping center. Johnson's response to all this? "Let's do it," he said.[88] Thus, the stage was set for one of the most incredible individual performances in NBA playoff history. Carrying out his best impression of Superman in high tops, Johnson exploded for 42 points, 15 rebounds, 7 assists, 3 steals, and a blocked shot in a stunning 123–107 series-clinching Lakers victory in Philadelphia that had seasoned basketball scribes like Bob Ryan dropping their jaws in abject awe. "From the first period when he scored 13 points on five baskets that were not even distantly related, to the last period, when he brought out his hammer and bucket of nails to do with coffin-closing honors, this was Magic's Extended Moment," Ryan wrote.[89]

Even the usually eloquent Dr. J struggled to find the right words to describe what he had just witnessed. "Magic was outstanding. Unreal," he said. The performance was rendered all the more amazing by the fact that Johnson was confused about how to properly position himself in the center circle for the jump ball at the start of the game. "I didn't know whether to stand with my right foot forward or my left," he said. "Didn't know when I should jump or where I should tap it if I got to it."[90]

Johnson, of course, eventually was able to figure things out, but dealing with his newfound fame was an entirely different nut to crack. The irrepressible point guard, just three years removed from high school, suddenly found himself the most celebrated athlete in North America playing in the entertainment capital of the world. That reality took some getting used to, however flattering the flood of attention. "It's nice," he told an interviewer from *Sport* magazine. "It's different. It's, like you say—*Hollywood*. You always dream about it, and say wow! And here I have the opportunity to experience it, to actually *meet the stars*. You can come out here and be in Hollywood, but you maybe never get a chance to meet nobody. But I've got the chance. I met some already. Muhammad Ali, Richard Pryor, Jane Fonda, Jayne Kennedy—here I was with *them*. I got invited to this private party with all these big celebs, and I said, 'Wow!' It's like even when standin' there talkin,' you wanna get away and call everybody at home, just to tell 'em. It's great, and it's only gonna get better."[91]

Yet things nosedived in the opposite direction for Johnson during his sophomore season. Suffering from a cartilage tear to his left knee in November, Johnson underwent surgery and spent the next several months on the sidelines, undergoing a drawn-out, oftentimes painful physical rehabilitation process that ended up keeping him out of 45 games. "In my darkest moments," he confessed, "I wondered what would happen if I couldn't come back at all. What if I turned out to be one of those guys who played in the NBA for only one season? In that case, maybe I should be thankful that my rookie year had ended on such a high. But I didn't *feel* thankful. I felt ripped off. And very angry."[92] His spirits did not improve when he returned to the Lakers lineup. In his absence, the team had continued to play well with former first-round draft pick Norm Nixon capably handling the playmaking duties. But now Nixon saw his minutes in the backcourt cut back to accommodate Johnson's reinstallment at point guard, causing open resentment on his end. "Norm's biggest thing was always he wanted to be bigger than Magic," a teammate revealed. "He had a little man's syndrome. You're little, but you wanna be big. Well, you're not going to be bigger than Magic. It's impossible."[93] The underlying locker-room tensions did not aid the Lakers in their title defense later that spring. They were upset by the Moses Malone–led Houston Rockets in the opening round of the Western Conference playoffs. "Pettiness killed us," Lakers forward Jim Brewer concluded. "We didn't think Houston could stay with us, and we got petty with each other. That's the kiss of death."[94]

Team harmony was similarly out the window at the start of the 1981–82 campaign. Many Lakers took exception to a new $25 million, 25-year contract that team owner Jerry Buss had awarded Johnson in the off-season. It gave off a stench of favoritism that was hard to shake. "Nobody, not even Kareem, had ever had a twenty-five year contract," Johnson conceded. "So what did this mean? Was I now part of management?"[95] Abdul-Jabbar certainly thought so and convened a press conference to publicly vent his displeasure.[96] He also openly speculated whether he would be better off taking his big man talents elsewhere. "I've always felt the people in New York appreciate quality basketball and I could provide that," he said.[97] Only when the Lakers gave the disgruntled center a new contract with a hefty salary increase did Abdul-Jabbar back off his criticism.[98]

All the while, Johnson struggled to regain his All-Star form on the floor. "Magic was still trying to work out some physical difficulties from his surgery," Paul Westhead said. "He didn't have the same quickness and movement that he'd have in the past, so he was being jammed up by defenders where normally it would be easy for him to control. I think he was both physically and emotionally distraught because he wanted to be and was the best."[99] Johnson's frustrations with his own play boiled over into an ugly personal feud with Westhead when the latter decided to change the team's up-tempo, freewheeling offense into a more deliberate half-court one featuring Abdul-Jabbar in the low post. "I tried to tell Westhead that I thought he was on the wrong track, but he didn't want to hear it," Johnson maintained.[100] Nor did Buss's "favorite child," as Abdul-Jabbar described him, want to hear Westhead's criticism that his rebounding totals could stand improvement. "I asked him how he expected me to do that when he had me playing thirty feet from the basket," Johnson angrily retorted.[101] The final straw for both came in a late-November road game against the Utah Jazz in Salt Lake City when Westhead became enraged that Johnson appeared to be tuning him out during a time-out in the team huddle. "I'm tired of your horseshit attitude," Westhead told Johnson. "I'm not going to put up with it anymore. Either you start listening to me, or you don't have to play."[102]

Shortly thereafter, Johnson announced to reporters his desire to be traded. "I can't play here anymore," he said. "I have to leave."[103] That was all team management needed to hear. Westhead was summarily dismissed and replaced by a then little-known assistant coach named Pat Riley. Johnson denied having any responsibility for the move, but he was hard-pressed to find anyone believing that claim, especially in the Lakers locker room. "Look, Magic knew there was no way the team was trading him," bench player Mark Landsberger later explained. "He and Buss were so close, there was no chance he was going anywhere. He handled it like crap. He wanted to get the coach fired—period."[104]

The firing initially did not go over well with fans and the media. Johnson was nightly serenaded with boos on his own home court, and local and national reporters went out of their way to portray Johnson as just another spoiled modern professional athlete putting his selfish needs above those of his team. Anthony Cotton of *Sports Illustrated* accurately summarized this point of view when he wrote, "The 20-year-old who had the ability to make everyone smile by walking into a room, onto a court or into a 7-Up commercial has turned into a greedy, petulant and obnoxious 22-year-old."[105]

Johnson was taken aback by the blowback. Hadn't he led the Lakers to a championship—only their second since the franchise moved to Los Angeles in 1960—just the season before? Wasn't he, according to a 1980 *Sport* magazine cover feature story, "that rarest kind of young athlete, who rises above his own gifts and glories to put some game back in everybody's game"?[106] For sure, Johnson could be forgiven for believing the "Magic" had disappeared from his NBA career. "I was really down," he said. "I was depressed. I slipped away from almost everyone. I kept wondering what was going on."[107]

Johnson later admitted he had to bite the inside of his own cheek during games to prevent himself from sobbing.[108] Not being able to sleep or eat did not help either. His thoughts turned to the then controversial baseball slugger Reggie Jackson for solace. "He was booed, all around the league, but that didn't stop him from hitting home runs," Johnson wrote. "I didn't know how it would happen, but I took some comfort in the idea that somehow this controversy would make a better person."[109] Johnson's anxiety was further eased by daily conversations with his father. Earvin Sr. assured him that he possessed the inner strength to see him through this fiery trial. "He told me to 'keep your head together and keep going.' But it wasn't easy."[110]

In spite of the soap opera theatrics, Johnson and the Lakers managed to regroup under rookie head coach Pat Riley and win 50 of their last 71 games to take their division and storm their way to another playoff matchup with Philadelphia in the Finals. Once again, they prevailed in six games with Johnson submitting a five-star caliber performance (16 points, 10 boards, and 8 assists per contest) to lock up series MVP honors. The victory was made doubly sweet when Johnson was unexpectedly approached by a middle-aged woman in the rowdy, champagne-soaked locker room following the series clincher. "I was one of the ones who booed you when the coach got fired," she solemnly informed him. "I wanted you to know that I'm sorry now, and I'll never boo you again. I thought I ought to tell you that. I thought you ought to know."[111] Johnson's response went unrecorded, but there is no question that he had turned an important corner in his professional life, even before his playoff heroics that spring. "Magic has become a great player," Jerry West said. "I've watched him go from one level to another, higher level this year. He's become solid, that's the big thing. He's in control out there. He knows what he's doing every minute he's on the floor. He's had a great, great season, especially under the circumstances."[112] The greatness was not easily earned. Johnson had been put through an emotional wringer and, as a result, he "definitely aged a little."[113]

But, according to courtly Lakers forward Jamaal Wilkes, this was all for the best. "He's a more likable superstar," Wilkes said. "He's had so much happen so fast . . . that he was unprepared to handle all of it. But now he looks at things a little more different. He's more contemplative. He's a little more ordinary. A little more everyday."[114] Johnson would make his third Finals appearance with the Lakers the following spring, but this time Philadelphia would not be denied, winning in five games. The loss stung, but Johnson could not get too downcast, for he was entering his prime as a player with the prospect of more Lakers titles in the offing. Whether one would come in 1983–84 remained an open question.

Larry Bird and the Celtics were entertaining championship thoughts of their own when the long NBA regular season drew to a close on Sunday, April 15, with a 118–111 home victory over the playoff-bound New Jersey Nets. With the starters sitting out a significant portion of the game, bench players like seldom-used rookie center Greg Kite (13 points on 6 for 9 shooting) were given the opportunity to shine. Wrote the *Globe*'s Dan Shaughnessy, "It was like the last day of high school, when the seniors show up late, everybody goes around signing each other's yearbooks, and you put your future on hold for one final moment."[115] Yet the Celtics had earned the respite. Since putting their disappointing February loss to the Lakers in the rearview mirror, the team had gone on a 24–9 tear through the remainder of their schedule to take the Atlantic Division by 10 games over a fading Philadelphia as well as earn home court advantage throughout the playoffs with a league-best 62–20 final record.

How dominant were they? Entering the fourth quarter of contests with a lead, the Celtics were 54–5; and when they shot 50 percent or better from the field, they finished with a 43–2 mark. In addition, they led all NBA clubs in wins at home (33) and on the road (29). "Sixty-two and 20 is not bad," Red Auerbach apprised. "It says a heck of a lot about these guys here on the team. . . . They had to deal with a new coach and a new system. They have really played together and responded to each other, and that's the most impressive thing about this club."[116] Still, even the longtime Celtics boss had to admit that none of this success would amount to a hill of Boston baked beans if the club stumbled to another early exit from the postseason. Having a Bird in hand, however, greatly reduced the likelihood of that happening.

CHAPTER FIVE

The Eleanor Rigby of Pro Basketball

THE OPENING ROUND OF THE 1984 PLAYOFFS SAW THE CELTICS TAKE ON the Washington Bullets, who finished the regular season with a 35–47 record, including 11 losses in their final 16 games. Despite the uninspiring showing, hope sprang eternal in the heart of Washington coach Gene Shue, a former All-Star guard with the Detroit Pistons in the early 1960s who went on to become a two-time NBA Coach of the Year. "I personally believe anything can happen in a playoff situation," Shue told David Dupree of the *Washington Post* on the eve of the best-of-five series. "Obviously, we don't have the talent of [the Celtics], but in a short series like this, if you start out playing well and get up your confidence, you have a chance." However, to realistically expect the Bullets to topple the Eastern Conference's top-seeded team appeared as plausible as the Loch Ness monster swimming along the banks of Boston's famed Charles River. All the same, Shue insisted there was reason for optimism. "We've played them well in the past and they have respect for us, but it's still if, if, if."[1]

The biggest if concerned whether the Bullets could stop the Celtics' running game by forcing turnovers and getting them to perform at a slower, more deliberate pace. "We want to make them take the outside shot, and if they miss, we have to rebound the ball," Shue said.[2] That's where the frontcourt duo of Jeff Ruland and Rick Mahorn came in. Dubbed "McFilthy and McNasty" by Celtics broadcaster Johnny Most for their body-pounding, intimidating style of play, the two beefy musclemen were being counted on to disrupt the C's offense by beating them up in the paint and not permitting any good looks to the basket. "They are a very physical pair, perhaps the two toughest in the league," Washington teammate Greg Ballard said. "They aren't just dumb brutes either—they're students of the game. And they're team players all the way, more interested in wins than statistics. I'm glad they're on my team."[3] Of the two "Bruise Brothers," Ruland was the more accomplished player, averaging 22 points, 12 rebounds, 3.9 assists, and nearly a steal a game in 1983–84. His 55 percent shooting the previous season had ranked him 10th overall in the NBA. "He's the heart of their club," Detroit Pistons coach and former Boston College head Chuck Daly said. "He's as solid as a rock. He might be the best power forward in the league right now. He *is* the best post-up power forward in the league."[4]

Jeffrey George Ruland did not appear bound for *any* kind of basketball success when he gravitated toward the sport as a gangly, woefully uncoordinated teenager living on New York's Long Island in the mid-1970s. "I stunk. Couldn't even make a layup," he once admitted to an interviewer. Playing in local pickup games with a group of highly competitive adults proved particularly galling. "I did everything wrong and all those old men . . . used to laugh at me. I wore these ugly green sneakers that my mom bought for me. *Green.* Damn, can you believe that? They were the ugliest shoes I ever had." But from that humiliation arose a burning determination to wipe the smiles from his tormenters' faces. No effort was spared. "I remember him being out there [practicing] every day, rain or snow," recalled his mother, a widowed, blunt-spoken tavern owner. "I used to see him go out there and I'd say, 'What's with him?' He'd be out there in the freezing cold and people would come by and say, 'Hey, dummy's out there again.' But I'd just tell them that it was a hell of a lot better than him running around the streets getting into trouble."[5]

Ruland presumably had ditched the unsightly green sneakers later in high school and transformed himself into a certifiable baller, talented enough to earn a scholarship to Iona College and lead the Gaels to two NCAA tournament appearances as well as a number 19 ranking in the national polls. Yet when it came to entering the 1980 NBA draft, the third-team All-American with a pocketful of Iona school records, including most career points scored (1,855), received minimal interest.

The main reason stemmed from Ruland having gotten himself entangled in a highly publicized scandal before his senior season that resulted in the NCAA stripping him of his remaining college eligibility. His unwise hiring of an agent and the acceptance of a significant cash sum from the same individual prompted the severe penalty. "I know I made a mistake, but what I did, signing with an agent, is something that about 200 guys do every year in college," Ruland claimed. "The only difference is that I got caught."[6] Ruland received an even ruder awakening on draft day when the Golden State Warriors selected him as the 25th overall pick in the second round. "I guess everybody thought I was racketeer," he said. "They must have figured I was some kind of shady character. It cost me a lot of money."[7]

Before Ruland had the opportunity to log a single minute with the Warriors, he was trundled off to Washington in exchange for another second-round draft pick. The situation was hardly ideal, for the team had a veteran starting frontcourt of Wes Unseld, Elvin Hayes, and Mitch Kupchak that the Long Island native knew he could not crack. "There just would not have been much playing time for me," Ruland said.[8] He opted to try his luck in Europe instead, where he plied his talents for a team in Barcelona. It was a decision he lived to regret. "The whole European thing was weird," he recounted. "The referees were terrible and some of the games were really bad. I ended up getting into a lot of trouble." Indeed, in an exhibition contest against a club from Italy, Ruland was sucker punched in the face by one of their players, a fellow American named Bruce Flowers who had played his college ball at Notre Dame. Never an adherent to Mahatma Gandhi's principles of nonviolence, Ruland retaliated in kind and had to hastily exit the venue in the company of heavily armed security guards.[9] "I came pretty close to going over the deep end," he said of his Barcelona experience.[10]

Back in the States, Ruland returned to the Bullets for the 1981–82 season and ended up seeing lots of action in the wake of Hall of Famer Wes Unseld's announced retirement and the trade departures of Elvin Hayes and Mitch Kupchak. Coming off the bench, the 6–10, 240-pound rookie with a round face and stubby, Popeye-like arms played in all 82 games and shot 56 percent from the floor despite having a mediocre jump shot. His numbers ticked further upward the following year when he was promoted to a starter's role, averaging 19.4 points and 11 rebounds while securing NBA Player of the Month honors in March. "When he gets down low, there is absolutely nothing you can do to stop him," All-Star Phoenix Suns forward Maurice Lucas said. "There are only two things that will happen when he gets the ball: He will score or you'll foul him. Sometimes you do both."[11] For Ruland, such high praise represented a long overdue validation after so many had written him off. "I always had confidence in myself," he said. "As far back as I can remember, I had my sights set on being a basketball player. I got sidetracked by a few things on the way, but there was never any doubt in my mind that I had the ability. I knew I could do it if I worked hard enough."[12]

Like Ruland, Derrick Allen Mahorn did not have an easy path to the NBA. Born shortly after the conclusion of World War II, he had to tread lightly around his childhood home in Hartford, Connecticut, when his mother was away at work. That's because his older brother, Owen, took special delight in physically abusing him at every opportunity. "As soon as she got out of the house, he'd beat me up," Mahorn remembered. As painful as those encounters were, Owen did stick up for his then chubby little sibling when the latter encountered other boys from the neighborhood intent of delivering further beatings. "What are you doing here, fat boy?" they sneered. "I can beat him up," Owen would interject, "but you will leave him alone."[13] Fortunately, young Ricky did not have to worry about bullies by the time of high school graduation, as he had grown into a strapping, 6–7 multisport athlete, starting on the varsity football and basketball teams. Curiously, he was better on the gridiron than he was on the court. "Even when I finally made the [basketball] varsity . . . the NBA was the farthest thing from my mind," he said. "If I was going to become a pro, I thought it was going to be in football. I was a defensive tackle and end . . . for three years and made the all-conference team as a senior. Football, and not basketball, was really my game."[14]

But a late growth spurt opened up new undreamed-of possibilities for Mahorn. "I was about 5 feet 11 and much too heavy the first two years I went out for basketball," the future NBA All-Defensive Team forward told the *New York Times*. "But then I grew around six inches between my sophomore and junior years and finally made the team, although I sat on the bench most of the season." Mahorn became a starter in his final season on a club that came within pair of baskets of winning the state championship. "I had a pretty good year, averaging about 12 points and between 10 and 12 rebounds, but I don't think many colleges were interested in me as a basketball player," he said.[15] Hampton Institute (now Hampton University) proved the exception. A historically black college in southeastern Virginia that was founded after the Civil War to provide newly freed black slaves with the moral and practical educational means to attain economic self-sufficiency, Hampton appeared the perfect landing spot for Mahorn. "I just wanted to get my college education and go on from there," he explained. "A future in the NBA? You got to be kidding me."[16] Ironically, the joke was on him. Mahorn shattered all expectations, establishing 18 records at the small Division II school and scoring more than 27 points a game his senior year. In hindsight, it should not have come as a surprise that he became the first player in Hampton history to make basketball's major league, taken ten spots below Ruland in the second round of the 1980 draft. "It's all a dream," he said at the time.[17]

After playing sparingly as a rookie, Mahorn became a regular in his second season, averaging a career-high 12.2 points with 8.8 boards. More significantly, he developed a reputation for being, as the *Washington Post* put it, "one of the meanest, toughest, and yes, dirtiest players in the National Basketball Association." Mahorn vehemently denied the characterization, in spite of having loosened the front teeth of many opponents with his swinging, sharp-edged elbows. "People are going to put a jacket on you one way or another and it's going to stay with you long enough until they've been around you long enough for them to see what you're really like," he said. "I do like contact, though, don't get me wrong. I set a lot of picks and get hit all game long, but those hits make my adrenaline flow and get me into the game. This is a contact sport anyway, and I'm just playing the game the best way I know how."[18] Referees were unconvinced, assessing Mahorn a combined 684 personal fouls over the next two seasons, separate from the fines that the commissioner's office had handed him for fighting and other various and sundry misdeeds. "I just think some of the guys think they can push me around," Mahorn said. "When I give it back to them, they don't like it."[19] But Mahorn did receive an unexpected endorsement from one rival big. "He does the things they want him to do, which is rebound, block shots and score when he has to. The main thing he does, though, is set picks," Milwaukee center Bob Lanier said.[20] Mahorn needed to perform all those things and more if the Bullets were to stand a chance against the Celtics.

It did not happen in the series opener on Tuesday, April 17. A sold-out home crowd of 14,890 witnessed the Celtics score a 91–83 victory that had *Washington Post* reporter and future Pulitzer Prize–winning author David Remnick conjuring visions of perdition's flames. "Not long from now," Remnick wrote in the lead paragraph to his game story, "some smart-aleck Harvard kid with equal passion for the Celtics and Dante will ferry across the Charles River and nail a sign above the door to ancient Boston Garden: 'Abandon hope all ye who enter here.'"[21] Why all the glum imagery? Perhaps Gene Shue offered a clue in his post-game comments. "We controlled the tempo and brought it down to a half-court game," the Washington coach said. "We played hard and we played well. It's the type of game we can win." But they didn't. And that was the point. The Celtics were able to adapt and beat the Bullets at their own game, being physical and not turning the ball over. "Sure, it's satisfying," said Cedric Maxwell. "We know we are going to beat this team because we come out and play hard. If it's half-court game they want, then we're ready for that. This is physical, setup basketball—the kind you have to play if you want to go all the way."[22] Still, big offensive stalwarts like Kevin McHale and Robert Parish were silenced as the suffocating Bullets defense limited them to fewer than 10 shots each. What the star spangled–clad Washingtonians could not account for, however, was the outside shooting of Larry Bird, who somehow found enough open spots on the floor to score a team-high 23 points while handing out 12 assists. "This is the way it's going to be," said Bird of the reduced pace of the contest. "People will have to realize that. We're going to have to be very patient against this team."[23]

Neither Bird (12 rebounds) nor his teammates deviated from this plodding strategy two nights later in Game 2 when the Celtics beat the Bullets again at the Garden, 88–85. Jeff Ruland's desperate, last-second attempt to tie the game with a three-point bomb at the buzzer fell wide of the mark. Ruland, who nearly succeeded in pulling off a triple-double with 16 points, 10 rebounds, and 8 assists, stood in stunned disbelief on the parquet afterward as the Celtics filed past him to the locker room. "I was asking myself, 'How did we lose this bleeping game?'" Ruland said. The brawny center was also fuming over a foul he had been assessed moments earlier on a loose ball that sent Parish to the line. Ruland had dived to the floor on the play and made contact with Parish. "I thought it was a jump ball," Ruland claimed. "And if there was a foul called, it should have been Parish. He hit me right in the jaw." Although the Chief converted only one of the two free throws, the Celtics were able to gain a three-point lead they would not relinquish. "They've got to be sitting down there saying, 'What do we have to do to beat these guys?'" Kevin McHale said. "I don't think they can beat us, to tell you the truth. I don't think they're capable of playing any better than they did tonight."[24]

McHale was forced to eat those words as the series shifted to the Capital Centre in suburban Landover, Maryland, for the next two games. Before a disappointing home audience of only 8,359, the Bullets rode to a 111–108 overtime victory in Game 3 on the wide back of Ruland, who finished with a personal playoff high of 33 points with 13 rebounds and 5 assists. "They were going to try to put us away," crowed teammate Greg Ballard. "They seemed confident and cocky. But there was no way we were going to give up."[25]

The Bullets did come perilously close to handing the game away. After squandering a 15-point fourth-quarter lead, the Bullets steadied themselves in OT with Rick Mahorn (14 points, 15 rebounds) supplying the biggest basket down the stretch—a hurried 15-foot jumper as the 24-second clock expired that somehow found net and ensured Washington the win. "I knew it was off," Parish said. "That's why it went in." Par for the course for the series, there was plenty of roughhouse play all around, including Washington guard Ricky Sobers's hard shove of M. L. Carr on a breakaway that sent Carr flying into a sideline television camera. "I'll never say anything's dirty," Carr told the *Washington Post*. "Anything to stop me is okay. He can throw me downtown, into Pennsylvania Avenue, and I'll say it's a good play." Cedric Maxwell refused to abide by Carr's speak-no-evil approach. "There's bad blood between these two teams," he confirmed. "They can be dirty and hit you with cheap shots. It's just brewing, and the longer this series goes, the worse it's going to get."[26] That concern notwithstanding, Maxwell expressed no doubt that the Celtics would ultimately prevail. Bird (27 points), on the other hand, was not so sure. An encroaching sense of doom pervaded his thoughts. "Truth is," he said, "we should have been blown them out by 15, 20 points. If we don't straighten things out and just wake up, there's going to be a fifth game. And that scares me because I don't even like to think about the possibility of three straight losses. We went through an experience like that last year."[27]

Bird's fear never came to pass. The Celtics managed to close out the Bullets with a 99–96 win in Game 4, despite missing their first six shots and No. 33 being held to fewer than 20 points for the first time all series. The principal difference maker was Robert Parish, who broke out of the scoring rut he had been in in the previous three contests with 20 points on 8 for 13 shooting. "I wasn't concerned about individual match-ups," Parish said. "I just knew I had to do more offensively because too many of my teammates were getting backaches from carrying me [in the series]."[28] The primary reason for the turnaround had to do with Parish finally breaking the defensive code of his mustached antagonist in the pivot. "He'd had a lot of trouble with Ruland," M. L. Carr confirmed. "The Chief had to figure him out, and he did. Ruland was moving Chief out from the places where he likes to shoot. Tonight, Chief moved back to those places."[29] Maxwell was not surprised. "I knew this would happen," he said. "It's an ability you have when you play with someone for awhile. Being around a teammate so long is almost like being around your wife: You can tell the moods. He was pumped up. Everybody was."[30] Parish also contributed to a key stretch in the second quarter when the Celtics turned up the defensive heat beyond half court and held the Bullets scoreless for almost a full six minutes with seven missed shots and four turnovers. "They took us out of what we wanted to do," Gene Shue said. "We rely on executing plays and we didn't do very well."[31]

Meanwhile, the Celtics went on an inspiring 15–0 run during the same span to build a 52–41 lead by halftime. They never trailed again, even though the Bullets kept it interesting with a furious, late-scoring onslaught that fell short. "We had our offensive screens working well," said Quinn Buckner, who contributed nine points off the bench. "And for some strange reason I got it going. I took some shots I normally wouldn't simply because I had my timing going."[32] Perhaps fitting, given the bruising back-and-forth physicality displayed by the two clubs throughout the playoff, open violence broke out on the final play as time expired. Gerald Henderson objected to the sumo wrestling-style techniques that Washington guard Frank Johnson had employed against him and uncorked some haymakers. "It was no big thing," Henderson said. "It was just tough to ignore the things going on. It was just something I couldn't continue to tolerate. I don't want to say anything more about it."[33]

Gratifying though the victory was, the Celtics received even better news two days later when they learned that the defending champion Philadelphia 76ers got swept in the first round by the upstart New Jersey Nets. Now there would be one less major obstacle in the East standing between them and a return to the NBA Finals. Bird expressed remorse that the Celtics would be denied the opportunity of facing their longtime archrivals in the postseason for the fourth time in five years ("It was always a good series, and it was fun getting excited about it."), but his teammates shed no tears. "Yeah, I'm real disappointed," Gerald Henderson said sardonically of his fellow Virginian. "I sent a telegram to my school (Virginia Commonwealth) for a scholarship award function there Friday, and I put, 'P.S. Moses Malone may show up, since he's on early vacation.'" Cedric Maxwell voiced even less sympathy. "I'm happy to see the chumps out of the way," he said. "Get 'em out the way, that's what I say."[34]

One team threatening not to go away was the Celtics next opponent. For the Hubie Brown–coached New York Knicks had wrapped up their regular schedule with 47 wins while giving up the third-least points (103) in the league. Four-year veteran center Bill Cartwright (17 points, 8.4 rebounds per contest) had a standout year along with speedy 6–3 guard Ray Williams (14.8 points, 5.9 assists), a Knicks first-round draft pick who had been traded and then reacquired in a savvy off-season pickup from New Jersey by the team vice president and director of basketball operations, Dave DeBusschere. But the main story line coming out of Gotham concerned the night-in, night-out heroics of Bernard King, the unstoppable All-Star scoring forward and reformed alcoholic who had come perilously close to flushing his career down the drain years earlier. "I knew [the series] was not going to be easy—if only because of Bernard King," Larry Bird wrote later. "This was Bernard at his best."[35]

During the Knicks' five-game takedown of the Detroit Pistons in their opening round playoff series, King hit a scorching 60 percent on 84-for-139 shooting while averaging 42.6 points a game. The performance earned him a coveted spot in the NBA record book for most points scored in a five-game playoff (213). "What impresses me," retired two-time NBA champion Knicks coach Red Holzman said, "is how he shoots with such quickness and such accuracy. Other teams overplay him, they try to deny him the ball, they double-team him and triple-team him. But he keeps scoring."[36] That was certainly the case in the deciding Pistons contest as King overcame a bout with the flu and dislocated middle fingers on each hand to tally 44 points, including almost half of the Knicks final 30 points in the closing 10 minutes. As Bruce Newman of *Sports Illustrated* wrote, "Whether he was thundering down the left sideline on a fast break—his back arched so extravagantly he sometimes looked swaybacked—or twisted like a pretzel around some helpless defender trying to establish position in the low post, King was always magnificent."[37] For King, this unsurpassed run of sustained hoop excellence was simply par for the course. "Down the stretch, I wanted the ball," he explained. "I wanted it to be on my shoulders. If you're a player, you're supposed to want the ball in that situation."[38]

King's long and bumpy ride to NBA superstardom began when he was a tall but physically awkward third-grader at P.S. 67 in the tree-lined Fort Greene section of Brooklyn in the early 1960s. "I'd be mercilessly teased by the class bullies," he later revealed in his autobiography, *Game Face* with Jerome Preisler. "Even the girls got into the act, calling me Blueberry Hill, after the Fats Domino song, because of my large, high-browed head."[39] But all the mean-spiritedness was forgotten when he had a basketball in his hands while staring up at the hoop in his school's cafeteria that doubled as a gym. "I was drawn to that rim, and kept returning with my classmates," he wrote. "One by one, they took turns trying to make the shot. And one by one, they became exasperated. They either couldn't throw the ball up as high as the hoop or couldn't get it to go in. After a few tries, they all walked away in discouragement." Except King. He became determined to succeed where his peers failed. Approaching the problem with the single-mindedness of a mathematician solving a complex equation, King experienced a hoop epiphany. "I finally realized the begin-point was touch," he related. "That meant getting a feel for the ball in my hands, then figuring how much upward thrust I needed to cover the height and distance between me and the basket."[40]

His life would never be the same. Henceforth, he devoted countless hours in the gym to perfecting his shot while feeling liberated from the daily drudgery that was the Walt Whitman Housing Projects where he spent the bulk of his childhood along with his five siblings. Times were tough. As transplants from the South, King's parents struggled to make ends meet on his father's modest building superintendent's salary. While King found his work ethic commendable, he thought his distant, authoritarian manner less so. "Dad was inflexible," he wrote. "He had his rules, and everyone obeyed. Every Sunday morning, we would get into our dress clothes and take the bus over to the Evergreen Baptist Church on Carlton Avenue, near our old walk-up. Once we were home, the kids couldn't go back outside. We were forbidden from going to the movies or listening to the radio. We weren't allowed to see our friends."[41] His mother was even worse, subjecting young Bernard to physical beatings with a strap and kitchen broomstick that left ugly, painful welts on his skin. He often puzzled over what provoked these outbursts of violence but never came up with a definitive answer other than she had been abused by her own parents growing up.[42] The resulting emotional scars made King embrace the game of basketball with even greater fervor. "The game was—almost literally—his life," award-winning author and journalist Joe Klein wrote.[43]

Yet for all his labors, which included daily conditioning runs on the Brooklyn Bridge, King did not begin to blossom as a player until his senior year at Fort Hamilton High School when he earned All-City honors. His younger brother, Albert King, who would go on to play in nine

NBA seasons, was considered the *real* basketball star in the family. As one of King's former high-school teachers observed, "Albert was surrounded by people, protecting him, driving him from game to game. Bernard had to struggle more. He took the subway to games."[44] King's hoops stock skyrocketed, however, when he played in a number of high-profile out-of-town tournaments like the Boston Shootout in 1974, which had been founded two years earlier by Ken Hudson, the NBA's first African American referee. The *Globe*'s Bob Ryan, the eminence grise of Boston sportswriters over the past half century, was unprepared for what he witnessed. Against premier high-school talent, King scored 20 points or better in every contest while displaying a polished, all-around game. He won the tourney MVP award going away. "I may get arguments from Ken Hudson and others," Ryan later wrote, "but I feel that King is the best *player* ever to grace the Shootout. Technically, there have been better shooters, better rebounders and better passers. But I doubt there have been any better defenders, and I absolutely insist there have been no better thinkers. Even at age 18, Bernard King knew exactly what he was supposed to be doing out there. Believe me, there were a few people in the NBA All-Star game who could not make that statement."[45]

In college, King continued to make statements with the University of Tennessee Volunteers, exploding for 42 points in his first game and becoming a three-time Southeastern Conference Player of the Year and All-American. Teamed with fellow New Yorker Ernie Grunfeld, a gifted, thickset naturalized Romanian forward whose parents had survived the Holocaust, the "Bernie and Ernie Show" vaulted the Vols to national prominence and a SEC championship in 1977. Recounted King, "Our skills and physical strengths were complementary. Neither of us could be blocked, we both had high basketball IQs, knew how to handle the ball, and could get around any defense you threw at us."[46]

The 6–7, 205-pound King was clearly the superior talent. Tennessee coach Ray Mears called him "the most competitive athlete" he had ever coached. To back up this claim, Mears cited a contest against archrival Kentucky during King's sophomore season. The Wildcats had built a seemingly secure 14-point lead with eight minutes remaining, prompting Mears to call a timeout. "[King]," Mears recalled, "came into the huddle and said, 'We're going to win this game.'" That was all the Vols needed to hear. "[King] was just unstoppable," Mears said. "We kept stealing the ball—he had the whole team pumped up—and feeding it to him. He put us ahead with a lob pass, falling back, off-balance. I think he was flat on his back when he shot. It was the most incredible thing I've ever seen."[47]

But for all the success King found on the court, trouble found him off it. He had frequent run-ins with the law in Knoxville, which he attributed to a racist local police force who resented his fame and success. Mears, in fact, relayed to King a confidential conversation he had with the Knoxville police chief, in which the latter revealed that his officers "don't like that uppity nigger."[48] Bill Bates, a defense attorney who represented King in several of these legal dustups, later confirmed that the police had it in for King. "One time," Bates said, "[King] was arrested for possession of marijuana. He had come out of a club and was sitting in a car. The officer came up and shined the light in the car and said he saw some marijuana seeds. He didn't bother to recover them, though, and when he was asked what they looked like, he said popcorn kernels."[49]

Unable to cope with the situation and still suffering the psychological effects of a difficult upbringing, King descended into alcohol and drug abuse, a disturbing behavioral pattern that followed him into the NBA when the New Jersey Nets made him their first-round draft pick in 1977. "I began to drink more heavily then," he confessed. "Part of it was coming away from a close relationship in college, two years with the same woman, and there was the pain of breaking up. But it was also . . . well, you dream about something all your life and then, suddenly, you're there—playing in the NBA—and it's not what you thought it would be. My friends and family were a lot happier for me than I was for myself. You can score 30 points and grab 15 rebounds, but then the game is over—and you find yourself taking that drive back to the apartment alone."[50] Despite his growing addiction problem, King managed to record 22.5 points per game and make the NBA All-Rookie Team. However, cracks were beginning to show. He alienated Nets coach Kevin Loughery and veteran teammates by showing up chronically late for practices and displaying an overall lack of maturity and discipline. Legendary *New York Daily News* sports columnist Dick Young, once described by a rival newspaperman as "the epitome of the brash, unyielding yet sentimental Damon Runyon sportswriter," informed his legions of loyal readers that King was "a spoiled star" at risk of throwing away a bright basketball future.[51] "They come and they go, these young men who think their talent is a license to abuse," he wrote.[52]

King lived down to that reputation in the seasons to follow. He remained a volume scorer, but his personal life spiraled increasingly out of control. Particularly embarrassing was his 1978 arrest on charges of driving under the influence and possession of cocaine that made front-page headlines. "There were times he came to practice and seemed really out of it, like he hadn't been to bed all night," said Nets general manager Charlie Theokas. "Both Kevin [Loughery] and I tried to talk to him about it, but he said he could handle it."[53] Nor did it help that King had a haunting premonition that he would die young. "I was living very dangerously in the sense that I'd drive with a quart of alcohol in my system," he explained. "I'd get in my car to drive home and I wouldn't remember the ride."[54] The Nets finally ran out of patience and shuffled King off to the Utah Jazz before the start of the 1979–80 season. "You are going to regret this," an angry and disappointed King told Loughery out the door.[55] But King (9.3 points per game) proceeded to flounder in Utah, a terrible team that finished 24–36 under head coach Tom Nissalke.

Feeling hopelessly lost and at loose ends, King finally sought help to tame his inner demons on New Year's Day 1980. With the help of his agent and friend Bill Pollack, he admitted himself into an intensive six-week alcohol rehabilitation program at St. John's Hospital and Medical Center in Santa Monica, California. "He wasn't cured," said Gerald Rozansky, his attending psychiatrist at St. John's. "There is no cure. The program is merely an introduction to the disease. We try to give people the words to understand their problem." Nevertheless, an important corner had been turned on his personal road to recovery. Meanwhile, the unsympathetic Jazz had suspended King indefinitely before unceremoniously packing him off to the Golden State Warriors in the 1980–81 preseason. Remembered King, "The thing that hurt the most was that the Jazz came to Los Angeles when I was in the hospital and not one of them—[players, coaches or front office personnel]—called to see how I was. . . . I'm in the hospital, fighting for my life, and none of them guys give a damn."[56]

King found a warmer reception in San Francisco, where he was able to resurrect his stalled basketball career. Performing at an All-Star level, King averaged more than 20 points a game in Warrior blue and gold while walking away with the Comeback Player of the Year award in 1981. "I loved the Bay Area," he wrote. "I'd gain a sense of who I was. This does not mean I'd dug down to the root of my problems. Some things can't be solved overnight. But I was no longer on a self-destructive course."[57] It showed on the court. After dropping 50 points on Philadelphia in a mid-season contest, Warriors coach Al Attles was floored by the ease in which King got them. "That was as good a 50 points as I've ever seen," Attles said. "You didn't even notice him scoring—it was all done within the team concept. He certainly didn't know it until I told him he needed only two more hoops for 50, and to go ahead and get them."[58] King would have been content to remain a Warrior for the rest of his career, but the team was in rebuilding mode, and King yearned to play on a winner. The Knicks afforded him that opportunity when they acquired the uber-talented 26-year-old from Golden State in a trade for guard Michael Ray Richardson and a fifth-round draft pick in 1982.

King's impact on the Knicks was not unlike that of Hall of Fame baseball slugger Reggie Jackson when he joined the New York Yankees lineup in the late 1970s: he became the proverbial straw that stirred the drink. Indeed, sparked by King's 26 points a game, the Knicks transformed themselves from an also-ran into a serious playoff threat by 1984. "He does not freelance or razzle-dazzle, or break plays or call for the ball or yell at his teammates," said Knicks coach Hubie Brown of his star forward. "He just takes good shots when they are there. Still, every couple of days in practice he does something I've never seen before. He's got so much to give. Yet he remains in touch with the entire picture. All he wants to do is win."[59] His mirthless, dead-eyed stare said it all during games. "King," wrote "Sports of the Times" columnist George Vecsey in the *New York Times*, "is the Eleanor Rigby of pro basketball—wearing a face that he keeps in a jar by the door. Who is it for? To intimidate the opposition with his silent scowl."[60]

The host Celtics did not appear intimidated heading into Game 1 of their best-of-seven semifinal matchup against the Knicks on Saturday, April 29. "Bernard has scored his last forty points," promised M. L. Carr. "He won't get any forties here. We've got somebody that can stop him." That somebody was Cedric Maxwell, who approached the task of covering the league's most dynamic offensive force with all the studied indifference of a Beacon Hill aristocrat reviewing his investment portfolio. Nothing to get too worked up about. Sporting an "I Love New York" T-shirt in practice, Maxwell cockily informed *Globe* reporter Dan Shaughnessy that King should not expect to rain down jumpers on the Celtics the same way he had against the Pistons. "We're going to stop the bitch," he said.[61] Maxwell proved prophetic—at least in the opener, holding King to "only" 26 points on 12-for-22 shooting in Boston's 110–92 pasting of the Knicks at home. "This may have seemed pretty easy, but guarding King was anything but," Maxwell later wrote. "He got his shot off so quickly that we couldn't double-team him. Heck, you couldn't even count to two before he released it. If he got you on his hip, he'd leverage you. The way I guarded him was to play circle defense and never let him lock me down in the post. His guards wouldn't throw him the ball those times. So at least it slowed him down."[62] King was not the only Knick to have an off night. Bill Cartwright had six points while Ray Williams sleep walked through a dismal two for eight shooting night. "All this talk about Bernard's numbers is overblown," an exasperated Hubie Brown said. "He never breaks an offensive set. He doesn't ruin our continuity. If the guy is shooting 60 percent, then, of course, we're naturally going to get the ball to him. Otherwise, how we do depends on the play of other individuals and how we perform as a team."[63]

Meanwhile, the Knicks had no counter to Kevin McHale (25 points, 8 rebounds, and 5 assists), who had little difficulty shredding New York's pressing defense. "You live by [the press] and you die by it," McHale said. "We tried to skip the guard-to-guard pass to break through. We used the long pass to just over half court to relieve the pressure. Then, when we got the ball in their end, we had an open court waiting." Robert Parish (17 points) and Larry Bird (23 points) also had their way while Danny Ainge came off the bench in the second quarter to connect on four of his first five shots to help give the Celts an insurmountable 20-point advantage at halftime. "Boston had a 40 percent success rate against our press in the regular season," Brown said. "Today they were something like six for eight against our first unit. There wasn't much to say. Boston had executed very well. But anyone who's been around the playoffs knows this is just one game."[64]

The lone discordant note in Boston's blowout victory was Bird turning over his right ankle after a successful driving layup in the closing minutes. Why Bird was still in the game led many in the media to question the soundness of K. C. Jones's judgment. "The Celts were on fire, but they were also playing with fire by letting the incomparable Larry Bird play out the string in the final quarter," noted one local writer.[65] Dave Anderson of the *New York Times* went so far as to describe the incident as a potential "turning point" in the series if Bird hereon in was unable to perform up to his optimum level. "The Celtics . . . might be vulnerable," he wrote.[66] For his part, Jones did not duck responsibility, instead opting to confront the issue head-on. "I thought about [taking Bird out] too late," he said. "I just made a boo-boo."[67]

Despite the admission, Celtics players rallied around their embattled coach afterward. "I don't think you can second guess [Jones] in a situation like that," Carr said. "The Knicks are a very capable team. What would've happened if we'd taken Larry out earlier and New York made a dramatic comeback? Everybody would've have said K. C. took him out too soon." Bird, who had injured the same ankle in the clinching game of the Washington series, did his best to diffuse the controversy in his own inimitable way. "I was hoping to play 47 minutes," he said. "It's a situation where you want to play as much as you can. But it's my fault that I didn't come out earlier. Hopefully, I won't have to take that kind of chance again. K. C. asked me two or three times if I wanted to come out, but the more I played the better I felt. It's easy to say [it was wrong to keep playing] when the game is over, but when the game is going on, you want to play. What happened was just a freak accident, but, next time, I think I'd come out [earlier]."[68]

Bird exhibited no lingering ill effects from the ankle injury in Game 2 as he torched the Knicks for 37 points while leading the Celtics to a resounding 116–102 win to go up 2–0 in the series. "Bird was everywhere at the Garden," wrote *New York Daily News* columnist Mike Lupica, "playing a sort of basketball that may have kids all over America going out today and spraining their ankles."[69] The offensive outburst notwithstanding, Bird had nothing but praise for the unfortunate Knick assigned to guard him, claiming that he was "a good defensive player" and that "guarding [me] shouldn't tire you out any more than guarding anyone else."[70] When apprised of Bird's comments afterward, a bemused Bernard King smiled. "Tell him I said to try it some time. Be my guest," he remarked.[71] That was the only bit of levity King (13 points) allowed himself the entire evening as he could not penetrate the suffocating defensive blanket the Celtics had wrapped around him. He connected on only 4 of 13 shots and went scoreless for a crucial 20-minute stretch in the middle of the game. "Every once in a while, not often, I'll have a bad day at the office," King explained. "This was my bad day at the office."[72]

Maxwell was once again his chief tormenter, hounding King from baseline to baseline while preventing the glum-faced New Yorker from setting up in transition and unleashing his patented stop-and-pop jump shot. "My job is to contain him," Maxwell said. "To hunt him. He's got little spots on the floor where he's been taking his shots from all year. We tried to keep him out of there. We did an excellent job. Basically, it's like a hockey series. We try to limit him to as few shots on goal as possible."[73] McHale, submitting another stellar performance with 25 points, 8 rebounds, and 4 blocked shots, agreed. "The idea is that we're taking away the biggest part of their offensive game," he said. "They can switch and make Bernard a decoy and have other people take the shots, but they're not geared that way. A guy takes five shots on their team and right away he starts worrying that Bernard isn't shooting. He has to get the ball to Bernard."[74]

King's frustration with Maxwell's Venus flytrap defense boiled over late in the fourth quarter when he swung an elbow directly at the trash-talking forward's head. Although King denied any malicious intent ("I don't take it home with me," he claimed), his coach was more honest and forthcoming.[75] "You would be [ruffled] too," Hubie Brown told reporters, "if guys were beating the hell out of you out there and they weren't calling any fouls. Then you look at the other end of the floor, you look at your guy and they call a foul. You don't have to be Bernard King to get upset about something like that. You can be Joe Shmoe down at the Y, and if that kind of stuff is going on, you're going to get frustrated, too."[76] Of course, the Knicks did themselves no favors by turning the ball over 27 times and allowing the Celtics to convert them into 31 points. Bird played a crucial role here, making four steals and putting on "the best stripping exhibition since Gypsy Rose Lee," according to one New York beat writer.[77] "He was a part of every double team or so it seemed," Brown said. "Every time somebody got a piece of the ball down low, it was Bird. He kept getting off his man and playing the passing lanes incredibly well. He really was like one of those roving middle linebackers in football. The monster man. A Killer 'B.'"[78]

The Knicks played like Killer Bs over the next two contests when the series shifted to New York City's venerable Madison Square Garden. "We didn't hang our heads after the two losses in Boston," Bernard King said. "They were supposed to win at home. They played great. They shot the lights out. Now we're in New York and we're supposed to win."[79] Indeed, in Game 3, the team received 22 points from Ray Williams to bull their way to a 100–92 triumph over the men in green. Williams, who had teamed with Kevin McHale in the mid-1970s on a great University of Minnesota Golden Gophers team, was at the peak of his hoops powers. "I feel so happy for him, the way he responded," said King, who contributed 24 of his own points in the winning cause. "This game doesn't always come down to what physical abilities you have as much as it does to what you have inside you. Ray showed tonight what he had inside him."[80] King was not talking hyperbole. Only days earlier, Williams's 40-year-old sister Martha Taylor had succumbed to a battle with pancreatic cancer, necessitating the grief-stricken Knicks guard to miss the second Boston game to attend the funeral. "Ray didn't say anything in the locker room tonight and that's not normal for him," teammate Roy Sparrow revealed. "Losing somebody that close to you has to have a profound effect on you, but Ray was able to adjust somehow. He was a true professional. I have no idea whether he dedicated this game to his sister [Williams elected to stay mum on the subject], but it's a tribute to him that he could play so well in a situation like this."[81] In spite of Williams's inspirational play, the Celtics managed to enter the locker room with a 52–50 halftime advantage behind the steady offense of Bird and Robert Parish (12 points each). But the Knicks rallied in the third quarter to grab a 77–70 lead, which the Celtics were never able to surmount due to a collective team scoring drought. "We shot 38 percent from the field and 68 percent from the free throw line. My mother and the four friends she has tea with could have beaten us tonight," McHale said.[82]

Game 4 was likewise no tea party for McHale and the Green. King (43 points on 17 of 25 from the floor) finally broke out with a big-time scoring performance that had Maxwell and other would-be Boston defenders backpedaling all evening in a 118–113 Knicks victory to tie the series at 2–2. "The Celtics threw everything they had at me," King remembered. "Switches. Double and triple teams. The [physical] hits got harder and more frequent. But it didn't slow me. I had everything working."[83] For certain, King established his dominance early with 12 points in the first quarter. "When I saw him making [a basket] driving down the lane, I said to myself, 'Oh boy, it's going to be a long night,'" McHale said.[84] It only got worse from there. In the second quarter, King received a pass from Ray Williams only to find himself surrounded by a sea of green jerseys bearing the names of Bird, McHale, Maxwell, and Ainge. No sweat. "I quickly saw the break point to the middle, drawing contact," King wrote. "I wasn't passing off the ball that close to the basket. Worst-case scenario, I'd go to the line. But I sank a short fadeaway jumper and came away with a 3-point play."[85] A few minutes later, he caught a high, arcing lob pass from Williams in the paint and delivered a thunderous dunk over a befuddled Maxwell that drew a foul, which the old Brooklynite effortlessly sank for another three-point play. "In the playground, we'd have called that sweet revenge," King gloated.[86] To further rub salt in the wound, King convinced a friendly reporter after the game to hand a stat sheet to Maxwell showcasing his gaudy offensive numbers. "Man, was I pissed," Maxwell recalled. "In my mind I was like, *This motherfucker . . . I'm going to kill this guy!*"[87]

Having blown a 2–0 series lead, the Celtics traveled back to Beantown for a pivotal fifth game on Wednesday, May 9, with their confidence badly shaken. Gone were any smug references of King being unable to drop 40 points on them. It had become a real series, and anything was possible. Said McHale, "We thumped 'em twice good in Boston, dug 'em a grave and put 'em in it. They've thumped us twice [in New York] and crawled out of their grave. Now we're fighting over the shovel."[88] The Celtics won that later skirmish with a 121–99 smackdown of the visitors in orange and blue before an appreciative Boston Garden crowd of 14,890. "As blowouts go," Mike Lupica informed his Manhattan readership, "this was top of the line. This was the Rolls Royce of blowouts. 'The Great Gatsby' of blowouts, the Michael Jackson or Frank Sinatra or Willie Nelson of blowouts, depending on your basic musical preferences."[89] A "Thriller" it was not. The Celtics burst out of the gate with an up-tempo running offense, scoring 16 first-half points off fast breaks while shooting a red-hot 64.6 percent from the field. Bird (26 points and 10 assists) became the key here, connecting on six of his first eight shots and narrowly missing a game triple-double by one rebound. "We were on an emotional high," Maxwell said. "There was the prospect of us losing in Boston, and we . . . didn't want that to happen."[90] Nor did it as the Celtics built a comfortable 20-point lead in the second half and coasted to the finish. McHale scored 22 points following a subpar performance in Game 4, and four other teammates (Maxwell, Parish, Johnson, and Gerald Henderson) all cracked double figures. "We were aggressive from the start," K. C. Jones said. "That aggressive play carried us through the entire game."[91]

The only bit of drama came late in the third quarter when Danny Ainge struck Knicks rookie guard Darrell Walker in the throat and chin with a double forearm shiver as the former Arkansas Razorback was driving toward the basket. "Darrell's head snapped back," King wrote. "It's the kind of move that can put someone in the hospital, or worse."[92] The incident, which Maxwell claimed produced "a better brand of football than the USFL," touched off a wild bench-clearing brawl between the two clubs that resulted in the ejection of Ainge and Walker after they grappled like a pair of fist-flying barroom drunks on the parquet.[93] "I didn't mean to hit anybody," said Ainge, who eventually would be fined $750 by the NBA for his misdeed. "I was trying to prevent [Walker] from getting a 3-point play. He stopped and I couldn't. I wouldn't call what I did hitting him with a forearm shot."[94] Walker, a recipient of NBA All-Rookie team honors that season, begged to differ. "It's the second time [Ainge] has done that to me," he said. "There are ways to foul, but that ain't one of them."[95]

Controversy always seemed to swirl around Daniel Ray Ainge. Just the previous spring Ainge had his right middle finger nearly bitten off by Wayne "Tree" Rollins of the Atlanta Hawks after he tackled the 7-foot center in a home playoff game. Ainge claimed Rollins had earlier unleashed a vicious elbow to his head prompting the response. "I couldn't let him get away with it, and no one was doing a thing about it," he said.[96] As the two combatants rolled around at mid-court exchanging punches, they were joined by their teammates in a wild pileup that saw arms and legs flying in all directions. "I didn't want to see Danny hurt," McHale said. "He may be a wimp but he's also my friend."[97] Be that as it may, Rollins took the opportunity to literally make a meal of Ainge's finger at the bottom of the pile—a gruesome sight captured on television replays that compelled the *Boston Herald* to run the instantly classic "Tree Bites Man" headline the next day.[98] "We were down on the ground and he had me wrapped up and I had him wrapped up and people were on top of him," Ainge said. "Then he just stuck my finger in his mouth. . . . I thought he was going to bite it off. I was trying to pull my hand away but he just stuck it in his mouth and chomped on it really hard."[99] Ainge received a five-stitch cut for his troubles along with a tetanus shot. What he did not receive was any kind of apology from Rollins then or years later when their paths occasionally crossed. Nor did he expect any. "It's just something that happened," Ainge said. "The bite was unique to it, but if there hadn't been the bite, it was still a brawl, and those are no big deal." Besides, he hastened to add, he did not think his finger tasted "too good."[100]

The product of a tight-knit, middle-class Mormon family, Ainge spent his formative years in scenic Eugene, Oregon, during the height of the Vietnam War and Watergate scandal. Neither of these generation-defining events appeared to have made much of an impression on young Danny, as his main focus was competing in whatever sport was in season on the baseball diamonds, football fields, and basketball courts that dotted his hometown. "A lot of people said football was my best sport in high school," he recalled. "But I was six feet four and kinda skinny, and I thought there was too much risk for injury if I played in college. So I told football recruiters I wasn't going to play in college."[101] He decided instead to concentrate on basketball at Brigham Young University in Provo, Utah, a middling Division I program that he would help elevate to lofty new heights in the early 1980s. But the thought of playing the sport professionally held no interest for him. "The NBA didn't really inspire me as much as Major League Baseball," Ainge said. "Playing in Yankee Stadium and Fenway Park, those were inspirational places for me."[102] To this end, he signed with the expansion Toronto Blue Jays after they had targeted him in their first amateur draft in 1977. "We drafted him and wanted him to play baseball," longtime Blue Jays GM Pat Gillick said in a 2020 interview. "He could play [basketball] at BYU, but then he would come and play baseball for us [during his summer breaks]."[103] Although Ainge rapidly ascended through the Toronto minor league system to make the parent club in 1979, he had trouble with breaking pitches and ended up batting an uninspiring .237 and .243 over the next two seasons, mostly as a second baseman and center fielder.

Ainge achieved greater acclaim and success back in Provo, where he averaged slightly more than 24 points a game as a senior and was instrumental in BYU advancing to the Elite 8 of the 1981 NCAA Tournament after making the game-winning basket at the buzzer against a heavily favored Notre Dame squad in the East regional quarterfinals in Atlanta. He accomplished this feat by streaking downcourt past five flat-footed Irish defenders for an electrifying layup. "I just wanted to keep going until they stopped me or I was so close enough in to get off a shot," Ainge related. "As it turned out, I was able to take it from only three feet out."[104] Legendary Notre Dame coach Digger Phelps, who would finish his college career with 419 wins in 21 seasons, stood in disbelief at what had transpired. "It's a tough way to lose a ballgame," he said. "We wanted to contain Ainge and we did that until the last eight seconds. We knew he was going to get the ball. We tried to stop him getting it but he is just too good an athlete."[105] BYU lost to Ralph Sampson's University of Virginia Cavaliers in the next round to deprive them of a Final Four berth, but Ainge's spectacular play was not forgotten when they handed out the hardware at the end of the season. He won the coveted John R. Wooden Award for being the top collegiate player in the country.

Ainge did not have much time to savor the honor. He had to report back to Toronto, where his struggles at the plate continued. Doubts now crept into his mind whether he had made the right choice in pursuing a baseball career over basketball. "Basketball was in my blood," he later said. "Giving it up was tough."[106] His reservations only intensified when the Celtics selected him in the second round of the NBA Draft that spring. Ainge felt that was an opportunity he simply could not pass up. He informed the Blue Jays that he was quitting baseball and heading to Boston. The move did not sit well with Toronto management, who proceeded to take legal action against Ainge and the Celtics. "When we signed him, we signed him to one of the tightest, most restrictive contracts in sports," Pat Gillick said. "If they drafted him, it would be infringing upon our deal." The Blue Jays ultimately prevailed in court, forcing the Celtics to cough up $500,000 to free Ainge from his hardball obligations. "We won the case," Gillick said. "We lost the player."[107]

Joining the Celtics for the 1981–82 season, Ainge quickly discovered he was not going to be the next coming of Magic Johnson, let alone Tiny Archibald, who then held a lock on the club's starting point guard position. "I thought I was pretty much a hotshot and I was going to tear the NBA up," Ainge remembered. Then reality hit him like a two-by-four to the head. "One of my first games, Larry had the ball on the wing, and I made a slash to the basket. I thought I had an advantage on the post, so I stopped. Larry just looked at me and goes, 'What are you doing? I have the ball right now. Get out my way. This is my ball game.' So then I did again. At halftime, he started yelling at me. 'Get out of here! What are you doing? When I've got the ball on the wing, you stay over on the weak side, you stay on the weak side. If your man leaves, I'll find you.' So I was humbled right away."[108] Ainge's self-regard took a further beating from Bill Fitch. The crusty, old-school Celtics coach let him know in no uncertain terms that he was a basketball bust, shooting at a rate equivalent to his anemic batting average in Toronto.[109] "He buried me and I became a whipping boy," Ainge said. "I had no confidence for the first time in my life. I had no rhythm. My game was a disaster." One out-of-town writer dubbed him "Danny Aint." "I thought [the nickname] was really funny and clever," Ainge said. "But it was true. I wasn't a player."[110] He averaged only 4.1 points a game that campaign and spent most of his time riding the pine. He modestly increased his scoring output and minutes over the next two seasons but continued to fall short of expectations. "I'm definitely not satisfied," he told writer Steve Barnfeld. "I set goals for myself coming in. There are places I wanted to be. I don't feel I've come as far as I should."[111]

Nevertheless, Ainge's hoops travails were trivial compared to the tragic loss he experienced off the court in his second season. His mother Kay took her life after suffering from years of depression, devastating Ainge and his family. "That was a time in my life where I didn't receive help when I could have used some help," he later said. "I wished I had talked with a counselor to help me deal with it."[112] Interestingly, this was also around the same period that Ainge acquired the reputation for being the "Angry Young Man" of the NBA.[113] Working through some unresolved personal trauma, perhaps? Sam McManis of the *Los Angeles Times* invited such speculation when he wrote the following on the troubled guard for a 1985 feature: "There always seems to be a distressed look on Danny Ainge's face when he's on the basketball court. It varies from merely a wince, when he misses a shot or commits a turnover, to a full-scale scowl when he feels he has suffered an injustice. Maybe that is why Ainge, more than any other Celtic regular, is disliked in every National Basketball Assn. city. Fans, even in his native Utah, boo Ainge. They taunt him. They look at that scowl and can't help themselves."[114] Ainge himself never disclosed the underlying root cause for the behavior, preferring instead to note that other players like Bird and Kareem Abdul-Jabbar made similar emotional displays while competing. "I guess if you're not a superstar, you're not allowed to act like that," he said.[115]

Magic Johnson and Larry Bird taking in the action
STEVE LIPOFSKY LIPOFSKYPHOTO.COM

A successful team: Auerbach and Harry Mangurian
STEVE LIPOFSKY LIPOFSKYPHOTO.COM

Bird at ease
STEVE LIPOFSKY LIPOFSKYPHOTO.COM

A Bird in Flight
STEVE LIPOFSKY LIPOFSKYPHOTO.COM

A familiar sight: Kevin McHale crashing the boards

Battle of the bigs: The Chief vs. Kareem
STEVE LIPOFSKY LIPOFSKYPHOTO.COM

Bird takes a spill

A mediocre defender: Philly's Julius "Dr. J" Erving gets the jump on Bird

Robert Parish tangling with future teammate Bill Walton of the San Diego Clippers

Bernard King: The Eleanor Rigby of Pro Basketball
STEVE LIPOFSKY LIPOFSKYPHOTO.COM

Always looking for an opening: Sydney Moncrief of the Milwaukee Bucks
STEVE LIPOFSKY LIPOFSKYPHOTO.COM

Under the banners at the Old Boston Garden
STEVE LIPOFSKY LIPOFSKYPHOTO.COM

A pensive Pat Riley
STEVE LIPOFSKY LIPOFSKYPHOTO.COM

Keeping their eyes on the prize in Game 7 of the NBA Finals

Kurt Rambis throwing his weight around

Bird caught in some L.A. traffic

An ancient rivalry rekindled
STEVE LIPOFSKY LIPOFSKYPHOTO.COM

Cedric "Cornbread" Maxwell celebrating with Celtic patriarch
Red Auerbach after his spectacular Game 7 performance
STEVE LIPOFSKY LIPOFSKYPHOTO.COM

The archrivals mixing it up
STEVE LIPOFSKY LIPOFSKYPHOTO.COM

CHAPTER SIX

Bucking for Revenge

HOLDING A 3–2 PLAYOFF SERIES EDGE, THE RESURGENT CELTICS JOUR-
neyed back to the Big Apple with the intent of closing out the Knicks
in Game 6, despite having gone winless in their previous two attempts
there. "We just have to come out with our blue collars on and get the
job done," a self-assured Gerald Henderson said.[1] Bernard King was of
a different mind-set. While driving in to Madison Square Garden from
his New Jersey home before tip-off, King suddenly became seized with
the conviction that the Knicks would not lose, could not lose. "I was
determined to carry the team to victory that night," he wrote.[2] King made
good on the pledge, exploding for 44 points in a 106–104 Knicks win
that was not decided until the final buzzer.

"I never would've thought it would come down to a seventh game,"
Kevin McHale said. "But it was the same thing [in New York]. We were
continually behind and we had to use an incredible amount of energy to
come back. And it was such a fragile thing, because every time we'd come
close, they'd get it back up to seven or eight. We fought back and fought
back but couldn't make it all way back."[3] Indeed, after reducing what had
been a 13-point Knicks lead early in the fourth quarter to two with just
six ticks left on the game clock, the Celtics appeared poised to pull out
a dramatic come-from-behind victory or at the very least force an overtime period. Larry Bird, looking to add to his team-leading 35 points,
had the ball in his hands, but his 12-foot bank shot from the right side
bounced off the rim and into the tangled embrace of McHale and Cedric
Maxwell. "I had the ball and had an easy shot," McHale said. "I had an

easy shot, a foot and a half, up and in. Then I saw Max fighting me for it. Didn't know it was me. I decided to let him have it."[4] It was not a wisest of decisions. Maxwell let fly an off-balance prayer that failed to land on target as time expired. "I didn't have control of it all the way," Maxwell explained. "I just got in position to shoot it and thought it might fall in."[5]

The Knicks would live to fight another day. "The burden is squarely on [Boston's] shoulders," King said afterward. "They're supposed to win this series. They won 60 games in the course of the season. This series was not supposed to go as long as this. But it did. And I think the pressure is squarely on their shoulders."[6] "Saint Bernard" received no argument from the other sideline. "It's time to see who chokes," Maxwell said.[7]

Choking had never been part of Larry Bird's lexicon, but even the Hick from French Lick copped to having concerns going into the series-deciding seventh game on Sunday, May 13. "I knew that if Bernard stayed hot, it would go down to the wire," he wrote. "The only thing making me feel good at all was that we were playing in the Boston Garden."[8] Assuredly, the sold-out, ear-splittingly raucous Mother's Day crowd did not let him down. Bird was dominant from the opening frame, accumulating 15 of his game-high 39 points while lifting the Celtics to a 36–26 lead. "Some days everything just clicks and I could tell early in the first quarter I was going to play really well," he related. "I was in the kind of groove where I knew I could do anything I wanted to at any time and my main thought was simply to get myself in a position to receive the ball as often as possible."[9] Bird did not lose that rhythm all afternoon as the Celtics marched to an easy 121–104 victory. Under the headline "Bird is the Word," even the normally unsparing *New York Post* columnist Peter Vecsey found himself gushing like a starstruck 10-year-old fanboy about Bird's performance, which included 12 rebounds, 10 assists, and 3 steals. "Call Boston's semifinal tournament liquidation of New York an 'Ode to Larry Joe,'" he wrote. "Bird was so fervent, so venerable, so sumptuous, so in control and so venomous in raking the Knicks . . . he definitely owes it to himself to renegotiate—with his agent."[10]

M. L. Carr knew something special was in the offing the moment he saw his superstar teammate enter the locker room before warmups: "Usually Larry and I crack jokes on each other and goof around, you know?

But today I stayed away because there was a solemn mood about him. Other guys were loosening up and Max was doing his thing, laughing and jiving, because that's what Max does to get ready, he likes to keep that pressure away, until we reach the floor. But Larry was quiet, as if he had already started to play the game in his head, and when you see that look in his face you simply stay away, because you don't want to break his concentration."[11]

Maintaining his own focus proved problematic for King, thanks to an ugly incident that occurred in the blowout's opening moments. Cutting through the lane, the forward was greeted with a forearm shot to the face by Robert Parish in front of his own bench. Disoriented and furious that no foul was called, King's immediate reaction was to physically retaliate against the 7-footer but then thought better of it. "The Celtics would have liked nothing better," he maintained. "If I got tossed for fighting, it was game over for my team. Parish would have cut the head off a dangerous snake."[12] Regardless, King was a nonfactor the rest of the way, making only 8 of his 17 shot attempts. "He never recovered," Hubie Brown said.[13] But even if King had been able to deliver another Game 6 kind of performance, he later conceded it might not have mattered. As he wrote, "Just as I'd refuse to lose the series in New York, [Bird] was determined not to go down in Boston and brought the full aggregate of his basketball prowess to the court. He rained three-pointers that hit nothing but net. He passed the ball off the dribble like Pistol Pete Maravich in his prime. He controlled the game's tempo and would not be denied."[14]

With the Knicks out of the way, the Celtics advanced to the Eastern Conference Finals, where the Milwaukee Bucks—the same squad that had ignominiously swept them 4–0 the previous spring—awaited. Wrote the *Globe*'s Dan Shaughnessy, "You've heard of the Revenge of Dracula, Montezuma's Revenge and the *Revenge of the Pink Panther*. Well, prepare for the Revenge of the Celtics." Only the team professed not to see it that way. "I don't think revenge will be as much of a factor as everybody is saying," Cedric Maxwell contended. "That's basically for other people to say. A lot of the revenge factor is missing with Bill [Fitch] gone and some of the others who are gone. I think we'd like to beat them, but not necessarily because they beat us last year."[15] M. L. Carr appeared to accede to this viewpoint as well. "We're not out for revenge," he said. "We're out to win a championship. They just happen to be the next team in our way."[16] Whether these soft-pedaling comments were genuine, there was no denying that the Bucks were a talented veteran ballclub under the leadership of former Celtic Don Nelson, having won 50 games on the regular season while making their second straight trip to the conference championship with playoff victories over the Atlanta Hawks and New Jersey Nets. They meant business, especially with their own Midwestern version of the Big Three in forward Marques Johnson (20.7 points per game), guard Sidney Moncrief (20.9) and Hall of Fame–bound center Bob Lanier.

A third overall pick in the 1977 NBA draft, Johnson was blessed with graceful athleticism and a nose for the basket that made him a dangerous threat to score anywhere from the floor. "He has an incredible feel for where he is in traffic," said former Bucks assistant coach Dave Wohl. "He'd drive the baseline, disappear into a tangle of bodies under the hoop, and somehow find the invisible seam between defenders and make the shot. When you first see it, you say, 'Well, it was a lucky shot.' But after a while, he keeps doing it. Unbelievable."[17]

Marques Kevin Johnson's basketball roots stretched back to the predominantly African American community of South Central Los Angeles of the late 1960s, where he learned to play the game from his father, Jeff, a local high school math teacher who named his son after the great Harlem Globetrotters point guard Marques Haynes. Every day Jeff Johnson drilled the future NBA star on the fundamentals of the game on a concrete basketball court he had constructed in the backyard. So late and noisome did many of these sessions become that their neighbors grew upset, complaining that the sound of the ball constantly bouncing prevented them from getting a good night's sleep. Marques gave it no thought. "[My father] took the time to teach me the right way, but he also made it enjoyable," he said. "We always played one-on-one in the end and it wasn't until I was an 11th grader that I finally beat him. He was only 5–11, but was a real dirty player." And Johnson was just warming up. He was named Los Angeles High School Player of the Year in 1973 and was tapped by legendary college basketball coach John Wooden to play

for a great UCLA team that was led by future Hall of Fame center Bill
Walton. "I made the statement when we recruited Marques that he very
well could be the finest forward UCLA ever had," Wooden later said.
"He very definitely was one of the best, only had him for two years, but
you could see that he was developing into an excellent forward."[18] By his
sophomore year, Johnson rewarded Wooden's faith in him by taking the
Bruins to the 1975 NCAA championship in what became the "Wizard
of Westwood's" swan song season. Johnson earned College Player of
the Year honors two years later under new coach Gene Bartow before
the Bucks snatched him up as the number three overall pick in the
1977 NBA Draft.

Although initially not crazy about having to perform in conservative, white bread Milwaukee ("I was pretty lonely and I stayed in my
apartment a lot and watched TV," he said), Johnson was slowly able to
adapt.[19] It helped that he had a former five-time NBA champion in Don
Nelson as coach. He knew all the preparations and nitty-gritty details
necessary to sustain a long and successful career. "Nelson worked a lot
with me," the 6–7 wingman said. "He showed me some things about
shooting that I'd never been told before. Not that he changed my method
of shooting: he just refined my release so I got the ball away the same way
every time. I was a good shooter in college at times, but I was very spo-
radic. Now I study films of myself in games, so I know right away when
I'm doing something wrong."[20] Johnson did not do many things wrong
on the court, scoring 20 points or better in five of his first seven seasons,
making him one of the elite offensive forces in the league. "He's great in a
different way than Bernard King," Cedric Maxwell said. "He creates even
more problems. He doesn't post up as much, but he drives better and has
more range and quickness."[21]

These latter qualities also made him a beast on the offensive glass
and an adroit defender. Yet his most underrated skill might have been
his ability to create as a playmaker, taking advantage of his superior ball-
handling skills and intelligence. In fact, Johnson is credited with coining
the now broadly used term "point forward" during Milwaukee's earlier
playoff series win against New Jersey. "Their pressure was killing us," he
recalled. "So Nellie . . . told me he had a new approach offensively. He

wanted me to kind of bring the ball up the court and set up the offense. Johnson immediately grasped what was being asked of him. "So instead of a point guard, I'm like a 'point forward,'" he told Nelson. A big lightbulb went on above Nelson's head. "Yeah, you're my point forward," he said. "I like that. My point forward."[22]

Sidney Moncrief was the "other" guard in the 1979 NBA draft that the Los Angeles Lakers almost took over Magic Johnson as the number one pick. "Life is funny," Moncrief later said of the episode. "One decision—any decision—can change everything." Indeed, instead of going to glamorous Tinseltown, "Sir Sid" ended up in drab Brew City where the beer was cold and the winters colder. Moncrief, though, claimed to have no regrets. "Honestly, I didn't have a strong preference," he claimed. "Detroit, Chicago, Milwaukee, Los Angeles and New York all expressed interest, and only L.A. was warm. So I guess that was preferable. But, really, I just wanted to be drafted."[23]

While Magic was heroically leading the Lakers to their first championship since 1972, Moncrief experienced a bumpier ride that rookie year, fighting for playing time in the Milwaukee backcourt and averaging less than 10 points. "I came into this league not knowing if I could really make it," he admitted. "A lot of players come in rocky, thinking they will be an All-Star. I came in a little scared. Really. I came in hungry, but I tried to progress slowly to make sure I did not peak in my first or second year. I wanted to peak later on in my career."[24]

Moncrief did not have long to wait. By his third season, the sleek 6–4, 183-pound post-up guard with a gap-smooth smile had become a key member of Milwaukee's starting rotation, leading the club in scoring (19.8 points), rebounds (6.7), and assists (4.8) and minutes played per game (37.7) while earning the first of five career NBA All-Star selections. "In the past, he was a blender," Nelson said. "He would fit into the tempo of the game, and we didn't call on him to dominate. We knew how good he was, but his ability was hidden to a certain extent because of the way he was called on to play." Those days were long over. "Now we like to have the ball in his hands. We want him to handle the ball early in the play, and we also want him to have it at the end of the play. He does everything for us now."[25] And that was just on the offensive side. Moncrief also proved himself to be a tenacious lockdown defender, assigned to cover the opposition's best, including the GOAT himself. "When you play against Moncrief," rookie Michael Jordan said in a 1986 interview, "he'll hound you everywhere you go, both ends of the court. You just expect it."[26]

Sidney Alvin Moncrief came of age in a struggling black single-parent household in East Little Rock, Arkansas, during an uncertain period in the late 1960s when the traditional barriers of legal segregation were beating a slow, steady retreat throughout the "Toothpick State" and the rest of the old Confederate South. White resistance to the change was often quite fierce and violent, but greater social, economic, and political opportunities opened up for many of the region's blacks. Just not for Moncrief's mother, Bernice Perkins. She labored long, arduous hours at low pay as a hotel maid, exhibiting a gritty stoicism that was not lost on her son. "As tired as she was," Moncrief told *Sports Illustrated*, "she always took the time for discipline. She never let conditions defeat her. I had to do things right or do them over until they were right."[27]

This no-excuses approach paid off for the future NBA star in high school as he overcame early classroom struggles to become an honor roll student and achieve academic eligibility to play basketball at the University of Arkansas.[28] "You've got to have confidence in yourself and I do," he explained.[29] In college, Moncrief distinguished himself further by becoming one of the best college players in the country and lifting what had been a mediocre program upon his arrival on campus to three Southwest Conference championships and a NCAA Final Four appearance in 1978. He might have made it to another Final Four the following year, but the Razorbacks were edged out by Larry Bird's Indiana State Sycamores in the Midwest Regional.

Still, Moncrief earned high praise for the superb defensive job he performed on Bird in the closing 10 minutes of the contest when Arkansas coach Eddie Sutton decided out of desperation to put him on the explosive forward. The result? A stymied Bird was limited to a pair of field goals. "I was more of a scorer in college but [Moncrief] still did a number of me," Bird recalled. "He does everything you're supposed to do on defense and doesn't take any short cuts. Plus he does it every night."[30] Of course, it helped that Moncrief had the leaping ability of a kangaroo treading on hot coals, making it extremely difficult for opponents to shoot over him. "I do it by timing, which I've developed by certain drills I do," Moncrief revealed. "During the summertime I have a drill in which I hit the floor with the ball and then dunk it. I do it ten times maybe once or twice a day. That helps my timing, and also my quickness."[31] Such obsessive commitment to personal improvement was the hallmark of Moncrief's greatness, according to Sutton, who coached the Razorbacks from 1974 to 1985. "Sidney has always had the big valentine," he said. "He played so hard it just made the whole state proud."[32] Presumably, Moncrief induced Bucks fans to feel the same way.

Johnson and Moncrief were at or near their primes, but Bob Lanier was well past his, struggling with bad knees and declining production. Nonetheless, Lanier—"Milwaukee's samurai warrior," according to hoop maven Bob Ryan—was still a formidable presence in the pivot, capable of giving the Bucks a double-double in games.[33] The problem was that such performances had gotten fewer and far between. Don Nelson preferred to take a glass-half-full perspective. "Bob Lanier is doing a hell of a job," the coach insisted before the playoff opener with Boston. "I can't ask any more than he's given me."[34] Against the Nets in the conference semifinal, the 35-year-old led all Bucks starters in field goal percentage (.552) and rebounds (46) while keeping in step with the younger and more explosive Darryl Dawkins. "As far as I know," Robert Parish said, "Lanier has had a great year. He really knows how to protect himself . . . he stays close to the hoop. He'll give anyone trouble because he's got a strong inside game."[35]

Born and raised in Buffalo, New York, during the economic boom times following World War II, Robert Jerry Lanier Jr. appeared an unlikely candidate to become a professional athlete. Although he had sprouted to 6–8 in his early teen years, he was so awkward and clumsy that his high-school basketball coach told him thanks but no thanks when he tried out for the team in his sophomore year. That did it. Being cut "inspired me," Lanier said later.[36] Going to a local gym where he labored around the clock on his game, he was able to progress enough as a player to go back to a new coach a year later and secure a spot on the varsity. He had learned such nose-to-the-grindstone perseverance from his demanding father Robert Lanier Sr., who owned a local trucking and hauling business. "My dad was about work," Lanier remembered. "He came from a family of 12 and had a fifth-grade education and couldn't read. You could not please him. But my dad was instrumental in my life with sports. He'd be one of the dads that would always take us to the games. He was always there. We weren't well-to-do, but we weren't suffering."[37]

Upon graduation, Lanier accepted a basketball scholarship from St. Bonaventure University, a small Franciscan school south of Buffalo in rural Allegany, New York. In three seasons with the team, "Buffalo Bob" averaged 27.6 points and 15.7 rebounds and transformed the Bonnies into a major collegiate powerhouse, leading them to a 25–3 record and a Final Four appearance in the 1970 NCAA tournament. He was at the top of the wish list for every pro team, including the then New York Nets of the ABA whose owner, Roy Boe, earlier had offered him $1.2 million to quit school and join his club. Lanier's father was adamantly opposed. "Stay in college and get your degree," he instructed his son. "I know you're gonna be a superstar but I don't want you to be a *dumb* super-star."[38] Lanier followed Bob Sr.'s advice and earned a bachelor of science diploma in business administration.

Next stop was the NBA, where the Detroit Pistons made him their top selection in the 1970 draft. Still feeling the lingering effects of a knee injury that he had sustained at the end of his final season with St. Bonaventure, Lanier struggled in his rookie year. "It was a year that was an embarrassment," he lamented. "If I had been smart, I wouldn't have played that year."[39] Many in Detroit viewed him as a disappointing bust, but the hulking 6–10, 250-pound center with a shoe size 22 dispelled their doubts over the next nine seasons, becoming a seven-time All-Star and averaging more than 20 points and 10 rebounds a game. "He understood the small nuances of the game," teammate Dave Bing said. "He could shoot the 18- to 20-footer as any guard. He had a hook shot—nobody but Kareem had a hook shot like him. He could do anything he wanted to do."[40] What he could not do was make the Pistons into title contenders. The organization was perennially out of the playoff mix due to poor coaching, a dysfunctional front office, and an ingrained loser mentality. It all got to be too much for Lanier. "The whole idea in this sport is sacrifice—getting players to think about 'we' instead of 'I,'" Lanier once reflected. "Just one time I was on a Detroit team that thought 'we,' and we won 52 games. The next year six of those players were gone. That's the story of this franchise."[41]

Lanier finally caught a break in the middle of the 1980–81 season when the Bucks acquired him in a trade for underachieving center Kent Benson and a first-round draft pick. "We feel Bob is just exactly what our team needs," a jubilant Don Nelson told reporters. "When you feel you're close to being a contender, you have to make the move that will make you one."[42] Lanier came as advertised, boosting the Bucks to the 60-win level and pacing them on several deep playoff runs. "Bob makes us all better players," Marques Johnson said. "He told me, for example, I should wait another beat before I roll off when he sticks a pick for me. Boom! I'm clearer to get a pass for a shot than I ever was before. And talk about intimidating. He can just scowl at somebody and it makes an impact."[43] The Bucks were hoping Lanier had enough left in the tank to have a similar effect on the Celtics.

Fat chance of that happening. The intrepid Cs held Lanier to two points while overwhelming Milwaukee, 119–96, to take the first game of the conference final at Boston Garden on Tuesday, May 15. "It just seemed like we were out of synch offensively, like we couldn't get things going," said Lanier, the focal point of Celtics double-teams all contest.[44] For sure, the Bucks shot a sluggish 42 percent from the floor, with Sidney Moncrief and Marques Johnson connecting on only 13 of their combined 29 shots.

"We came out lethargic," Johnson acknowledged. "And it was something that carried over for the rest of the game We tried to slow the pace down, but that kind of backfired. . . . We were flat. We didn't have a particularly good performance from anybody." There was little evidence of inertia on the Celtics side, even though the team was coming off an emotionally draining, seven-game tilt with the Knicks just two days prior. They pushed the ball up-court every chance they got, forcing the Bucks out of their normal rhythm to open up several Boston fast-break scoring opportunities. Larry Bird finished with a tidily efficient line of 24 points, 6 rebounds, and 5 assists with Cedric Maxwell and Robert Parish contributing 17 points apiece. Each team had 11 turnovers. "We were just a little less sloppy than they were," Bird assessed afterward. "There's no reason for us to feel cocky because of this, that's for sure. We got by, that's all."[45]

Things continued to trend positively in Boston's direction for Game 2. Five Celtics scored in double figures while Bird (32 points) gave another master class on offense to crush the Bucks, 125–110, to take a 2–0 series lead. "We came in here with confidence," declared an exasperated Marques Johnson, Milwaukee's leading scorer with 29 points. "But to be beaten as badly as we've been beaten? We need a team meeting, a chapel service, or something to get our spirits back up. I think everybody is down right now. They basically kicked our behinds these past two games." Everything that could seemingly go wrong did go wrong for the Bucks, including Don Nelson's short-lived defensive strategy of putting inconsistent, 6–11 third-year power forward Alton Lister on Kevin McHale (24 points) early in the contest. McHale, named the league's Sixth Man of the Year just before the start of the series, responded to Lister in the same manner as a shark would to chum in the water—he devoured him whole, reeling off six points in rapid succession to send a befuddled Nelson back to the coaching drawing board. "The idea was I would match up with McHale [in terms of height]," Lister explained. "It's really hard to tell what happened, it happened so fast. All I know is it didn't work out."[46]

Neither did the match up that pitted Sidney Moncrief against fellow All-Star guard Dennis Johnson. Johnson lit up Moncrief for 26 points on 9 for 17 shooting. "DJ likes big challenges," McHale said. "Tonight was just another one of those times. Moncrief was in foul trouble and DJ just fought for position down low. He wanted the ball. He wanted to post up, and just took it to him."[47] Moncrief did not dispute the analysis. "DJ had a great game," he said. "He makes them a better ballclub."[48] In point of fact, Johnson's performance throughout the entire postseason—averaging more than 15 points a game with All-NBA caliber defense—conjured memories of 1979, when his star turn in that year's Finals as a member of the Seattle SuperSonics earned him an MVP trophy. Johnson had a simple explanation to reporters when the subject of his elevated play came up. "I guess at this point, everybody's adrenalin[e] is at a much higher level," he said. "If you're on a team with a legitimate shot at the championship, it always makes you work that much harder. I think experience helps. There's not many times the pressure's gonna get to me."[49]

Dennis Wayne Johnson had not always been so confident. As a diffident, undersized high-school point guard, Johnson had competed for varsity playing time with fellow teammate and future major league outfielder Ken Landreaux in the bright sunny climes of Compton, California. Once a thriving middle-class black community located a few miles south of downtown Los Angeles, Compton had fallen on hard economic and social times by the time Johnson reached adolescence in the early 1970s, the eighth of 16 children born to a stone mason and a social worker. Deindustrialization, surging unemployment, gang violence, and the defunding of beneficial Great Society antipoverty programs had all taken their toll. In spite of that, Johnson maintained that he had a relatively happy, if imperfect childhood. "We weren't rich, but I wouldn't call us poor, either," he once told an interviewer. "I guess you could say we were scraping by, just like everybody else. I know sometimes I'd ask for a quarter and my mom would give me one. I'd get some candy, go home, hide it, and eat it later. Sometimes I had pants with a hole in the knee." When Christmas rolled around, however, there were always gifts under the tree, whether they be a new pair of Chuck Taylor high-tops or a crisp new shirt. "My father worked a little longer and a little harder and we'd have some money to buy presents," Johnson said.[50]

DJ was not so fortunate on the basketball court. At 5–9 and possessing the speed of an aging tortoise with mobility issues, he was lucky to see more than a fleeting minute or two of action as a senior. "It was like a challenge," he said. "I had to prove to myself I could play."[51] But with no college recruiters lining up on his doorstep, his options were limited after graduation. In lieu of this sobering reality, he decided to take a job as a forklift operator at a local warehouse for $2.75 an hour while spending the bulk of his off-hours playing in a rough-and-tumble summer recreation league. "At the time, [defense] was the only thing I knew how to do," Johnson said. "Run up and try to steal a couple of balls. That was how I got my points. I wasn't no great shooter."[52] But good enough to attract the notice of Jim White, the struggling head coach of Los Angeles Harbor College, a two-year community college in neighboring Wilmington. "Actually," White remembered, "a referee saw him score 44 once and told us about him. In that league, once you scored 20, there'd always be some guys who'd make sure you didn't score anymore. Knowing that, we were even more impressed with Dennis."[53]

And why wouldn't they be? Johnson had shot up several inches in height and exhibited a gritty new edge to his game, raw though it was. "He was totally undisciplined," White said. "But God, he could do some great things. He had the same sense of timing Jerry West had."[54] Johnson did not need much coaxing from White to enroll at Harbor, where he ended up averaging 15 points and 10 boards while leading his team to a junior college state title his second season. "He turned our program around," White said.[55] But this success was not arrived at easily. Johnson was often a disciplinary problem, blowing off practices and prone to outbursts of anger on and off the floor. He also took a decidedly laissez-faire attitude toward his academic studies. White did his best to curb these tendencies, especially when it came to hitting the books. "What we did was make sure he did some of his schoolwork," the coach said. "We got a room here on campus. My assistant talked to all the teachers. We guaranteed he'd do his work. We checked on him every day. For three or four weeks, we had him spend two hours a day in there studying. . . . Before that, he got through school by hook or crook."[56]

Johnson moved on to Division I Pepperdine University from Harbor and once again demonstrated his basketball worth by helping the Wave to a 22–6 record and a berth in the 1976 NCAA Tournament. Although Pepperdine was ousted by a higher-ranked UCLA team featuring Marques Johnson in the second round of the West Regionals, Johnson received accolades for his overall fine defensive play, particularly when he made a spectacular block on an attempted turnaround jumper by 7–2 Bruins center Ralph Drollinger. "After the game," Johnson recalled, "we're going back to the hotel and these agents were coming up to me and asking what I was going to do."[57] In his mind, the answer was obvious and unequivocal. He was returning to Pepperdine for another year. At least that was the plan until the Seattle SuperSonics—at the direction of head coach and former Celtics great Bill Russell—unexpectedly selected him early in the second round of that spring's NBA Draft. The hard-knocks kid from Compton saw this as a thrilling, once-in-a-lifetime opportunity he could not refuse. But sticking with the Sonics was an altogether different matter, as Johnson had to outbattle former Washington State star shooting guard Norton Barnhill for the final roster spot. "Barnhill was a great player and we were both running, diving, and doing what rookies do," Johnson said. "Finally, Russ picked my defense over Barnhill's offense."[58]

Johnson saw significant action in the backcourt that first season, subbing for veteran starters Slick Watts and "Downtown" Fred Brown. He scored just shy of 10 points a game in what turned out to be Russell's final year behind the Seattle bench. "I wasn't sure I belonged," Johnson later reflected to author Michael D. McClellan. "Having Bill Russell as my coach was intimidating, but he did a good job of pulling me aside and pointing things out. We talked a lot. That's how I started learning the pro game, and my defense became very good. I started analyzing other players' moves and tendencies and figuring out how to counter them."[59] What Russell could not provide his impressionable, freckle-faced protégé with reddish hair was valuable postseason experience as the Sonics fell short of the playoffs by a single game. Johnson was not all that surprised. "We didn't have a team," he said. "We had a cast. Let's just say that a lot of guys were not enthused about winning and played only for themselves."[60] A bored and increasingly disengaged Russell did not exactly foster team unity either, constantly demeaning his players with sarcastic comments and a smug, condescending attitude. "You're all assholes," he told them.[61]

The situation greatly improved in the seasons to follow with the arrival of Lenny Wilkens as head coach. A former nine-time NBA All-Star point guard who had led the league in assists in 1970, Wilkens played a central role in molding the Sonics into serious playoff contenders. "Lenny got more involved in the offense by running me into the low post," Johnson said. "He also encouraged me to take the dribble to the hole. Overall, Lenny got us together as a team."[62] By the '79 Finals,

Johnson and the Sonics were finally ready to have their champagne shower, beating the Washington Bullets in five games. Although he had been crowned Finals MVP after averaging 22.6 points a game, the season had been a challenging one for Johnson due to an ongoing contract dispute with club management. For sure, his sense of frustration spilled over onto the floor the following year. "Dennis would often dog it," said a teammate. "He'd walk the ball up-court when we needed to run. He'd force shots and try to squeeze his dribble through traffic. He thought that scoring more points would earn him more money and he was very difficult to play with. Then he'd complain that nobody passed to *him*. But I must admit, whatever his mood, Dennis was always dynamic in the clutch."[63]

The sullen behavior and inconsistent play did not end when the Sonics finally rewarded him with a lucrative new pact. His once solid relationship with Wilkens deteriorated to the point where Wilkens thought it best to part ways with his star guard following the 1979–80 season. Johnson, whom Wilkens had uncharitably labeled a clubhouse "cancer," was traded to the Phoenix Suns for former Celtic Paul Westphal.[64]

Johnson always maintained that his differences with Wilkens were overblown. "Sure, Lenny and I got into some heated arguments," he once offered. "Maybe I missed a couple of people or took some shots I shouldn't have. That's all it ever was."[65] With Phoenix, Johnson made two All-Star teams and cemented his reputation for being one of the finest all-around backcourt talents in the business. "Before Magic Johnson came into the game and reinvented the guard position," Hall of Fame center and future Boston teammate Bill Walton posited, "Dennis Johnson had been the best guard in the league for a number of years. His teams *won* the damn game. He could move, defend, pass, and he had leadership qualities. There was none better."[66] Yet, as was the case with Seattle, Johnson clashed with the Phoenix coaching staff and front office to the point where the team was willing to give him away for pennies on the dollar to Boston for the forgettable Rick Robey. Johnson could not have been happier. "I think anybody would feel great being traded here," Johnson enthused afterward. "Anybody would want to be part of this team [with the winning interaction of Bird, McHale, and Parish]. That's not the way it is with every team. I don't have more pressure with this team than any other one, it's just that everybody seems to notice you."[67] Johnson still had his momentary lapses of misbehavior. He would get angry at Jones or some teammate for a perceived slight and moodily retreat into a shell. "But," noted Danny Ainge, "DJ would always come around. He might hurt our chemistry, and crazy stuff would happen for that game. But then the next day was an apology, and the next day was fun and games. He had a great personality, sense of humor, and it was really easy to get him back. And I would take him on my team."[68]

The Bucks finally gave the Celtics a competitive contest in Game 3, but the results were the same. Overcoming a 15-point deficit early in the second half, the Celtics rallied behind Larry Bird to escape with a physical 109–100 road win at the aging, barrel-roofed Metropolitan Milwaukee Exposition and Convention Center and Arena, otherwise known as the MECCA to fans and players alike. "I got banged around more in this game than I have in most games this year," Bird complained afterward to *Globe* columnist Will McDonough. "But their banging wasn't vicious. They weren't out to hurt me, like some teams. As long as they don't undercut me and things like that, I can deal with it. But they did let me know all afternoon they were going to double-team me. Every time I made a move there was someone there to push or shove me." An enraged Bird finally had enough by the beginning of the fourth quarter and went on a tear, scoring 11 of his team-leading 28 points in helping the Celtics pull away. "When Larry wheeled in . . . we knew that was it," commented M. L. Carr. "We knew he was really ticked off at what was happening to him." That was especially true at the 4:33 mark when Bird raced down the baseline to deliver a rim-rattling, adrenaline-fueled reverse dunk. "With the dunk I just wanted to do something with authority," the forward said. "I do not like to dunk the ball, but that time I wanted to do it." The play helped take the air out of Milwaukee's sails and force Don Nelson to figuratively hang his head. "What is there about Larry Bird that hasn't been said before?" bemoaned the Bucks coach. "He just took over the game at the end."[69]

Now one win away from completing a sweep, the Celtics brimmed with confidence heading into Game 4, which was scheduled to get underway at the MECCA on Monday, May 21. "It's a nice feeling," Parish said. "I think it's the first time since we clinched best record in the regular season that there is absolutely no pressure."[70] In point of fact, the pressure was all on their opponents, who were seeking to avoid the embarrassment of an early playoff exit—a complete role reversal from the situation the two clubs faced the previous spring. "We know what it's like to be down 3–0," McHale said. "It's really a fragile feeling. You start thinking about all kinds of things. You feel vulnerable. You try to wipe 3–0 out of your mind and get back into it by increments—win the first quarter, the second quarter and so on—but it's very hard to do."[71] Maxwell agreed. "It'll be worse for them; they're at home. They'll be tighter than us. They've got to be a little cautious."[72] Even the Bucks appeared to concede the point. "Seems like it would take a miracle, huh?" Bob Lanier confided to a Boston reporter.[73]

Whether it was by divine intervention or some other, more earthly reason, the Bucks were able to pull out a 122–113 victory to keep the brooms at bay and send the series back to Boston. "The Bucks played very well, from their starters right down to their bench," M. L. Carr said. "You could sense they were ready. We were like the little kid who teases a Doberman who is on a chain. I guess we wandered a little too close and got bit." The dog, or in this instance, the Buck with the biggest bite was Bob Lanier. "The Great Grabber," as the Celtics called him, scored 15 points while frustrating Parish (six points on two for seven shooting) on the offensive end. "Chief just got manhandled by Lanier," Maxwell said. "He'd get the ball four feet from the basket and by the time Lanier finished pushing and holding, Robert ended up with a 15-foot shot." Unsurprisingly, the Bucks came away with a somewhat different take. "Bob Lanier wanted this game tonight," Bucks backup center Paul Mokeski said. "He kind of picked us all up."[74]

Bird—a game-leading 32 points with 10 rebounds and 8 assists—did everything short of handing out towels from the bench to keep the Celtics in the game, but he received little help from the rest of the team apart from Maxwell and Gerald Henderson, who each had 18 points. McHale was the biggest disappointment here, making only two shots from the field and looking out of sorts all evening. "I should have stayed in the hotel and put on a movie," McHale said. "It seemed like everything I threw up came back at me. The worse things went, the harder I had to work, and the harder I worked, the worse things went."[75]

The Celtics regained their bearings two nights later at the Garden, delivering a 115–108 death blow to the Bucks that earned them their second Eastern Conference title in four seasons and a berth in the NBA Finals against the Los Angeles Lakers, the soon-to-be-crowned Western Conference champions. "I'm relieved," K. C. Jones said. "If we'd lost this ballgame we'd have been in trouble, because I felt if we went back to Milwaukee, we'd have been in for a seven-game series, and anything could happen in a seventh game."[76] To ensure that that outcome did not come to pass, the Celtics went to their inside power game, making 29 of their 34 baskets in the first three quarters on an array of layups and jams, much to the delight of the deafening sold-out home crowd. "The place was really rocking," said Gerald Henderson (17 points), who was among five Celtics to score 15 points or better. "I was just happy the noise didn't bring the rats out."[77]

What it did bring out instead was the best in Larry Bird with another MVP-like performance of 21 points, 13 rebounds, and 4 assists. "We got a lot of easy shots because we made things happen on offense," Bird said. "We didn't do that well in Milwaukee, even in the game we won, but tonight we kept moving, we got the right men posted up at the right time and we didn't let Milwaukee double up with any amount of success."[78] The key sequence in the contest occurred in the middle of the third quarter when the Celtics went on a 13–0 run to take a 20-point lead. Dennis Johnson threw a dart to Maxwell under the basket, which the North Carolinian then shuffled to Parish for a two-handed dunk that brought the building to its collective feet. "For a split second I saw Robert, and I just knew he would be there," Maxwell said. "I can pat myself on the back and say it was a great pass, though I'm not Larry Bird. But it was that chain reaction of moving the ball, one of the greatest moments all night, because it got everyone involved, including the crowd."[79] To their credit, the Bucks battled back late in the fourth quarter, getting to within seven points with 2:52 left. But Henderson put the brakes on Milwaukee's comeback with a clutch jumper and a smart feed to an open

Maxwell (19 points) in the paint for the conversion. The Bucks began making their offseason plans at that point while Jones could breathe a little easier from the Boston bench. "When the lead got up to 20, we started to relax," the Celtics coach said afterward. "We acted like it was over and played some very ugly basketball."[80]

Indeed, it was the sort of lackadaisical effort the Celtics could ill afford against the battle-tested, purple and gold high-wire act they would be facing in the upcoming championship round.

CHAPTER SEVEN

Showtime

THE LAST TIME THE CELTICS HAD MET THE LAKERS IN A BEST-OF-seven championship series, the country was embroiled in an unpopular land war in Southeast Asia, the Beatles were on the verge of breaking up, and Neil Armstrong and his intrepid Apollo 11 crewmates were in final preparations for a historic landing on the moon. Fifteen years later, the country was at peace, the surviving Beatles band members were enjoying highly successful solo careers, and no astronaut had visited our planet's closest celestial neighbor in more than a decade. One thing did remain unchanged, however. The Lakers were still looking to defeat their greatest rivals on pro basketball's biggest stage.

Going back to 1959 when the franchise had yet to make the fateful jump from Minneapolis to Los Angeles, the Lakers had gone toe to toe with the Celtics seven times in the NBA Finals, and each time they had come away disappointed. There were always good reasons. In 1962, guard Frank Selvy missed a crucial jumper as time ran out in Game 7 that would have put the Lakers over the top. "I'm sure poor Frank still wakes up in the middle of the night and sees the ball hit the rim and go up," Celtics Hall of Famer Bob Cousy recalled. "I was so relieved. I don't think Frank had missed that shot since 1928."[1] Three years later, the team attempted to make do without the services of high-scoring forward Elgin Baylor, who had severely injured his knee at the start of the play-offs following a fantastic regular season in which he averaged 27 points. The result? Boston in five games. Finally in 1969, the Lakers suffered the most devastating loss of all. In another tense seventh-game standoff, the

Celtics were able to pull out a last-minute victory on a "ridiculous rim shot" by future Hall of Fame coach Don Nelson at the "Fabulous Forum," the Lakers' palatial home arena in the neighboring city of Inglewood that then team owner Jack Kent Cooke had erected with considerable fanfare two years earlier. "Sometimes luck does play a part," Nelson said. Luck and overconfidence. For prior to the contest, the Celtics learned that a smug Cooke had planned an over-the-top postgame celebration involving thousands of balloons being released from the rafters in the certain event of a Lakers victory. Bill Russell and Co. could not have asked for better motivation. A humiliated Cooke ended up sending the unused balloons to a local children's hospital. "The kids had a great time with them," he said, "certainly a better time than I did."[2]

No balloons were in sight when the Lakers deplaned in Boston after a long flight from the West Coast on the eve of Game 1 of the 1984 Finals. Now known as the "Showtime Lakers" for their fast-breaking offense led by resident superstar Magic Johnson, the team was coming off a surprisingly close six-game matchup with the Phoenix Suns in the Western Conference Finals in which All-Star Phoenix shooting guard Walter Davis—a former Olympic gold medalist and first-round draft pick out of the University of North Carolina at Chapel Hill—had shredded the Laker defenders with 24 points a game. "It took a lot of effort to beat Phoenix," said Laker forward James Worthy, "but it will take a double or triple effort to beat Boston."[3] Indeed, billed as underdogs by many to win the championship, the Lakers were in need of more than just the sweat off their collective brows to bump off the Celtics. They required another big playoff out of Johnson, whose offensive numbers on the year stood out with 12 triple-doubles and a career-high 875 assists, as well as a significant contribution from 37-year-old center Kareem Abdul-Jabbar, a three-time NBA champion.

Although less spry than he had been in his glorious prime with the Milwaukee Bucks in the 1970s, Abdul-Jabbar was nevertheless a major headache for any opponent trying to defend him with his signature sky-hook—an unorthodox shot involving the full extension of his shooting arm above hishead with a fluid sweeping motion toward the basket from a perpendicular angle. He had copiously employed this unique offensive weapon over the years to surpass Wilt Chamberlain's NBA all-time career scoring mark of 31,419 points in April. "If anyone deserves to break the record, it's definitely him," a magnanimous Chamberlain said at the time. "It's no fluke of a record. It's something that took a lot of years, a lot of time, a lot of two and three guys hanging on him—and he has done it."[4]

Kareem Abdul-Jabbar was born in New York City on April 16, 1947, at the height of the postwar economic boom in American society. Named after his jazz musician turned transit cop father, Ferdinand Lewis Alcindor Jr. grew up in a tight working-class Catholic household in upper Manhattan that placed a premium on education. "My father was interested in my report cards, and my mother [the former Cora Lillian] was vitally concerned," Abdul-Jabbar remembered. "She wanted the best of everything—for her, for me, for our family—and saw schooling as the key to my future."[5]

Abdul-Jabbar did his best to live up to his parents' expectations, performing well in the classroom and showing real talent as a writer. But it was on a basketball court where he really excelled. At nearby Power Memorial Academy, an all-boys Catholic high school, he became the stuff of legend, scoring 2,067 points overall while ushering his team to 71 straight wins and 3 city Catholic championships. The game came easily to him and he attracted the attention of the game's heavyweights like Wilt Chamberlain, who frequently took him out to dinner and invited him over to his home. "I went up there about a dozen times," Abdul-Jabbar confirmed. "He had the most beautiful women in the *world* up there. Every time there'd be this I-mean-stunning woman in a Danskin. And there I'm 17 years old and just dying—in the *throes* of puberty—and here are all these beautiful women."[6]

On a more serious side, Abdul-Jabbar also found himself confronting the ugly face of racism up close and personal when his Power Memorial coach—Jack Donohue—called him "a nigger" in the middle of a game during his junior year, supposedly, so Donohue later claimed, to "motivate" him.[7] "He meant I'd been playing lazy and slow, like something and someone I didn't want to be," Abdul-Jabbar later reflected. "But was that what he thought about blacks? Was I shiftless, too, couldn't be trusted with the game? Didn't I smile enough fo' the fans? Should be twirling the basketball like an ol' watermelon?"[8] Understandably, Abdul-Jabbar lost all respect for his coach and contemplated transferring to another school but thought better of it when he realized he would lose a year of eligibility. "I was trapped," he wrote.[9]

As his illustrious schoolboy career drew to a close, Abdul-Jabbar decided to attend the University of California at Los Angeles over the hundreds of other schools recruiting him for the opportunity to play under legendary basketball coach John Wooden. Already a two-time national champion by the time Abdul-Jabbar arrived on campus in the fall of 1965, Wooden had impressed the eager young phenom with his straightforward personality and emphasis on academics over athletics. "He was more concerned about our long-term happiness than our won-loss record," Abdul-Jabbar noted. "He didn't treat me as a basketball player, but as a student who would be playing basketball on the side."[10] Nevertheless, there was no denying Abdul-Jabbar's remarkable ability between the baselines as he averaged 26.2 points and 15.5 boards a game while leading the Bruins to three straight NCAA titles from 1967 to 1969. But he also became a figure of immense controversy when he joined 50 other black athletes in boycotting the 1968 Olympics over the longstanding mistreatment of people of color in America. "That was the first time that something like that was ever really tried," Abdul-Jabbar said in a 1975 *Ebony* magazine interview. "Being a young man, you're so tired of looking back on our history and seeing that people haven't done anything, and that they were never going to find out something worked because they wouldn't do anything. 'Niggas' just sit around and talk and say 'this might' and 'that might' and 'maybe' and 'wait' and 'plan.' So this was something we could do. We *could do it!*"[11] Less publicly at first, Abdul-Jabbar also became a convert to the Sunni Islamic religion after reading the autobiography of slain Muslim leader and human rights activist Malcolm X his freshman year. He had been particularly moved by Malcolm's transformation from "illiterate street hoodlum to articulate spokesperson for hundreds of thousands of black Americans."[12] "I read that [book] and it made everything clear to me as to what was happening and what it was about," Abdul-Jabbar said. "I've always had a belief in, well just knowing that there's something more to the universe and existence than the things we can see here on Earth."[13] As a result, he dropped his Christian birth name, which estranged him from his parents for a time.

With graduation, Abdul-Jabbar mulled over offers to play in the NBA and ABA after he was made the first overall pick for each respective league in the 1969 draft. "I really wanted to play in New York," he recalled. "Unfortunately, the Knicks hadn't won the rights to draft me, the Milwaukee Bucks had. However, the New York Nets of the ABA were in real pursuit, and all things being equal, I would have been more than happy to play for them. The ABA was a new league, without the tradition and composure of the NBA, but I was no great fan of tradition and composure."[14] The problem was that the Nets bungled negotiations, offending Abdul-Jabbar by their initial low-ball offer and what he called "bozo business dealings."[15] "The Nets had had the inside track and had blown it," he wrote. "I signed with Milwaukee."[16]

He made an immediate impact in Brew Town, scoring 28.8 points a game to win the 1970 NBA Rookie of the Year Award and lifting the second-year expansion club to a 56–26 record and championship contention. In 1971, he did himself one better, leading the Bucks to their first NBA title after the team picked up Hall of Fame point guard Oscar Robertson in a trade to complement their young superstar. Abdul-Jabbar easily won the first of what would be six NBA MVP Awards over the course of what would be a long, distinguished career. "He's probably the most active center in the game," Milwaukee coach Larry Costello told *Sports Illustrated*. "He moves from a low to a high post, from one side of the lane to the other. He brings the ball downcourt when he has to. He exerts far more energy than most big men. Even when we get the ball in to him on the post, he herky-jerks around and uses moves—not just muscle—to work in. But he doesn't get tired. You know a funny thing? He's gained weight during the season."[17]

Abdul-Jabbar continued to thrive on the court in the seasons ahead, picking up two more MVP awards and appearing in another Finals—a seven-game loss to the Celtics in 1974. "In all the years I've seen professional basketball," an impressed Bob Cousy observed, "I don't think I've seen a center like Abdul-Jabbar. He has the qualities of Chamberlain and Russell, who were the two best. He uses the great mental concentration of Russell with the overpowering strength and ability of Chamberlain. It's really impossible to stop him. There's not a lot you can do."[18] Especially against his nearly indefensible skyhook. "The only way is to go at him from the blindside when he's winding up for the hook," said Bill Sharman, Cousy's former backcourtmate in Boston who coached the Lakers to a title in 1972. "It is the most effective and hardest shot to stop in the history of the game. He is incredibly accurate within a range of 12 to 15 feet."[19] This success was neither effortlessly achieved nor easily replicated by others. "A normal shot is easier to triangulate," Abdul-Jabbar maintained. "The three corners of the triangle are your eyes, the ball and the rim, and most players shoot from near their eyes. But on the skyhook the ball is way up here, and that difference in triangulation keeps most players from getting the coordination of it. . . . It's almost exactly like Zen Buddhism—you center on your inner calm and your target, isolate everything else until you and your object become one."[20]

Despite the dominance, Abdul-Jabbar found himself increasingly disenchanted with the long winters and suffocating provincialism of Milwaukee, which then did not have much of a black community, let alone a Muslim one. "I would stay home, read, get into my music," he said.[21] All these factors added up to one unmistakable conclusion when he entered his final contract year with the team in 1975. Wrote Abdul-Jabbar, "Although they offered to buy me a townhouse in New York City and even suggested that I could commute to the games if I would re-sign with the Bucks, it was time to think of a change of venue. I asked to be traded and the Bucks obliged."[22] Although his preference was to play for the Knicks, Milwaukee GM Wayne Embry was dissatisfied with New York's offer of aging veteran stars Willis Reed and Walt Frazier. "They may have provided instant success, but that was not what I wanted," Embry later revealed. "I wanted high draft picks in the ensuing years."[23]

The Lakers stepped up with the desired draft capital, and Abdul-Jabbar once again found himself performing in the City of Angels. But the Lakers reminded no one of the dynastic UCLA teams he had been such an integral part of under John Wooden. They were a fairly drab, mediocre outfit regardless of Abdul-Jabbar's night-in, night-out outstanding performances, which resulted in back-to-back MVP seasons in 1976 and 1977. But for many local media members and fans, this was not remotely good enough. If Abdul-Jabbar was so great, they asked, where were all the championships? "I recall being the scapegoat," Abdul-Jabbar later told writer Roland Lazenby in his 2006 book *The Show: The Inside Story of the Spectacular Los Angeles Lakers in the Words of Those Who Lived It.* "I was the best player on the team. I got a lot of things done, so they just used me as the focus for why the Lakers weren't successful. That was very frustrating. It was one of the worst times in my basketball life because I couldn't win."[24] Sometimes these frustrations carried over onto the court with the prime example being his violent reaction to being elbowed in the stomach by Milwaukee's Kent Benson in the 1977 season opener. Abdul-Jabbar knocked the rookie center unconscious with a single punch to the face while breaking his own hand in the process. "I can understand how the punch happened," Abdul-Jabbar later said. "He was a rookie, he made a mistake. When he did that I thought of all the times I was provoked, abused, bullied, scorned and I was not going to take one more [provocation]."[25]

Abdul-Jabbar's overall disposition improved with the arrival of Magic Johnson during the 1979–80 season. For the first time since he had paired up with Oscar Robertson in Milwaukee, Abdul-Jabbar had a topflight playmaker who intuitively knew how to run an up-tempo offense and get the ball to him anywhere on the floor. It was a marriage made in hoops heaven and produced Lakers titles in 1980 and 1982. More importantly, the intense glare of the media spotlight, a fact of life Abdul-Jabbar had been reluctantly forced to live with since his days at Power Memorial Academy, had now shifted to his younger, more charismatic teammate. He could breathe easier, secure in the knowledge that he no longer had to shoulder the burden of carrying the team all by himself. "I've had to [learn] to take things in stride," Abdul-Jabbar later said.[26] Indeed, this new loose attitude could be seen in his ability to poke fun at himself. In 1980 he won rave reviews for his cameo role in the 1980 comedy spoof *Airplane!* Playing ill-fated copilot Roger Murdock, he is hounded by a young passenger named Joey Hammen who insists that he is the real-life Kareem Abdul-Jabbar. "I think you're the greatest," Hammen innocently tells him. "But my dad says you don't work hard enough on defense . . . [a]nd that you don't really try, except during the playoffs." Affecting rage, Murdock roughly grabs Hammen by the shirt and announces that he's been "busting buns" for 48 minutes every night against the NBA's finest.[27] The scene elicited huge laughs from theater audiences, who appreciated the meta touches.

Abdul-Jabbar was again in top form when the Lakers captured the opening game of the 1984 NBA Finals with a 115–109 victory over the Celtics on Sunday, May 27. As a disappointed Boston Garden crowd of 14,890 looked on, the UCLA product made good on 12 of his 17 attempts from the field for a game-high 32 points while tacking on eight rebounds, five assists, and two blocked shots. "I grew up in L.A. watching Kareem," said teammate and NBA-All-Defensive First Team guard Michael Cooper, "and it seem like he's been getting the job done for so many years I can't count 'em all. He's simply a professional through and through. And I don't think I've ever seen him play any better than today."[28] Indeed, Abdul-Jabbar made a mockery of a much-anticipated matchup with Robert Parish by consistently hitting his skyhook over the increasingly frustrated Boston center, who had only 13 points and fouled out late in the fourth quarter. "We cannot win without Robert Parish," opined Cedric Maxwell, who did not distinguish himself either with six points. "He is the most important person on this team. If Robert neutralizes Kareem . . . I think that's half their offense."[29]

For his part, Abdul-Jabbar downplayed his oversized role in the victory. "I usually do well with one-on-one coverage," he said. "That's no secret."[30] Neither was the Lakers ability to run, as they jumped out to a 20–6 lead at the start of the contest with Magic Johnson (18 points, 10 assists) directing their fast-break attack the same way Leonard Bernstein conducted an orchestra: with consummate skill and brio. "We wanted to make a statement," Lakers coach Pat Riley said. "The first period was as good a period as we've ever played in a big game."[31] The Celtics did go on 14–3 tear late in the third quarter to cut the lead to 92–88 as Abdul-Jabbar and Johnson took an extended breather on the Lakers bench. But when the two franchise players were reinserted into the Lakers lineup during the final period, the LA lead grew again to scotch any Boston comeback hopes. "That's the best I've ever seen a team run," said Larry Bird, who contributed 24 points in the losing cause. "We like to run, but there's no way we can run as good as they can."[32]

The Celtics looked like they were destined to take another on the chin in Game 2 as they trailed 113–111 with 13 seconds left in regulation and with the Lakers in possession of the ball. "We were in major trouble," Maxwell later wrote. "If we lost this game, we'd go out to LA down 2–0 and on our way to a quick series loss."[33] But then the "Miracle of Causeway Street" occurred. Invoking memories of John Havlicek's famous steal against Philadelphia in the 1965 playoffs, Gerald Henderson intercepted a sloppy James Worthy cross-court pass and then proceeded to convert it into an uncontested layup to tie the score. "I was about to go home," K. C. Jones joked afterward, "but then I found out I was sitting on the bench as a coach, so I decided to stay."[34] There was still enough time remaining in regulation for the Lakers to get off a final shot, but Magic Johnson decided to dribble out the clock—a bizarre decision that Maxwell claimed forever earned the Lakers guard the appellation "Tragic Johnson."[35]

Thus reprieved, the Celtics went on to take the game, 124–121, in overtime. "I knew it was a bad pass as soon as I let it go," said Worthy, who claimed he was going to have a tough time sleeping that night. "Henderson was in a gambling defense and I tried to get the ball over to [teammate Byron Scott]. Byron sort of drifted away, and Henderson doubled back and just stole it. I saw it coming, and my heart went from my throat right down to the bottom of my feet. It wasn't a good play."[36] Unless your last name was Henderson, that is. "I saw the pass and it didn't have any zip on it," Henderson said. "If Byron Scott had stepped in there, we would have had one heck of a collision. I was really moving toward the ball. I was like a race horse with blinders on. I had tunnel vision for that basketball."[37] In OT, Henderson would also shine, making a key pass to wide-open teammate Scott Wedman with 14 seconds remaining that the Kansas native coolly drained from the left baseline to put the Celtics up 122–121. "I was lucky," said Wedman, who had played sparingly in a reserve role all season. "Larry was double-teamed and my man was on him. It was just one play and I was trying to take care of business. [Henderson] threw the ball to me. I knew when it was coming that the shot was going up."[38]

Interestingly, Henderson later said that his assist to Wedman was of greater importance than his more celebrated steal due to the fact that it gave the Celtics a permanent lead. "It was a split-second decision and the pass had to be perfect," Henderson explained.[39] After the Lakers were unable to respond offensively, Larry Bird finished out the Boston scoring with a pair of free throws. Although Bird had led the Celtics in points and rebounds with 27 and 13 respectively, there was no doubt in his mind or the minds of his teammates who the true difference maker was. "Gerald is the one who gave us a chance to win," Bird later told biographer Bob Ryan. "If we had lost that game, we were staring at another Milwaukee."[40] Robert Parish agreed. "We were basically dead in the water until Gerald made that steal," he said. "It really changed the whole complexion of the season, not just the game."[41]

An undersized combo guard at a generously listed 6–2, 175 pounds, Henderson was born in the old Confederate capital of Richmond, Virginia, on January 16, 1956. Coming of age at the local Whitcomb Courts housing projects where a black ghetto once stood, Henderson expressed no nostalgia for his hometown in later life. "I go back there now and it's a strange feeling," he told *Boston Herald* columnist Joe Fitzgerald in 1984. "Many of the folks I knew then are still there. Whole generations of families keep turning over, staying in the same area, doing the same things. Then mothers and sisters have babies and it starts all over again." Yet something always drew Henderson back to his roots, if for no other reason than as a reminder of how differently his own life might have turned out minus a few breaks and a lot of hard work. "I look at it and I wonder," he said. "I mean who knows what kind of talent there is inside those people? That's why I like to go back. I'm sort of a role model to kids who look at me and say, 'Hey, he did it, and I'm just as big as he is!'"[42]

After being a three-year starter for Virginia Commonwealth University, Henderson was chosen by the San Antonio Spurs as the 64th player in the 1978 NBA Draft. But he became the last player cut in training camp. Undaunted, he hooked up with the Tucson Gunners of the minor league Western Basketball Association hoping for another shot at the big time. "A season of long bus rides, a season of playing in empty arenas, a season of staying in crummy hotels, a season of surviving on $10 a day meal money, it all has a way of motivating you every second you're on the court," Henderson later told Celtics broadcaster Johnny Most in a radio interview.[43] Henderson's situation improved when he signed on as a free agent with the Celtics the following year. Unsurprisingly, given his previous unheralded draft status, he was paid scant notice by the Boston media when a team spokesman blandly introduced him at a press conference. A sympathetic writer approached him with a few words of encouragement. "I suspect you plan to surprise a few people," the fourth estate member said. Henderson's face lit up as he gave his response. "They don't know me now," he answered. "But they're going to."[44]

First, though, he needed to harmonize his talents with those of the club, which operated an up-tempo offense with fellow rookie Larry Bird as the focal point. "My biggest adjustment will be learning how to be [a ball distributor] for this team," Henderson said. "I've always had a scorer's mentality. Here with Boston, I know I'll be the last option, the guy who shoots only because I'm not being guarded or because we're desperate."[45] He fortunately did not have to look far afield for a mentor. In Tiny Archibald he had the perfect guide to show him the ropes. "A lot of things I do now," Henderson later shared with *Basketball Digest* contributor Larry Whiteside, "I remember from the way Tiny did things. When we run and get out on the break, I'm all over the place. I'm penetrating, going to the basket. That's how I get a lot of assists. A lot of things I picked up from Tiny are coming to me now."[46] Henderson rewarded the Celtics' faith in signing him with a solid rookie season in which he averaged 6.2 points and made half his shots (191 for 382) from the field. Even the notoriously hard-to-please Bill Fitch had been happy with the results. "He's in a group of maybe eight or nine guys [in the NBA] with exceptional quickness," the Boston coach said.[47]

The steady improvement in Henderson's game continued in the years to follow as he became a reliable defender and outside shooter while consistently finishing among the team leaders in steals, including a then career-best 117 takeaways during the 1983–84 regular season. None of this resulted from some fluke accident. "I decided to do something when I was coming through school and my first couple of years here," Henderson explained. "I decided I would work on making myself a total basketball player, all aspects—dribbling, shooting the ball, doing this, doing that. Not just one thing well. That's been the key to my success. That I can do different things and do them well. I can play offense well and defense well. I feel like I'm well-rounded."[48] Yet nothing could prepare him for the outpouring of adulation he received for committing the most audacious theft in Beantown history since Anthony "Fats" Pino masterminded the robbery of a Brink's armored car depot near the Boston Garden in 1950. Said Henderson, "In my mind, I could hear Johnny Most screaming, 'Henderson stole the ball! Gerald Henderson stole the ball!' Fact was I had no idea the ball would be going to Scott. I was just running towards the nearest Laker towards me, trying to put some defensive pressure on them."[49]

A different kind of narrative would emerge when the Celtics traveled to the Greater Los Angeles area to play the Lakers in Game 3 at the Forum three days later. Once again unleashing the full might of their vaunted running attack before a sold-out Tinsel Town audience, the Lakers buried K. C. Jones's club in convincing fashion, 137–104, to go up 2–1 in the series. "Basically, we didn't stick to our game plan," explained Scott Wedman, who did his best to turn back the purple and gold tide with 16 points and 10 rebounds. "We didn't get back on defense. Regardless of what they do, you still have to get back. They got a lot of their points off the fast break, and when that gets rolling, everything works for them."[50] Indeed, with Magic Johnson at the controls, the Lakers offense dashed off 74 fast-break points to put Celtics defenders on their heels all contest. If that wasn't enough to draw at least a grudging nod of respect from the visitors, Magic also produced 21 assists to set a new single-game NBA Finals record. "They ran us off the floor," Robert Parish said. "Their halfcourt game doesn't hurt us that much . . . but they killed us from end line to end line. And they outrebounded us by a good margin because we didn't box out or help out. We were very complacent. Passive. I know I switched off a couple of times and Kareem [Abdul-Jabbar] was left wide open. And that third quarter was the worst period I've ever seen since I've been associated with the team."[51]

Ah yes, the third quarter. The Lakers scored more points that period—47—than the entire Celtics offense was able to muster in the first half. It was enough to make a certain annoyed Celtics' team captain, who claimed his club "played like sissies," speculate whether Red Auerbach would trade his treasured victory cigars for cigarettes if the Lakers' blitzkrieg scoring attack could not be slowed down.[52] "Am I disappointed?" Bird asked sarcastically. "No, I'm happy as hell. I love to get beat by 30 points. There are so many things we've got to do better, it's unbelievable. We are a good defensive team, but we are not good against the break. Let people write what they want. Let people read it and let's hope we get fired up."[53]

The Celtics appeared to take Bird's words to heart in Game 4, battling from behind for the better part of the evening to grind out a 129–125 overtime win to tie the series at two-all on D-Day, the fortieth anniversary of the historic Allied invasion of Western Europe during World War II. Although there was no formal storming of the beaches this time around, Kevin McHale did the next best thing late in the third quarter in front of an unprepared Forum crowd of 17,505 that included such Hollywood luminaries as the Oscar-winning actor Jack Nicholson, the Lakers' most high-profile and garrulous fan. Seeing his club trailing 76–70 and long-haired Laker forward Kurt Rambis threatening to add to the lead on a breakaway, McHale decided that the time was ripe to breathe new life into his fading club by delivering the cheap shot heard round the world. He took down the 6–8, 213-pound Rambis at rim level on a straight clothesline that would have earned the Minnesotan an extended stay in a jail cell had he committed the same shocking act of violence on Wilshire Boulevard.

Not that this likelihood would have deterred McHale very much. During the team shootaround before the game, he had lectured his teammates on the need to raise the bar physically against the Lakers in the series. "We can't keep letting them dunk all over us and get all those layups," he said.[54] Encouraged to take a personal lead in the matter by Danny Ainge, McHale did not disappoint against Rambis, setting up a wild scene on the court in which both benches emptied, and shoves and harsh words were exchanged. Bird and Abdul-Jabbar also got into it a few moments later when Abdul-Jabbar's elbow made contact with Bird's head. "I will fuck you up white boy," Abdul-Jabbar reportedly said.[55]

"I was not trying to hurt Kurt Rambis," McHale ingenuously maintained afterward. "I was trying to wrap him up [to prevent a clear layup] and he slipped out of my grasp, so it looked like a body slam. He came up mad and swinging, and he had every right to do that because of the way he went down. But I wasn't trying to hurt him." Pat Riley thought otherwise, accusing McHale and the Celtics of using thuggish tactics. "I didn't appreciate that kind of play," the Lakers coach said the next day. "There's an unwritten rule in the league. If you take someone out, you make sure he misses the shot, but you go out with him, set him down real gentle. But that was as bush a play as I've seen and I mean that."[56] Yet the play was also highly effective as evidenced by the Lakers scoring only three fast-break points for the duration of the contest after they had been permitted to gambol freely about the court in the first half. As Maxwell observed, "Before the Lakers were just running across the street whenever they wanted. Now they have to stop at the corner, push the button, wait for the light and look both ways."[57]

The Lakers were nevertheless still in a strong position to win the game in regulation, but Magic Johnson revived his Casper the Friendly Ghost routine from the second contest and disappeared, committing a turnover and whiffing on a pair of key free throws in the final minute of play to force the extra period. "I thought the free throws more than the pass were mistakes," he later recalled. "Those were things I—not the team—I should have taken care of. When you miss the shots, you go home and sit in the dark."[58]

Dennis Johnson contributed in a major way to the Lakers point guard's distress when K. C. Jones opted to put him on Magic over the slighter and less muscular Gerald Henderson, who had proven wholly inadequate in that defensive role up to that point. "DJ jumped all over him and really took it to him," Jones said. "He gave Gerald a chance to breathe." Magic did not disagree. "[DJ] really played good defense," he said. "He wasn't sagging; he was playing right on top of me."[59] Magic's troubles resumed in overtime as he struggled again at the free throw line and was forced to look on hopelessly as Bird buried a turn-around jumper over him on a defensive switch with 16 seconds left to ice the victory for the Celtics. But most of the talk after the game centered not on the Laker's uncharacteristic miscues, but on McHale's fateful encounter with Rambis. "We wanted to be physical," McHale insisted. "We wanted to play good, hard-nosed basketball. This was more our type of game."[60] And no one played it any better or tougher than Kevin Edward McHale.

Born on December 19, 1957, in the small town of Hibbing in northern Minnesota, McHale was the son of a miner who made his living digging iron ore from the nearby Mesabi Iron Range, which along with three other similar districts in the region went collectively by the name the "Iron Range." McHale had a happy childhood and later seemed to delight in the fact that he shared the same hometown with the internationally famous singer-songwriter Bob Dylan, whose music he was a big fan of growing up. In future years, McHale would joke that next to Dylan and former Minnesota governor Rudy Perpich, who also called Hibbing home, he was only "the third most popular person" to originate from the community.[61] Basketball became a consuming passion in his young life only after he realized that he was not cut out athletically for hockey, his favorite sport. "All of a sudden, one summer, I started playing [hoops]," he said. "I went out for the seventh-grade team and really loved it. It was cold as hell in the winter up there, sometimes 30 to 40 below. It was warm in the gym. That certainly had something to do with my decision [to focus on the game]."[62] But it was not the only reason. Blessed by the genetic luck of the draw, he sprouted to 6–10 by his senior year in high school. "It's a gift God gave me," he said. "My dad is 5–10, my mother is 5–6."[63] The extra inches in addition to the extensive mentoring of his high-school coach, Gary Addington, who stressed ballhandling and one-on-one skills, helped transform McHale from an average player to a force to be reckoned with on the floor. "I could have gotten into a rut . . . but Gary forced me to learn the whole game," he said.[64]

But despite being named "Mr. Basketball" for Minnesota in his final season for the Hibbing Bluejackets, McHale drew mild interest from major college programs around the country, who were skeptical that his odd barrel-chested build—complete with "broad but hunched shoulders that look like they swallowed a coat hanger"—could hold up to the rigors of top-flight competition.[65] None of this must have surprised McHale as his idea of being "incredibly successful" in the game involved being the best player on his high-school squad.[66] "I thought about college, but I didn't know my dad could afford it," he said. "I didn't want to take out a loan and be $10,000 in debt. At 18, that's not a way to start life."[67] Nor was the grim prospect of working in the mines as so many of his peers in Hibbing ended up doing. Then he received a lifeline in the form of an unexpected phone call from University of Minnesota Golden Gophers head coach, Jim "Dutch" Dutcher, informing him that he would be receiving a full basketball scholarship from his school. A grateful McHale was overcome with emotion and gratitude. "It was the most unbelievable day in my life," he said. "It was like going to the ionosphere."[68]

His next four years resumed along a similar upward trajectory as he became one of the best college forwards in the country, scoring 1,704 points and pulling down 950 rebounds in the rugged Big Ten Conference while leading the Golden Gophers to within a victory of the 1980 National Invitation Tournament championship his senior season. He lost out to Ralph Sampson's University of Virginia team in the final. Along the way, he made sure to have a good time, hosting all-night parties with teammate and future NBA star Mychal Thompson and acquiring the reputation on campus as a free spirit. "They'd have kegs stacked up," recalled Ray Williams, another Gopher destined for greater things when he first crossed paths with McHale as an underclassman. "I'd come back to the house and they'd still be at it. They'd be stretched on the floor with beer cans and wine bottles all over the place."[69] None of these extracurricular activities seemed to trouble Dutcher as the Michigan product possessed an easygoing nature himself. Remembered McHale, "Dutch and I would go pheasant hunting in the morning before practice and he'd say to me, 'You're not going to do bleep at practice today, are you?', and I'd say, 'No.'"[70]

The *Animal House* fun and games notwithstanding, McHale nursed a lifelong regret about spending his entire college career in a relative small-time program like Minnesota's. "From a basketball standpoint," he told biographer Peter May, "I should have transferred. All [my class-mates on the team] did. My junior year, there was no one left but me; we started four freshmen. My senior year, there was no one to comple-ment my game. I just kinda played. If I had gone to any of the fifteen or twenty schools that called, it would have been different. They had senior guards who got you the ball. But it goes back to the whole loyalty thing. I wasn't going to leave. The thought of quitting just didn't enter my mind. I thought it would be a cop-out. It's easy not to play when you're hurt. It's easy to leave. It's hard to stick it out."[71]

The Celtics had their own concerns about McHale's ability to stick things out after they made him the third overall pick in the 1980 NBA Draft following the famous trade with the Golden State Warriors that also brought Robert Parish to Boston. Unhappy with the team's initial three-year contract offer of $525,000, McHale decided to explore the idea of playing in Italy instead. To prove how serious he was, McHale took an eight-hour direct flight to Milan with his agent, Ron Simon, to discuss signing with the local professional team there. "It was the only option I had," McHale explained. "I liked the European attitude. Everybody was so mellow, it was interesting, although I don't honestly know if I would have found it six months interesting."[72] Red Auerbach, who had already penciled in the 6–10, 210-pound forward for the club's sixth man role, was not keen on McHale finding out. The Celtics improved their offer to $600,000, and although McHale still felt shortchanged, he grudgingly accepted the new terms. "The Celtics are very good business people and I don't think they wanted to lose their first-round draft choice," he told reporters. "As for me, it was a lot of mental anguish. I'm very excited about the signing. I've always wanted to play in Boston. I'm just sorry this has prevented me from being with the Celtics from the very first day of practice. I've got a lot of hard work ahead of me to catch up."[73]

If he had known exactly how much toil he was going to face, he might have decided to remain in Milan, for hard-nosed Celtics coach Bill Fitch was not of the mind to bring McHale along slowly, even though the Minnesotan was suffering from a severe bout of hemorrhoids that he had picked up during his transatlantic travels. "I saw McHale sitting in his own blood, with our stretching exercises," an unsympathetic Fitch remembered with sadistic delight. "He wasn't about to ask me for more time off! I don't think anybody had a worse case than Kevin . . ."[74]

McHale somehow survived training camp, but more challenges awaited him once the regular season started, as it quickly dawned on him that the NBA was not the Big Ten Conference and that he needed to raise his game to a higher level if he wanted to survive. "You come in here and you get your ass whipped for the first three weeks," he said. "You think, 'Holy shit! What is going on in this league?' In college, a lot of times, you use your jumping ability and your size to jump over people and get the rebound. Here people are as big as you are. You've got to box them out, stay between them and the ball, use your body on them. . . . In college I let the guy stand next to me and then I would outjump him. Here, you have to bump him and then go get the rebound. There is more *thinking* here."[75]

But he made the adjustment and thrived as the Celts' top choice off the bench, averaging 10 points and 2 blocks per game while making the NBA All-Rookie First Team. Even the eternally dyspeptic Fitch had to concede that he was impressed. "Kevin was so good at being the sixth man," he later said, "that if the quality of the team had remained the same over the years, he'd have had a ring on his hand every year. He could play forty minutes a game if he had to. He had the ability to come in and, without even throwing a warm-up pitch, throw a hundred-mile-an hour fastball. All things considered, Kevin should go down in history as the absolutely ideal sixth man. He could play any position up front. He could give you inside scoring, outside scoring. He blocked shots. That's such a luxury for a coach. You tell him, 'Tonight, Kevin, we need shot blocking.' Or, 'tonight, Kevin, we need scoring.' And that's harmful to the other team."[76]

Opponents would not have disputed this claim as word spread rapidly around the league that the versatile Boston rookie was something special—"a total package," as Larry Bird would later describe him.[77] "I was surprised at how big he was," said veteran Milwaukee guard Brian Winters, a two-time All-Star. "He is strong and smart, and his arms just keep going."[78] For sure, McHale's unusually long arms gave him the wingspan of a much taller player, which made him even more effective as a rim protector. Yet there was far more to the story than that. As Nets forward Buck Williams observed, "No question, McHale has got tremendous reach, but it's his great sense of timing that intimidates people. He stands there a couple feet away from you, daring you to take the shot, and then moves in at the perfect moment to make the block. Even if he doesn't block it, he usually makes you miss because you tend to miss."[79] Explosive Indiana Pacers forward George McGinnis found this out the hard way one evening when McHale was given the challenging task of guarding him. "He put a move on me and just as he was going by, I blocked his shot," McHale remembered proudly. "He didn't like that. He looked at me and said, 'OK, rookie.' The next time they got possession, you could tell the play wasn't for McGinnis, but he called for the ball anyway. He got me to foul him twice in the next few minutes, but I refused to give in to him. I think a mutual respect was born from that."[80]

In the playoffs, McHale continued to make his presence felt, especially on the defensive end. Down 3–2 in the Eastern Conference Finals against Philadelphia on the road, McHale helped preserve a slim Boston lead in the closing seconds of Game 6 with a dramatic block of a driving layup by rookie 76ers guard Andrew Toney. "I ticked the ball but I didn't want it to go out of bounds," McHale said. "It sort of went straight up in the air and I went up and got the ball and held it." Bird later described the rejection as the biggest he had ever seen in his career—one, in fact, that was pivotal in the Celtics going on to take the series and the championship in the next round.[81] "Andrew thought he was in the clear," Bird wrote, "but Kevin came over and made a huge play, knocking the ball off the glass and then retrieving it."[82] A stunned Toney could only acknowledge the obvious afterward. "I thought I had a shot," he said.[83]

McHale witnessed further improvement over the next two seasons, steadily increasing his scoring, rebounding, and minutes while comprising a third of the best frontcourt in the league with Bird and Parish. But unlike in his first year, when every day felt like a trip to Willie Wonka's chocolate factory, McHale was feeling increasingly jaded and restless. A big reason had to do with his uncertain status with the team. The original three-year contract he had signed as a rookie was coming to an end, and the Celtics front office were dragging their feet in inking him to a new pact. "I'll never be the kind of guy to carry a team, like Larry [Bird], Dr. J or Magic [Johnson]," McHale said. "That's too much pressure. . . . But I can perform a certain role."[84] And for that role he wanted significant financial compensation.

Another contributing factor to McHale's malaise was his worsening relationship with Bill Fitch, whom he had taken to calling "Laughing Boy." For Fitch had refused to let up in his relentless riding of the former Golden Gopher, and McHale resented the demeaning treatment. "We're both opinionated about the game and the way things should be run," McHale said. "Bill would say, 'You did this and it was stupid.' And I'd say, 'Christ, are you crazy? No I didn't.' A lot of people would've passed it off, which I should have done. But, hell, if you're competing and working hard, and somebody jumps on you, your first reaction . . . well, you're intense and stuff. So I guess we yelled at each other once in a while."[85] Fitch added more fuel to an already combustible situation when he told members of the team that McHale would "starve" in the event that he had to play center in the league. "I didn't like it and I still don't like it," McHale said.[86]

Fortunately, both the contract and coaching situations were resolved to McHale's satisfaction before the start of the 1983–84 season, but the same was not true of the smoldering tension that existed between he and Bird. Bird had come to view his teammate's laid-back personal nature, which one national magazine likened to that of "a guy who identifies strongly with beer, deer steak, Dom DeLuise movies and more beer," as an indication of a fundamental lack of seriousness toward the game.[87] "I think Larry resented it night after night he's out bustin' his butt for basketball, basketball, basketball, basketball, and there was Kevin with a totally different set of priorities," Celtics radio announcer Glenn Ordway told writer Jack McCallum in 1992. "On the court, Kevin is as fierce a competitor as anyone, but at other moments he's always talking about his family or his golf game or his fishing. That got to Larry at times."[88] So much so that Bird would often tell reporters or anyone else willing to listen that McHale could be an MVP if he only pushed himself harder— an opinion Robert Parish privately shared. "Larry just wanted it more," Parish said.[89]

The center later added in an interview with the author that a toxic brew of personal envy and wishful thinking on McHale's part also may have played an important role in the conflict. McHale "thought he was fucking Larry Bird!" he said.[90] McHale, in turn, resented the fact that Bird went public with his criticism and that the latter was inevitably portrayed in the press as more committed to winning. As a result, *Globe* columnist Dan Shaughnessy believed there existed "a bit of a Ruth–Gehrig dynamic" between the two, whereby McHale, like the "Iron Horse" before him with the New York Yankees, was always destined to play second fiddle to a once-in-a-generation talent, in this case basketball's answer to Babe Ruth. McHale's own greatness never figured into the equation. "Everyone assumed," Shaughnessy said, "because they were superstar white guys from the Midwest that they just must be besties and they weren't. But they didn't hate each other either."[91] Indeed, McHale believed their contretemps was only natural given the "unbelievably competitive environment" they worked in. As he said, "You butt heads with everybody at some point or another."[92]

If the Lakers had hopes of reestablishing control of the series back in Boston for the crucial fifth game, they were in for a rude awakening. For amid an unseasonable June heat wave that saw the mercury rise to 97 degrees inside the Garden—an arena with no air conditioning—the Celtics were able to cool down their unacclimated visitors, 121–103. When asked afterward by a reporter about how difficult it was performing under such sweltering conditions, the normally even-keeled Kareem Abdul-Jabbar became unusually demonstrative. "I suggest you go to the local steam bath with all your clothes on," he said. "First, try to do 100 push-ups. Then run back and forth for 48 minutes."[93] Indeed, Abdul-Jabbar was so overcome by the sauna-like atmosphere that he could be seen on the bench during timeouts sucking desperately on an oxygen mask. "I was having trouble breathing," he confirmed. "I wasn't sharp. All you had to do is jog up and down the court and you were covered in sweat. The coach had to take me out a couple of times because I wasn't able to get up and down the court fast enough."[94] Veteran NBA referee Earl Strom, whose esteemed officiating career dated back to 1957, likewise discovered that he needed to exhibit the stamina of a Boston

Marathon runner just to remain upright. "I've worked games here before when it was hot, but this is the worst," he said. "I can't ever recall it being this hot. I've seen guys have to [depart] because of injuries, but never heat."[95]

Leave it to Larry Bird then to rise above the hellish circumstances and produce a 34-point, 17-rebound gem to give the Celtics a commanding 3–2 series lead. "He's the leader," said Danny Ainge. "When he's playing like that and setting that kind of a tempo with that kind of confidence, he gets everyone fired up. He definitely showed a little more emotion tonight, kind of like Magic Johnson, and Larry isn't like that. But we can tell when he's fired up and it's contagious. He doesn't say much; he just goes out game after game and leads by example."[96] Upset by Lakers coach Pat Riley's characterization following Game 4 of the Celtics as being the spiritual heirs to *The Godfather*'s Luca Brasi, Bird was already in a ruthlessly aggressive frame of mind before the action even commenced. "I was emotional, into the game, and I didn't really feel the kind of heat everyone anticipated," he said. "The few times I came out I felt it, but not when I was on the floor. I wanted to be in the game."[97]

So on target was Bird (15 of 20 shooting, two three-pointers) that he permitted himself a rare bit of showboating after connecting on a jumper in the second half when he made like a stereotypical Old West gunfighter and pretended to blow smoke from his fingertips. "He has had fatter, larger, more glossy games inside a Celtics uniform," the *Globe*'s Leigh Montville wrote, "but he has never had a more determined one. Eyes? He had headlights on this night. He had fairy-tale saucers. He had eyes that could see through buildings, cornfields, all across America and deep into the scariest part of [popular Lakers in-game performer] Dancing Barry's silver soul."[98] In sum, it all added up to sweet victory for the side wearing green. "We don't win in the same way [the Lakers] do," posited Kevin McHale, another contest standout with 19 points and 10 rebounds. "They ground out a victory, it's prime rib. When we ground one out it's hamburger. Just twelve guys and three coaches against the world. Our theme is 'Don't Be Denied.' When you have the best player in the game sacrificing himself like Larry does, it makes everyone do the same."[99]

Dennis Johnson (22 points in a leg-buckling 40 minutes) was no exception. Since K. C. Jones had given him the primary responsibility of covering Magic Johnson two games back, the NBA All-Defensive First Team guard had responded with his best ball of the series, averaging more than 20 points and depriving the usually explosive Lakers playmaker of scoring opportunities by forcing him out of his comfort zone away from the basket. "Dennis managed to stay in front of Magic all night," McHale observed. "If he didn't score a single point all night, he still would have been one of the biggest contributors."[100]

CHAPTER EIGHT

Cornbread Maxwell's Spectacular Evening

WITH JUST ONE WIN SEPARATING THEM FROM CLINCHING THEIR 15TH NBA title in 27 years, the Celtics were unable to close out matters two nights later in Game 6 after coughing up a big lead down the stretch in a demoralizing 119–108 loss at a much cooler Forum. "We had an 11-point [advantage] and we blew it," said Gerald Henderson afterward. "They stole it from us. There's no way we should have lost this game."[1] For sure, the Celtics were ready to pop the champagne corks when they went on a 13–4 run with five minutes left in the third quarter to establish a comfortable 85–74 lead. What's more, they let the Lakers know this inconvenient truth by rolling out a line of trash talk that uncharitably portrayed their hosts as needing the Heimlich maneuver performed on them. "That's their style," James Worthy said. "They don't give you any respect. They abuse you physically and mentally. Verbally. All that choker stuff. They like to talk."[2]

Meanwhile, a CBS network television crew had dutifully set up cameras in the Celtics locker room in anticipation of the expected trophy presentation ceremony. "It was like a big party was being prepared in our backyard and we weren't invited," Kurt Rambis said. "It wasn't the greatest feeling in the world."[3]

Fortunately for the Lakers, they had a 7-foot not-so-secret weapon in their employ named Kareem Abdul-Jabbar, who overcame a painful migraine headache just an hour before tip-off to score a game-high 30 points, 14 of which came during his team's valiant second-half comeback. "You hear a lot about Celtic pride and tradition, but we got some of that here, too," the center said. "There was never any question that I was going to play. I was just going to have to be sick. I couldn't hold my breakfast, so maybe it was vapors I played on."[4] Whatever the explanation, the Celtics could have benefited from a similar sense of urgency as their offense lapsed collectively into hibernation, making only five shots in the remaining 17 minutes. "It was a lot of fun until the third quarter," K. C. Jones said. "Then, all of a sudden, it became a job. Thereafter they got their fast break going and cut the lead down to zilch."[5]

Inexplicably, Bird (28 points, 17 rebounds, 8 assists, and 3 blocked shots) did not receive his usual allotment of touches during crunch time and this volte-face annoyed him no end. "My own teammates just wouldn't give me that ball," he grumbled. "I would have liked to have had the ball when we were up by 11 points. I know I could have made something happen."[6] In his anger, Bird also saw fit to lash out at NBA Commissioner David Stern for reportedly telling a fan in an elevator prior to the game that the league hoped the series would go the distance. The forward darkly hinted that the pronouncement was tantamount to instructing the referees to rule against the Celtics on close plays. "When Stern makes a statement like that, things are going to happen," he said. "The NBA wanted a seventh game because they wanted to make more money and they got their wish."[7] While a Stern spokesperson formally dismissed the accusation as "ridiculous," Bird's unfiltered comments nevertheless received the unbridled attention of Pat Riley, who was looking to rattle the Boston forward.[8] "I couldn't believe the statements coming from him," the Lakers coach said. "He was blaming his teammates, blaming the commissioner, blaming the fans. It was bizarre. I couldn't believe he'd say that. Usually, Larry Bird plays the game and doesn't worry about all that. He showed significant signs of cracking up."[9]

If so, the Celtics leader's subsequent breezy behavior belied that characterization. Driving to Boston Garden with M. L. Carr and Carr's then wife, Rhonda, before the start of the winner-take-all seventh game two days later, he calmly assured his teammate's visibly apprehensive significant other that things were well in hand. "Rhonda," Bird drawled in his familiar southern Hoosier twang, "don't worry about it. I'll take care of it. I can tell you right now we are going to win tonight. Just relax at the game and have a good time." Her worst fears now put to rest, Rhonda replied that his word was good enough for her.[10] Bird had spent his entire life and career making believers out of such skeptics.

A product of rural French Lick, Indiana, Larry Joe Bird was born on December 7, 1956, to economically disadvantaged parents who struggled to meet the basic needs for Bird and his five siblings. "All my kids were raised in an environment that was, well, tough," said Bird's mother, Georgia, who labored long, backbreaking hours, mostly as a short-order cook or as a waitress at local restaurants, to keep her family from falling into complete destitution.[11] At the end of the day, though, she did not have much to show for all her hard work. "The best she'd wind up with would be $100," Bird wrote. "I can remember whatever she made, she always needed an extra $20 or $30 for groceries. She'd go to the store on Saturday, but we'd generally start running out of things on Thursday. We really had to pinch those last two days. Mom never spent much money on herself; anything she ever made she spent on the kids."[12] Bird's father, Joe, was a different story.

A veteran of World War II and the Korean War, Joe was a heavy drinker who struggled with post-traumatic stress disorder stemming largely from his experience in Korea with his army unit. According to one family member's account, he once "ducked for cover" under the seats in a local movie theater when the film on the screen depicted bombs going off.[13] Transitioning to civilian life was not easy, and Joe had difficulty holding on to jobs due to frequent outbursts of erratic personal behavior. Family was apparently not high on his list of priorities as he spent a considerable amount of time associating with his friends at various drinking establishments. "He loved to buy his friends a round of drinks in return for the drinks they bought for him," Bird wrote. "As you can imagine, none of this sat too well with my mother."[14] This was especially true when Georgia and the kids were forced to constantly move from one home to another due to a chronic inability to make monthly rent. "I always felt sorry for my husband," Georgia once stated. "Drinking was something he had to do; it wasn't something he *wanted* to do."[15]

Young Larry found personal release from this less-than-ideal home situation in basketball. Starting around the age of five, he took up the game after receiving a basketball at Christmas—a common present for Indiana children of the hoops-crazed state. "I remember I was so happy," Bird later recalled in a firsthand account of his early years with Dan Shaughnessy for *Indianapolis Monthly* in 2000. "Remember those rubber balls they used to have? They were more like beach balls than basketballs. They were real light. We had a little goal outside, nailed to the side of the garage. It didn't have a net or anything. We didn't have any real driveway. It was sort of like a few rocks here and there. When it got cold, the ball wouldn't bounce. We had a potbellied stove in the middle of the living room, and every time you'd get real cold, you'd come in and put your ball there for about 20 minutes and it would warm it up and you'd go back out there and play."[16]

As far as learning the basics of the game, Bird had able teachers in his older brothers Mike and Mark, who kept him in constant tow growing up. "We always needed another player, so we got Larry," Mike once said.[17] Their pickup games were always ferociously competitive and notable for the extreme amount of sweat and energy expended during them. "We used to play at 9 or 10 at night," Bird recalled. "It would be dark out, but we had a streetlight off to the side, and it gave us just enough light to barely see the rim. My brothers beat me all the time."[18]

The losing would end when Bird grew more than four inches one summer and started suiting up for the local Spring Valley High School team. His legendary work ethic was already becoming apparent. "I never wanted to leave the court until I got everything right," he said. "I would practice different kinds of moves for hours on end, and worked very hard to make my left hand as strong as my right."[19] His progress as a player seemed to stall, however, when he broke his ankle as a sophomore and missed most of the season. But then something interesting began to happen. "When I came back," he said, "I began throwing these fantastic passes that I had never thrown before. I have no idea where it came from, but there I was, throwing all kinds of passes. I remember being in the locker room after the first day back and guys saying, 'God, Larry, where did you learn to pass like that?' Suddenly, I had a whole new way to play."[20]

Bird finished out his Spring Valley High career on a high note, averaging 31 points, 21 rebounds, and 5 assists as a senior, but came away mostly empty-handed when statewide awards for individual excellence were handed out that off-season. "I heard what they said about me," he later said. "Too slow, can't jump. Country kid, never had the big-city competition. I went to the state all-star game my senior year, and I got in the first five minutes. I wondered if I was really that bad."[21]

When it came time to decide where he would go to college, Bird was initially torn between Indiana University, Indiana State, and Purdue. But IU won out after a furious recruiting push by celebrated Hoosiers coach Bobby Knight, who had journeyed to French Lick to see the phenom play as a senior and came away impressed with his hands, leaping ability, and competitive desire. "Bird is a special player, one of the best," he said. It was not a hard sell on Knight's part to convince the pride of French Lick to become a Hoosier. He occupied a near demi-god status in Indiana hoop circles in the 1970s, and Bird's family was completely enamored. "We were all IU fans," Mark Bird said. "My dad was probably the biggest IU fan ever. He'd say to Larry, 'Boy I seen this red jacket the other day, and I sure would like to buy it and wear it to one of your ball games.'"[22]

Things went south quickly, however, when Bird first set foot on the nearly 2,000-acre, tree-lined Bloomington campus. "The school was way too big for me," he reflected in his memoir. "There were too many students. One of the classrooms could have held half of [my place of birth]—or so it seemed to me. Thirty-three thousand students was not my idea for a school—it was more like a whole country to me. It was too far to go to your classes. I'd be thinking, 'Which building do I go to next?' I walked around for two days, trying to figure out where I was going."[23] If that wasn't bad enough, Bird felt painfully out of place with many of his upwardly mobile classmates with their fancy cars and fashionably trendy clothes. "I roomed with [teammate] Jim Wisman and we shared a closet," he said. "I had a few pairs of pants, a few shorts and not much else. His stuff took up 95% of the closet and it was not like he was all that rich. Everywhere I looked it was like that. I couldn't cope."[24]

Bird felt similarly lost on the basketball court where he struggled to fit into Knight's motion offense, which required split-second timing with precise down picks. "He wasn't anywhere near cracking the starting lineup," Wisman remembered. Unhappy with his performance, Bird would retreat into a sullen shell after practice and shoot baskets alone back at his dorm. "That's where he really felt at home," Wisman said.[25]

Bird received no support or encouragement from the abrasive Knight, who treated Bird as he did all the underclassmen on his roster with a combination of haughty contempt and dismissiveness. When Bird attempted to strike up a casual conversation with him at a campus restaurant, Knight gave him a cold shoulder, making the callow youth feel even more insecure than he already was.[26] Bird left IU for good not long afterward, bringing his entire stay at the school to less than a month. "It just wasn't what I expected college to be," he said. "Plus I was just seventeen years old and hadn't been out on my own before. I guess all that just got to me."[27] In retrospect, though, Georgia Bird believed the experience may have been a fortunate break for her son. "Bobby Knight might have put him in a slot and not given him the freedom he needed on the court," she explained.[28]

Bird was not feeling so lucky at the time, however. Returning home to French Lick represented a tremendous humiliation as many of the same people who had enthusiastically cheered him on in high school now saw him as an embarrassing failure to be shunned. Even his old high-school coach, Gary Holland, could not hide his disappointment. "I think we all looked at him and thought, if he doesn't go back to school, it's going to be a big waste of talent," Holland said.[29] To earn some spending money while pondering what to do next, Bird went to work on a local garbage truck. "I loved the job," he later told Frank Deford of *Sports Illustrated*. "It was outdoors, you were around your friends. Picking up brush, cleaning up. I felt like I was really accomplishing something. How many times are you riding around your town and you say to yourself, Why don't they fix that? 'Why don't they clean the streets up?' And here I had the chance to do that. I had the chance to make my community look better."[30]

Off-hours, Bird remained active in basketball, playing for an American Athletic Union (AAU) team in the neighboring city of Mitchell fifteen miles way. But his participation failed to stoke the old competitive fires. "I just couldn't really get the adrenalin[e] flowing for the AAU games," he confessed. "It was the same kind of feeling I have in practice, not like a game situation where you're playing for something."[31] He knew deep down that only returning to college would satisfy that nagging urge.

Yet before he could act on it, he received the devastating news in the winter of 1975 that his father had taken his own life with a gunshot to the head. The passage of years had not been kind to Joe Bird. His stormy marriage to Georgia had resulted in a divorce, and his finances were in such disarray that he was unable to satisfy any of his creditors or make court-ordered child support payments. Facing imminent arrest by local law enforcement officials for the latter oversight, Joe decided to end it all. His death did not come as a complete surprise to his family. "We all knew what he was going to do because he came right out and told us," Bird wrote. "Not that he wanted sympathy or anything. He simply said, 'I'm not going to be around much longer. No use me living this way. You kids would be better off if I was gone.' It sounded pretty casual, but that was just the way he was brought up. It's just the way around French Lick; everyone is straightforward and matter-of-fact about everything."[32]

In the midst of processing his grief, Bird was approached by then 32-year-old Indiana State assistant coach Bill Hodges about the prospect of playing basketball at the small Terre Haute school, which had come up short recruiting him previously. It was not an easy sales job. Bird initially appeared distracted and unwilling to talk to Hodges. But through patience and no small amount of native small-town Hoosier charm, Hodges was able to wear Bird down and convince him to accept a full ride. Georgia Bird, for one, was relieved. "I'm glad [Hodges] didn't give up," she said. "His coming was like an answer to a prayer, because I knew that Larry had an awful lot of talent and he wasn't using it. He was just hanging around town, picking up garbage . . . and that wasn't the way I wanted him to spend the rest of his life."[33]

Returning to college was not the only momentous decision that Bird made during this period. He also tied the marital knot with Janet Condra, a former cheerleader whom he had dated since his junior year at Spring Valley High. "She came from a nice middle-class background,"

Bird wrote. "Her parents were nice people, and they treated me great. We had nice times together, but we always seemed to be arguing about something stupid and we'd break up and then get back together again. This went on all the time."[34]

The marriage unsurprisingly failed after a year but not before Condra became pregnant with their child, an infant girl named Corrie, which later became a taboo subject for friends and journalists to raise with Bird. "Larry never, never talks about it," his one-time agent and close confidant Bob Woolf said.[35] Still, the enforced silence did not prevent a trailblazing young female sports reporter named Diane K. Shah from later breaking the news in a feature story on Bird for *Inside Sports*, an edgy monthly sports magazine that *Newsweek* started publishing in 1979 along with the even lesser-known fact that his father had committed suicide. "I wrote my story with the information and Larry Bird went nuts," Shah recounted. Indeed, Bird became so enraged that he told the *Boston Globe*'s Bob Ryan that if he ever saw Shah again, he would "spit in her face."[36] That never happened, but for Bird and Condra the pain generated from the episode left a lasting imprint on their lives. "We just got married too young," Condra told writer Seth Davis in 2009.[37] "It was my decision to get divorced. There was so much stress with him playing basketball and me feeling like I always came last. I thought if I filed for divorce it might shock him into trying to change a little bit, but it didn't work out that way."[38] For his part, Bird felt shame and regret over his actions. "When I was a kid I thought people who got divorced were the devil," he said. "And then I go out and do it myself right away. Getting married was the worst mistake I ever made. Everything that ever happened to me I've learned from it, but I'm still scarred by it."[39]

Unlike his troubled brief tenure in Bloomington, Bird found Indiana State more to his liking as most of the students there sprang from similar less privileged socioeconomic roots as himself. "You have to find a place you can relate to," Bird later explained. "I had to be relaxed."[40] Equally important, he did not have to worry about competing for playing time as he did at IU with other top-shelf recruits from around the country, for he was clearly the only blue-chip talent on the Sycamores roster. Indiana State head coach Bob King, who had mentored Hall of Famers Don

Nelson and Mel Daniels at his previous coaching stop at the University of New Mexico, liked what he saw in Bird. "Larry's really fluid and quicker than he appears," King said. "He can handle the ball and pass it like any guard in the country. In fact, he can pass it better than most guards in the country. As far as I'm concerned, his strength is not in his scoring, but in his passing and rebounding."[41]

Due to his transfer status, Bird was compelled by then existing NCAA rules to redshirt his first year, but that did not preclude him from picking up a basketball. "I played more than ever before," he recounted. "In between classes I would go down to the gym and shoot. When [the team] went away on road trips, I played in that gym. The following summer I haunted the Terre Haute Boys' Club. I was always practicing there, always shooting baskets. I was a real 'gym rat.' I'd go home and eat, then come back to the gym and play some more. I mean, I practically lived in that gym."[42] He did experience a bit of a misunderstanding with Bob King, however, when the coach initially refused to use him in scrimmages with the varsity's first team. Bird interpreted the move as a lack of confidence in his own abilities. In fact, he became so distraught that he came perilously close to quitting school again, but King deftly stepped in to smooth over any bruised feelings. "Look Larry," he told Bird, "I can't get anything done with these other guys. They're scared to death of you. You make them look like idiots. Now how are they going to go out and play a game?"[43]

By the time Bird's sophomore year rolled around, he was chomping at the bit to see real game action at the recently constructed, state-of-the-art Hulman Center on campus where the Sycamores played their home games against Missouri Valley Conference opponents. "I've matured a lot and I'm ready to play," Bird said. "I know what I want out of basketball right now. As a 17-year-old I didn't know. Then last year, sitting out, I don't feel I improved half as much as I wanted, but I sat out two years waiting for this opportunity and I'm not going to blow it."[44] Nor did he. In his official college debut on November 27, 1976, the 20-year-old showed just how exceptional he was in a lopsided Indiana State victory over Chicago State by registering a triple-double with 31 points, 18 rebounds, and 10 assists. *Sports Illustrated*'s Kent Hannon wrote, "His first shot . . . , a rampaging slam dunk at the end of a fast break, alerted long-suffering Indiana State fans that a new era was dawning."[45]

And Bird was only getting warmed up. Over the next three seasons with the Sycamores, he continued to score and rebound with a similar abandon, even when rival clubs employed box-and-one defensive schemes—a thinly disguised zone designed to keep the shooter away from the basket. In such cases, Hannon noted, Bird "merely banged away with the same jump shot he developed in his backyard as a kid; head cocked slightly to one side like Jack Nicklaus as he prepared to hit a long drive, easy motion over the top, plenty of rotation on the ball upon release."[46] If worst came to worst and he did not have a clean look, Bird always fell back on his dazzling passing skills to distribute the ball to open teammates for easy scoring opportunities. "I've got to pass off for us to win," Bird said. "I know I'm going to turn the ball over. I have to figure on about four turnovers a game, squeeze passes inside and things like that. But I guess four isn't too bad considering how much I have my hands on the ball. I often find myself bringing the ball up the floor, and I will admit I feel better doing that because I like to be around the basketball."[47]

Long relegated to college basketball backwater status, Indiana State suddenly became a major national power, posting 23 wins or better from 1976 to 1979 with Bird's face now popping up regularly on magazine covers and newspaper front pages around the country. The massive media attention had established pro players like Philadelphia 76ers guard Doug Collins curious to discover what all the fuss was about. To that end Collins attempted to drive to Terre Haute in a blinding snowstorm during an off day with a then unknown assistant coach named Chuck Daly to witness Bird in action. But not far into the journey, their car skidded off the road and became inoperable. "We decided then we'd better forget about it and we rented a car and checked in to a Holiday Inn," Collins said. "We watched the game on TV and that was the first time I saw him. And all I could think of was, 'Oh, my word.'"[48]

That just about summarizes how Indiana State fans felt during Bird's final collegiate season when they saw the 6–9, 220-pound senior cornerman be named College Player of the Year and lead their team on a magical run in the 1979 NCAA Tournament under new coach Bill Hodges that ended with Magic Johnson's Michigan State Spartans defeating them in the championship game. When asked to comment on that final loss afterward, a physically and emotionally spent Bird remarked that he felt sorrier for his Sycamore teammates than himself. "I would have liked very much to win," he said, "but now I can look forward to next year."[49]

For certain, there was much to look forward to as he would soon be mentioned in the same breath as Russell, Cousy, and Havlicek as a Celtic in his first four seasons in the NBA, despite possessing at first glance an unathletic build with the beginnings of a paunch protruding from underneath his green-and-white jersey. Yet as teammate Tiny Archibald observed in a 1983 interview with *NBA Today*, the outward appearance was "very deceptive." "People are always saying [Bird] doesn't have any foot speed, but I've been with Larry for quite some time and he always gets out there on the fast break," Archibald said. "He's always running on guys and getting plenty of rebounds for a guy who supposedly can't jump."[50] Red Auerbach was in full accord, believing that at this early stage of his career Bird still had not reached his full potential as a player. "I honestly don't know when he'll stop improving," he said. "Here's the difference between Larry and a lot of other guys with talent. The average guy worked hard to get into the league. But once he got on top, he figured he'd made it. The work stopped—or lessened a lot. Now Larry, he didn't reach the All-Star level and give himself a rest. He'll spend an hour after practice working on a little move that might or might not work. The important thing is he's never satisfied. Even when it comes to shooting free throws—and he hits better than eight of 10—you'll see him working on that everyday."[51]

One area of Bird's game that needed no work was his uncanny ability to get under opponents' skins. As Philadelphia small forward Leo Rautins once observed, "I say this in the utmost complimentary way: Larry was a prick."[52] Indeed, Bird's trash-talking acquired a near mythic status around the league as he sought to psychologically destroy whoever he was matched up with, whether a certified all-star or bench scrub. "Larry has that Muhammad Ali kind of approach," K. C. Jones said. "He gets to you and your mind before the fight begins. By the time you step into the ring, you're already 20 points down. And he's able to back it up."[53] Future teammate Joe Kleine discovered this when Bird was taking the ball out in front of the New York Knicks bench late one game. "He looks over at [Knicks coach Hubie Brown] and goes, 'Kevin [McHale] is going to post up right there, I'm going to throw him a perfect pass, he's going to throw it back to me and I'm going to make a three.' And he did."[54] But Bird's most famous example of verbal denigration occurred during the NBA's first Long Distance Shootout (aka three-point shooting contest) before the 1986 All-Star Game at Reunion Arena in Dallas. "They had all of us in a room that measured six feet by eight feet and I told everyone I was looking for a second place finisher," he said.[55] That was enough to reduce fellow competitors like Leon Woods of the Washington Bullets, Kyle Macy of the New York Knicks, and Craig Hodges of the Milwaukee Bucks into quivering masses of Jell-O and give Bird a runaway victory. "I'm the new three-point king," Bird announced triumphantly to reporters afterward. "And the ones that didn't think I could win can go to hell."[56]

Bird, of course, did not need to resort to such crude psyche-out tactics as he had already established himself as a proficient scorer from behind the three-point arc, which measured 23 feet, 9 inches from the center of the basket. For sure, Bird boasted an impressive 40 percent success rate from that range as a rookie, slightly above his career average of 37.7 percent. Ironically, he had started out as no great admirer of the shot, which the NBA had adopted from the old American Basketball Association to generate more offense and fan interest. "I never thought I would be shooting one," he confessed. "The distance looked to be just too far out. I didn't even *like* the rule because I felt that a two-point lead at the end of a game should at least be enough to get you an overtime unless a player fouls you in the act of shooting."[57] But Bird gradually came around as he saw what a game-changing difference it made during a tight contest against the Atlanta Hawks his first season. Future 1984 assistant coach Chris Ford, who is credited with making the first three-pointer in NBA history, was playing guard and drained one from the corner. "When he got the ball back," Bird recounted, "we ran another play for him in the same spot and he hit another one."[58] To borrow a classic line from Humphrey Bogart at the end of the 1943 Academy Award–winning movie *Casablanca*, that moment on the floor represented the start of "a beautiful friendship" between Bird and the crowd-pleasing shot.

If Bird had one weakness, where no amount of practice or long hours in the gym seemed to help, it was on the defensive side of the ball. He had great difficulty containing taller players in one-on-one situations. "If he had to evaluate his game," posited Hall of Fame forward turned television broadcaster Rick Barry, "he'd say that."[59] K. C. Jones thought, however, this was vastly overstating the issue. "It's absolutely true that people have been known to exploit Bird by posting up during the first three quarters or so of games," the Celtics coach said. "It is definitely true Bird is a better overall offensive than defensive player and that he is not one of the top dozen or so individual defensive players in the game. But he is one of the truly intelligent team defensive players in basketball, and when it comes to crunch time, he even turns into a standout individual player. Many a posting up forward has learned to his dismay that he cannot establish the same position against Bird in the final four minutes that he did in the first 44. Larry Bird turns into a fabulous defensive player when it most matters."[60]

Bird certainly mattered to Boston fans as they packed the dilapidated old Boston Garden to capacity every night whenever the Celtics from the era had a game scheduled. Season-ticket sales alone jumped from 4,800 to 10,000 over the course of his rookie year. "Maybe the Garden isn't the House That Bird Built," postulated Gene Wojciechowski of the *Los Angeles Times* in 1993, "but at the very least, he strengthened its foundation."[61] Indeed, the dynastic Celtics of Bill Russell, who dominated their sport in a way that conjured memories of the lordly New York Yankees of Major League Baseball during the 1940s and 1950s had trouble filling seats during the interminably long winter months. "Folks were more interested in hockey," former player and coach Satch Sanders said. "We'd get 13,909 for the playoffs, but during the regular season it would be more like 7,500 or 8,000."[62] Although there is certainly merit to this statement, it does not fully explain why the Celtics suddenly became the hottest ticket in town during the 1980s.

The simple truth of the matter is that Boston and the surrounding New England area had a long-established history of preferring white star athletes to black ones on their teams. Bill Russell was a prime example. Despite having 11 championship rings in his jewelry collection, he was never accorded the same kind of respect as Ted Williams, who had no titles to speak of for the hometown Red Sox. In fact, when it came time to name a gleaming new highway tunnel under Boston Harbor in 1995, the lifetime .344 hitter easily got the nod over Russell. But this oversight was nothing compared to the indignities the great center suffered during his playing days. "Hey, nigger, how many crap games did it take you to win that car?" a local bigot once assailed him as he was driving around the city's streets in his convertible.[63] On another occasion he was peremptorily addressed as "boy" by a passerby when he was mowing the front lawn of his northern suburban Boston home in Reading. Apparently, the person wanted to know how much Russell charged for yardwork as it was just assumed that no black man could afford to be a homeowner.[64]

Sometimes the affronts involved elements of violence, such as when vandals broke into his house when he was away, destroying many of his trophies and spray painting the term "Nigga" on the walls. Adding further insult to injury, a petition was circulated within the community in protest of his family's efforts to move to a nicer section of town. When their garbage cans were also found knocked over due to what an unsympathetic Reading police force attributed to "raccoons," a fed-up Russell finally took action. He applied for a gun permit, and the problem magically disappeared. "He'd joke that the raccoons can read gun permits," his daughter Karen said.[65]

The situation was no laughing matter to other pro athletes of color. Russell's longtime teammate Satch Sanders remembered how next to impossible it was getting a taxi to come out to Roxbury—the predominantly black section of town—or finding an apartment in upscale white neighborhoods like the Back Bay. "Real estate people kept driving by me," Sanders said. "There were all kinds of incidents."[66] Mild-mannered K. C. Jones experienced his own brush with racial animus as a player when he had a cross burned on his front lawn after he bought a home in a nearby suburb.[67] "The neighbors said they didn't want any blacks to move into the house," Jones said.[68]

Outspoken baseball All-Star Reggie Smith, who patrolled center field for the 1967 American League champion Red Sox, often received letters addressed to him as "Dear Nigger." "Boston was clearly different from any place I ever played," he told author Howard Bryant in his critically acclaimed 2002 book *Shutout: A Story of Race and Baseball in Boston.* "It was the most divided city that I ever played in. In places like St. Louis, it wasn't like that. In Boston, you had to know the ground rules. There were places you could and places you couldn't go. It angered me, but it was the way it is. I dealt with it."[69] Compounding matters for Smith and many of his African American teammates was the fact he played for an owner with a well-deserved reputation for bigoted acts. Under the long stewardship of popular South Carolinian Thomas A. Yawkey from 1933 to 1976, the Red Sox became the last team in the majors to break the color line and passed on opportunities to sign all-time greats Jackie Robinson and Willie Mays. Not coincidentally, they never won a World Series during his tenure and, apart from an occasional pennant, were perennially mired in mediocrity. Yawkey "had his farmers on the team," explained Earl Wilson, a candid hard-throwing right-hander with the club in the early 1960s. "They were black. What other people call great is bad for other people. Some people probably thought Hitler was a great person. And they truly thought he was, but they wasn't Jewish and they didn't have to deal with it. But once you're in that little guy's empire—everybody's got cronies and junk. I don't know. I might have been a public pressure. You never know."[70]

The Celtics were not the Red Sox. In 1950, they became the first team to integrate their sport by drafting Duquesne All-American Charles "Chuck" Cooper as their first pick in the second round of that year's NBA Draft. When Celtics owner Walter Brown was pointedly asked if he knew that Cooper was a "colored boy," Brown responded, "I don't give a damn if he's striped or polka dot or plaid."[71] This progressive attitude on race continued as the championships began to pile up. During the 1963–64 campaign, the Celtics became the first professional basketball team to have five blacks on the floor at the same time. Three seasons later, they registered another milestone with the appointment of Bill Russell as player-coach, the first African American to direct a major league sports franchise.

Yet these history-making moves were not truly reflective of the kind of community Boston really was, especially since the outbreak of World War II when African Americans from the Deep South streamed into the mostly white city in unprecedented numbers. The demographic shift was part of a broad national trend that witnessed millions of blacks abandon their traditional rural homes below the Mason-Dixon Line and head to northern and midwestern urban centers for higher pay and greater economic opportunities in war-related industries. Problems soon arose, however, as ethnic blue-collar whites saw the newcomers as unwanted competition for jobs, housing, recreation, and education.

By the 1970s, these roiling tensions erupted into full-scale violence after Federal District Court Judge W. Arthur Garrity Jr. issued a ruling that required Boston public schools to desegregate by busing. The most notorious incident—and the subject of a famous Pulitzer Prize–winning picture by a *Boston Herald-American* photographer—involved a near fatal assault on a local black attorney named Ted Landsmark. In 1976, Landsmark was walking hurriedly through City Hall Plaza, late for a meeting, when he unexpectedly ran into a group of angry white antibusing demonstrators. Recounted Landsmark, "They shouted 'There's a nigger, kill him!' and I was hit. My glasses were knocked off and my nose was broken." The worst was still to come. One of the protesters wildly swung an American flag attached to a long metal pole at Landsmark and came perilously close to spearing him. "He missed me by about two inches," Landsmark said.[72] "The Soiling of Old Glory," as the infamous event became known, forever cemented Boston's reputation as a seething cauldron of racial hatred and intolerance—a damning image that still haunts the city well into the third decade of the 21st century, despite boasting a nonwhite majority and its first woman mayor of color in Michelle Wu.

Having waged a full-on basketball equivalent to the "War of the Roses" over the previous six games, the 1984 Finals now boiled down to one final clash of wills to determine who would be crowned the next champion. And the big day could not come soon enough for all the parties concerned. As Lakers forward Michael Cooper mused, "It's like we're kids waiting all year for Christmas and the big toy. You're good all year. You listen to your mother when she says you better not pout, you better not cry. Well, we've been good all year."[73] And although it was to be expected that nerves would be taut on both sides heading into the seventh game at a jam-packed, decibel-breaking Boston Garden, the Celtics took particular pains to disabuse observers of such an impression. Indeed, the atmosphere inside the home locker room prior to the start of the contest had the irreverent, carefree feel of a college frat house party. From Bird on down to the lowest bench player, the Celtics were a loose and confident bunch eager to have some fun at the expense of their more glamorous, high-profile rivals from the left coast, none more so than Danny Ainge, the club's enfant terrible. He ambled up to teammates with a stethoscope and half-jokingly started to check on their heartbeats as they were dressing. By the time he reached Cedric Maxwell, Ainge registered mock surprise. "Nah," he said, "your heart's not even beating."[74]

Ainge was not far off the mark as Max turned back the clock to the 1981 NBA Finals and delivered a vintage clutch performance with 24 points, 8 rebounds, and 8 assists in a rollicking 111–102 title-clinching victory over the Lakers that left thousands of hometown fans literally dancing in the streets. His showing even eclipsed that of teammates Dennis Johnson (22 points) and Larry Bird (20 points, 12 rebounds), the latter a unanimous choice for MVP of the playoffs. "I felt I had something to prove," said Maxwell who breezily informed James Worthy early on that the former collegiate all-American was incapable of guarding him.[75] Worthy's "a good ol' North Carolina boy like me, but I told him, 'this isn't the 2-A [high school] championship, this is the big boys, you have to deal with me.'" To drive home his point, Maxwell repeatedly blew by Worthy in the lane for easy Celtics baskets, leaving "Big Game James" with the befuddled look of Elmer J. Fudd after another humiliating encounter with Bugs Bunny. Twisting the knife further, Maxwell got Worthy into early foul trouble and forced Pat Riley to substitute in the slower Kurt Rambis, who fared no better. "Max was awesome," Kevin McHale apprised. "He was our hit man tonight. We just got him the ball, and he put it away for us."[76]

Apart from an understandable desire to add another championship ring to his finger, Maxwell was motivated by old-fashioned revenge. During the previous contest in LA, Worthy had rudely pushed Maxwell into a basketball support and did not appear too broken up over it. The provocation was all Maxwell needed to fire him up for Game 7. "All day, I was like a caged animal, just pacing around," he said. "I tried to play with my nephew, I couldn't even do that. I'm glad we took the team bus [to the arena] today. I had so much energy, I felt if I had to drive into Boston traffic I would have killed someone."[77] Instead, the only fatalities turned out to be Worthy and the Lakers. Maxwell made certain of that. "For a stretch of the game, it wasn't going to Kevin and Larry, who are first-ballot Hall of Famers," Ainge recalled. "The ball was going to Max. And it wasn't going to D. J., who was a multiple-time All-Star, a former Finals MVP. And it wasn't going to Parish, a top 50 of all-time. The ball was going to Max."[78]

Maxwell's scoring notwithstanding, the Celtics also greatly benefited from dominating the glass with a 52–33 rebounding edge—an advantage that puzzled the peerless Kareem Abdul-Jabbar, who led his team in scoring for the fifth time in the series with 29 points. "They got the long rebounds," Abdul-Jabbar said. "Whenever the ball bounced out, it seemed like they got it."[79] In spite of the glaring disparity, the Lakers were able to put together a courageous late fourth-quarter run after trailing for most of the game. With just over a minute left on the clock, the "Fakers," as caustic Celtics radio voice Johnny Most called them, pulled to within three points, 105–102, thanks to some timely scoring from Worthy (21 points) and the ever-reliable Abdul-Jabbar. But the Celtics weren't ready to assume the fetal position. They had progressed too far as a ballclub since the l'affaire Fitch of the previous season to let that happen. "I wasn't worried," Bird said. "When you got the lead in the fourth quarter, it shouldn't bother you. That's when teams choke up but as long as you have the lead, you should be OK."[80] And the Celtics were OK as the team's stalwart defense held on like Joshua Lawrence Chamberlain at Little Round Top, preventing the Lakers from scoring any more baskets. Meanwhile, the offense added six more points to put matters out of reach and send Garden denizens pouring onto the parquet in a state of unrestrained joy. It was an especially gratifying moment for Maxwell, whose inspired play had made the wild impromptu celebration possible. "I was on a mission from God," he said.[81]

Born on November 21, 1955, Cedric Bryan "Cornbread" Maxwell hailed from the sleepy small town of Kinston located in the coastal plain region of eastern North Carolina. Although the community of 20,000 outwardly resembled the fictional Mayberry from the popular television series *The Andy Griffith Show*, it was anything but in the early 1960s. Segregation ruled, and young Cedric learned not long after he left the crib that there were certain rigid lines of race, culture, and class in the Jim Crow South he dared not cross lest he or anyone sharing his skin pigmentation wanted a nocturnal visit from the local chapter of the Ku Klux Klan. "We literally lived on the other side of the tracks and had separate restaurants, water fountains, etc.," Maxwell recalled in his 2021 autobiography with Mike Isenberg. "Kinston had some beautiful beaches, but White folks had the run of the land, and we were left with what was left over."[82] Yet young Cedric was shielded from the most oppressive extremes of this apartheid society by his compassionate and caring parents, Manny and Bessie Mae. "Growing up," he wrote, "I always knew I was loved. The sun shone on my ass all the time."[83] Only decades later did he learn the unsettling truth from his mother that he was born out of wedlock and that his biological father was not Manny but Deford Small, a former Kinston resident who had moved to Greenville, South Carolina, when Maxwell was a toddler. "She said [Small] didn't want to marry her, so she took her baby and kept me clean," Maxwell revealed.[84]

It all worked out for the best as Manny provided a warm, stable home environment from which Maxwell and his two siblings could thrive. "A good man to look up to," Maxwell said of his adoptive father in a 1982 *Basketball Digest* interview. "He was a Marine drill sergeant until he retired. He [had] a way of getting his point across."[85] Bessie Mae was forceful in her own way, too. In fact, she bore primary responsibility for pushing her son down a basketball path. A former player herself at the historically black public college that became North Carolina Central University, she took time away from her busy homemaking and child-rearing duties to school Maxwell on the ins and outs of the game.

"So yes, I got my skills on the court from Mom," the future NBA star confirmed.[86]

Initially, though, the instruction appeared to make little difference. At 6–3, 140 pounds, Maxwell was no one's idea of a natural athlete. He lacked speed and was too skinny to make much of an impact under the boards. It came as no great shock then that he got cut from his high-school varsity squad as a junior just like, Maxwell would later jokingly point out, Michael Jordan before the former Chicago Bull became the most iconic basketball player on the planet. Paul Jones—the coach responsible for the decision—offered no apologies. "It just so happens that we had a few people back from the team before that had won a league and division championship," Jones recalled. "We were a running, gunning, pressing team. Also, I already had two seniors who looked like they were good centers. Max . . . really hadn't developed."[87] That hard truth, however, did not prevent Bessie Mae from calling up Jones and pointedly inquiring whether her son had somehow offended him, a reasonable assumption given Maxwell's irreverent sense of humor and jaded attitude toward adult figures of authority who were not Manny. Jones was unequivocal in his response, however. "I just told her no, and added that he couldn't help us on this club this year."[88]

A crushing setback, Maxwell contemplated ditching the sport for good, that is until the following summer when a sudden growth spurt combined with the discovery that he could now dunk with either hand forced Jones to rethink his earlier assessment. When the coach sought out Maxwell and asked him whether he was planning on going out for the team again as a senior, the young man voiced understandable confusion. "No," he replied, "you just cut me!"[89] Jones said not to worry; his luck was about to change. "I first noticed him in a phys ed class, and he was up to 6–6," Jones recounted. "I said, 'This kid is still growing,' and urged him to work on a weight program. I told him he needed to play basketball all the time. He was just the kind of kid who just worked and took a basketball with him everywhere. When he reported the next fall he was up to 6–8 . . . and his arms gave him an extra three inches."[90]

Observing that he was still slower than Ebenezer Scrooge handing out a check, Jones determined that Maxwell's talents would best be used playing the post. "There," Jones said, "he became fairly good because he worked at it so hard. We went to a double-post situation, and one post would break out. We kept Max around the basket, and if we got him the ball, there was no way they could stop him."[91] Though he averaged just 13 points, Maxwell was an absolute beast on the boards, grabbing 16 rebounds a game. He also established himself as an intimidating force on defense, averaging five to six blocked shots. "I was a late bloomer," he said.[92]

Despite the improvement, Maxwell discovered that no collegiate hoop programs were willing to offer him a full scholarship apart from the University of North Carolina-Charlotte, which was located four hours due west from Kinston. So, he packed his bags and headed for the Queen City. "I loved it there," he wrote. "None of us were big-time recruits, it was us against the world, and we all bought in. We were like the Rodney Dangerfield of college basketball. We'd play anyone anywhere. When we got to UNCC, the school had around 9,000 students. Today, enrollment is more than 30,000. We were a big part of building that."[93]

Maxwell was not exaggerating. The 49ers were the toast of the campus during Maxwell's four years at the school, going a perfect 58–0 at home and winning the 1977 Midwest Regional for the right to play Marquette in the Final Four at Atlanta, Georgia, where they dropped a heartbreaking 51–49 decision. Maxwell had tied the game with four seconds remaining, but a subsequent desperate inbounds pass from Marquette guard Butch Lee ended up in the hands of teammate Jerome Whitehead, who managed to lay the ball in for the winning basket. "Whitehead bumped me, but I was still able to partially block his dunk," remembered Maxwell. "The ball hit the backboard and bounced off the rim before dropping."[94] Marquette went on to take the title, but there was no doubt that Maxwell's hoops stock had risen through the roof, as the First-Team All-American averaged 22.2 points and 12.1 rebounds as a senior. The previous year he had led UNCC to the NIT Tournament championship while walking away with MVP honors.

One of the impressed spectators on hand to witness the occasion at Madison Square Garden was Red Auerbach. "His talent for dribbling caught my eye—behind the back and between his legs, an extraordinary feat for someone 6-foot-8," he said. "The kid was not showboating. I know when I see it. He had great body control, quickness and very fluid moves."[95] Auerbach remembered Maxwell when he became available at No. 12 in the first round of the 1977 NBA Draft after the Milwaukee Bucks decided to go with Ernie Grunfeld from the University of Tennessee the pick before. The latter move was no great surprise. Milwaukee had earlier arranged a predraft interview with Maxwell in Charlotte, only to find that he apparently had forgotten about it. He eventually showed up over three hours late, but the meeting went steadily downhill from there as an unapologetic Maxwell gave mostly one-word answers to the questions posed by Milwaukee GM Wayne Embry and coach Don Nelson. "He did a better job of interviewing us than we did of interviewing him," Embry later wrote.[96]

Maxwell, whom sportswriter and author John Powers once described as "an odd collection of arms and legs who could shoot and dribble and rebound and run," was the lone standout on an otherwise forgettable club when he made his debut in a Boston uniform for the 1977–78 season. "I had joined a team that suffered its first losing season in almost ten years," he said. "We had a collection of former all-Stars, but the chemistry wasn't right."[97] Although he averaged only 7.3 points and 5.3 rebounds off the bench, "Cornbread," a nickname Maxwell had picked up in college for his resemblance to the lead character in the 1975 film *Cornbread, Earl and Me*, impressed onlookers with his aptitude for the game. "He knew his strengths and weaknesses and just played hard 100 percent of the time," teammate Don Chaney said.[98] Less inspiring were his dietary habits, which could bring a nutritionist to tears. "They told me what he eats and most of it you put in a toaster," John Havlicek said. "And before a game, I've seen him drink grape sodas with a couple of Butterfinger bars on the side."[99]

Maxwell showed dramatic improvement in his second season when he was designated the team's starting forward. He led the league in field goal percentage (.584) and set personal career highs in scoring average (19.9 points per game) and rebounding (9.9). Player-coach Dave Cowens attributed his growth on the floor to learning how to position himself underneath the basket. "It's tough down inside," Cowens said. "There's a lot of traffic and when you're in there it becomes very physical. I had an adjustment to make myself. But Max has become our best offensive rebounder and our main threat in there." Maxwell saw things slightly differently. "I've always been an offensive player with pretty good moves inside," he told writer Larry Whiteside. "But in college I had a team that was built around me. Here, I had to adjust to the system. I think I have thus far, but the key to it all is confidence. I have more confidence in myself and in my teammates. I think I've matured . . . I can't explain it. It just happened that way."[100]

As Cowens, Havlicek, and the rest of the underperforming cast from this era faded from the scene, Maxwell provided a bridge to a newer, more talented generation of Celtics stars in Larry Bird, Kevin McHale, and Robert Parish. And while the Big Three rightfully earned most of the headlines and cheers, Maxwell did not exactly retreat into the background, providing consistent scoring and defense while demonstrating a propensity for coming up big in high-pressure situations. A case in point was the fifth contest of the 1981 NBA Finals when Maxwell personally took charge with 28 points to give the Celtics a crucial 3–2 series edge over the Houston Rockets.

"It's amazing how simple the game became that night," he said afterward. "If I took a step in one direction, the ball would come my way. If I took a step in another direction, the ball would also come that way. Everything seemed to be happening my way. Houston tried several players against me defensively, but not one of them could contain me. It was a magical night. It was like a Rembrandt. I couldn't have painted a better picture." Yet Maxwell was under no delusions about where he fit into the club's overall hierarchy. "On that team I was considered just the other forward," he said. "I understood that it was because Larry Bird was an excellent basketball player, but I had pride, too." For sure, that was why winning the NBA Finals MVP award that season meant so much to him. "It was not only a boost to my ego . . . it was also a tremendous experience that had a profound outcome on the rest of my career."[101]

There were plenty of ear-to-ear smiles to be found in the champagne-soaked Celtics' clubhouse following the team's historic seven-game triumph over the Lakers. None were broader than the one belonging to Red Auerbach—the venerable team patriarch who relished the opportunity of accepting the league championship trophy for a record 15th time. Of course, Auerbach being Auerbach, he could not resist taking a swipe at the alleged doomsayers in the media he believed were responsible for writing off the Celtics following their abysmal showing at the start of the series. "Whatever happened to the Los Angeles dynasty?" he playfully inquired between puffs on his trademark victory cigar. "Here's where it is, right here! That's the dynasty right here. We're the best team in the world right now!"[102]

Be that as it may, Kevin McHale preferred to frame the outcome in hyperbolic us-versus-them terms, reflecting the underdog self-image of many Boston fans. "It was a case of the Teamsters, the hard hats and the miners taking on the MD's in their Mercedes, the lawyers in their three-piece suits and movie stars of Hollywood and winning by getting their hands dirty," he said.[103] Larry Bird declined to go down that particular rhetorical route, choosing instead to emphasize the Celtics overall resilience as a team. "To be honest," he said, "[the Lakers] should have swept, and it was virtually over after that game they crushed us, but we came back and played hard and played together."[104]

The victory registered on a more deeply personal level with K. C. Jones. Previously dismissed as a coaching lightweight for his alleged mental lapse in the 1975 NBA Finals, Jones had impressed everyone by the grace and skill with which he brought the club together following one of the most tumultuous off-seasons in franchise history. "I can't explain how I feel," Jones said. "It's too great a feeling . . . my thought is that these guys, all these players, made me a better coach and I needed their help. I wanted this championship and they went out and got it for me."[105]

Equally elated but for reasons that had nothing to do with who won or lost that day was rookie NBA Commissioner David Stern, on hand to officially hand out the championship hardware. His long-term goal when he assumed office in February was to make the league a global entertainment enterprise; and if the television ratings for the 1984 Finals were any indication, he and his sport had taken a giant leap in that direction. For CBS, the television network tasked with broadcasting the event, the Celtics–Lakers dogfight was a massive ratings hit, drawing unprecedented numbers of viewers to the contests, including a previously unheard-of 40 million for Game 7.[106] "Those two weeks in June 1984," writes author L. Jon Wertheim in his 2021 best-seller *Glory Days: The Summer of 1984 and the 90 Days That Changed Sports and Culture Forever*, "a country was captivated by the drama and captured by the rivalry—two different teams led by two different players." Wertheim added that the series offered an early glimpse of what would become known as "reality television" in the not-so-distant future, complete with colorful characters, personal feuds, and unscripted moments of high drama.

The tone was understandably more somber in the losers' clubhouse. "The ending was not good," said Magic Johnson, who had delivered another stinker in the series-deciding contest with 7 turnovers and 16 points on 5 for 14 shooting. He had kept reporters waiting almost an hour by his locker before emerging from his postgame shower to take questions. "I felt like we handed it to them," he offered, "but I'm still going to party tonight because I'm a party guy. They are celebrating in there [the Celtics locker room], but so am I because we got here. We didn't get the title, but we came darn close. We deserve a party."[107] Kareem Abdul-Jabbar, who had his goggles ripped from his head by an obnoxious Boston fan as he was leaving the floor, was definitely *not* in a partying mood when he addressed the media. "How do I feel?" he asked with tears brimming in his eyes. "I'm disappointed. I thought we could've played better. Too bad we didn't. We came in here and we felt we had a shot, but we just came up short. I felt we were ready. It doesn't matter when people say you're a better team on paper, you have to prove it on the court. The Celts proved they were better."[108]

Fellow big man Kurt Rambis, the recipient of Kevin McHale's brutal takedown in Game 4, concurred, citing the Lakers' inability to secure second shots as the deciding factor. "The reason we lost was because we didn't do anything on the boards," he said. "When they were rebounding well and we were not, it kept us from running. Just look at the stat sheets, you'll see rebounding won them the series. We came in here knowing how well they rebound, so we knew we'd have to control the boards to win and we didn't."[109]

Feeling lower than Charlie Brown after he failed to kick the football yet again, the Lakers experienced one final blow to their dignity when they wearily boarded the team bus well past midnight to make it back to their hotel in downtown Boston. "Even though their team had won the series," Johnson recounted, "the Celtics fans were mad at us. Several hundred people surrounded the bus, and some of them threw rocks and bottles. It got pretty hairy when they started rocking our bus. We all ducked down with our hands over our heads in case they smashed the windows."[110] Local police arrived on the "mad scene" to prevent any further hair-raising mischief, but Johnson caught himself wondering what the mob's reaction might have been if his team had won.[111]

Cornbread Maxwell's spectacular evening thankfully spared him from finding out.

CHAPTER NINE

Requiem for a Champion

LESS THAN 14 HOURS AFTER WINNING ARGUABLY THE MOST EXCITING NBA Finals in history, an exhausted and somewhat hung over Celtics squad flew to Washington, D.C., to meet President Ronald Reagan for a celebratory White House Rose Garden reception. "You are the Celtics," the Gipper intoned, "and like the original Celtics, the great Irish warriors in olden times, you have fought for and won great victories with great glory."[1] It was a satisfying moment for fellow Washingtonian Red Auerbach, who relished the opportunity of rubbing elbows with the leader of the free world. "It's a thrill to have the President of the United States shake your hand," beamed Auerbach, who had made a regular practice of meeting commanders in chief going back to the days of Harry S Truman. "It was inspiring, the culmination of a fantastic year." Even though Reagan badly mispronounced the surnames of several ex-Celtics greats such as John Havlicek and Dave Cowens, whom he referred to as "Hava-lick" and "Covens," respectively, no Green Team members appeared to pay serious mind.[2] Everyone was having too good a time.

Indeed, a sunglasses-wearing Danny Ainge jokingly asked the president whether it could be arranged to have the team's playoff-winning shares made tax-free. Dennis Johnson also chimed in, wondering how Reagan did not sweat in the sweltering June heat during the ceremony. Still, the event was not devoid of controversy. That's because three of the most prominent contributors to Boston's victory were not in attendance: Larry Bird, Cedric Maxwell, and Robert Parish. Of the three, only Maxwell had anything approaching an understandable excuse. "I was getting married the next week," he later explained. "I was out getting a marriage license. I didn't have time. It wasn't anything anyone said. It wasn't that I didn't like the president." As for his other absentee teammates, the Chief kept publicly mum on the subject while Bird opted for a snarky response. "If the president wants to see me," the recently crowned 1984 NBA MVP said, "he knows where to find me."[3] Future megastar athletes like LeBron James, Mookie Betts, and Tom Brady who would shun similar presidential gatherings got into far deeper trouble in the age of Twitter, Instagram, TikTok, and Facebook. But in 1984, social media in its omnipresent modern form did not exist, and as a result, memory of the incident quickly faded.

Who did not fade away were the Celtics. They started the 1984–85 season in true defending champion form, blazing to a 15–1 start. Bird showed no drop-off in production. In fact, he seemed better than ever. "I honestly don't know when he'll stop improving," said Auerbach, who had formally given up his GM duties to become team president.[4]

In the middle of the hot streak, Bird managed to earn the ire of Julius Erving when he exchanged elbows with the aging Philadelphia superstar during a blowout victory at the Garden. Bird, who scored 42 points in the game, was whistled for an offensive foul, and he took out his frustration on Erving. "Larry was saying things to Julius," remembered Ainge. "Things like 'You better retire if that's the best you can do.' Or, 'Get someone else to guard me. You can't do it.'"[5] Tensions escalated from there with more harsh words and blows. Said Erving, "It was very uncharacteristic, you know, because we did Converse commercials together, we did Spalding commercials together, so we were kind of cool. But I thought something was going to happen, because [Bird] was definitely mad—but he was mad at the referee, he wasn't mad at me."[6] Bird was assessed a then record $7,500 fine by the league for his role in instigating the fracas, but it did little to detract from his on-court performance moving forward.

On March 12, 1985, he set the Celtics' single game franchise scoring record of 60 points against a hapless Atlanta Hawks squad on the road. "He told us at halftime that nobody could stop him so just give him the ball and get out of the way," Robert Parish said. "Then he went out and started taunting the Atlanta players on the floor, the ones on the bench, their coaches, even the referees. He was talking so much trash he was buried in it. It was one of those nights he could have drop-kicked the ball in. I loved it."[7] Just nine days earlier in a victory over the Detroit Pistons, Kevin McHale had taken home the honors with 56 points before prematurely pulling himself out of the contest in the final moments. Bird could not believe his eyes. "I told Kevin afterward that he should have gone for sixty," Bird later confessed to writer Peter May. "You don't give up. You do the best you can while you have the opportunity to do it. When he had the opportunity, he should have went for as many as he could. What's the difference if you come out two minutes before the game is over? You've already played the whole game. You might as well finish it up and have your greatest game you can and not worry about it."[8]

After wrapping up the regular season at 63–19, a one-game improvement over their previous year's mark, the Celtics once again steamrolled their Eastern Conference playoff competition to earn another NBA Finals appearance with the Los Angeles Lakers. But the team was missing a major 1984 contributor: Gerald Henderson. Henderson had been traded to the Seattle SuperSonics in October for Seattle's first-round draft pick in 1986. The reason? According to Auerbach, Henderson had shown up at training camp out of shape, therefore making himself expendable. A more likely explanation was that Auerbach resented the starting point guard's earlier holdout for more money in contract extension talks. "Gerald didn't have an ounce of fat on him," Maxwell maintained. "Red always had to make the guy he was trading away into a villain. He had to justify every move he made. The sad thing is that the fans in Boston believed everything Red said. If he said the moon was purple, there were people who took his word for it."[9]

Maxwell would have his own problems with Auerbach that season after undergoing exploratory arthroscopic surgery on his left knee in February. Slow to recover, Maxwell lost his starting forward's spot to Kevin McHale and was a shadow of his former self the rest of the way. Auerbach was unsympathetic. He believed Maxwell was dogging it and not seriously committed to his rehabilitation. He was not alone in this assessment; Bird expressed similar thoughts: "I don't know what's going on, but I can tell you that Max doesn't want to play for us anymore," he confided to Bob Ryan.[10] Maxwell, however, dismissed such speculation. "I've never had my integrity questioned before," he said. "I can be a happy-go-lucky person, and I have to admit that I don't work in practice as hard as I should. [But] I stated I was hurt and they just didn't believe me. For them to question it and say I didn't try, well, it was a bad situation."[11]

Minus Henderson and a healthy Maxwell, the Celtics were at a competitive disadvantage vis-à-vis the Lakers in the finals. Although the Celtics soundly thumped them in the series opener, 148–112, Los Angeles took four of the next five games to win the world championship and avenge their previous spring's heartbreaking loss. "There comes a time when you have to plant your feet firmly, take a stand and kick butt," an emotional Pat Riley said afterward. "That's what we did. They can never mock us, or humiliate us, or disrespect us, which is what they did last year."[12] Bird, who injured his right index finger in a Boston bar fight following the second game, was disconsolate. He made only 12 of his 29 shots in the deciding contest with an underwhelming .449 field goal percentage for the entire series. Meanwhile, Danny Ainge—Henderson's starting backcourt replacement—posted a .414 average, and Maxwell could barely make it down the floor. "Your goal is to win a championship," Bird said, "and if you don't win it, you're a failure."[13] Not even being named regular season MVP for the second year in a row could make up for that.

Bird's spirits picked up later that off-season when he visited Red Auerbach at his office. The wily hoops patriarch had a question for him. What did he think of Bill Walton coming to the Celtics?[14] Bird was stunned. A big fan of the supremely gifted but oft-injured veteran center, he could barely believe his ears. Walton was a former league MVP who had been the hub of an underdog Portland Trail Blazers team that had gone all the way in 1977. True, he had performed in relative obscurity the previous four seasons for the also-ran San Diego/Los Angeles Clippers, but he still had put up decent numbers in limited duty. Parish, meanwhile, had looked worn down in the Finals due to the heavy minutes he had logged during the regular schedule. He was in desperate need of an adequate backup, and Walton could more than adequately fill that role. "Go get him," Bird told Auerbach.[15]

A deal was struck just before the 1985–86 season began. Walton came to Boston in exchange for Maxwell and a first-round draft pick. Maxwell was beyond surprised. His knee was feeling better, and he thought a comeback season was in the offing. Instead, he got blindsided. "At that point I felt betrayed, hurt, all of the above," he later recounted. "It was like they had forgotten everything else I had done—and all those things were factual. We won two championships, and I was a leading contributor. And during the resurgence, I was a big part, too. And I was the person who had to make the sacrifices and change my role."[16] Whereas Maxwell believed that he was being discarded like "a worn-out pair of shoes thrown to the back of the closet," Walton regarded the trade as a great opportunity to prove that he could still be a valuable contributor on a title-contending ballclub.[17] "I'm honored to be part of this team," he said in his introductory Boston press conference. "I can't play 35 to 40 minutes per game. I think I can be a productive and complementary player for the Celtics. One of the nice things about playing with the Boston Celtics is that the minutes will be kept down—it could certainly prolong my career."[18]

Although Walton got off to a shaky start with his new club by committing seven turnovers in a season-opening overtime loss to the New Jersey Nets ("It was exactly the way not to play basketball," he said), the ex-UCLA star soon righted himself and played with a gung-ho brio that lifted the Celtics to another competitive level.[19] Observed Kevin McHale, "You watch an old, old guy like that, with the most hammered body in sports, acting like a high school kid—it's both funny and inspiring at the same time. Every game was a challenge, and he didn't let any of us forget it."[20] Coming off the bench, Walton shot a career-high 56.2 percent from the field while averaging 6.8 rebounds, 2.1 assists, and 1.3 blocked shots in just under 20 minutes per contest. He became an obvious selection for that year's NBA Sixth Man Award, an honor that had gone to McHale the previous two seasons.

"His style of play fit perfectly with mine," Bird wrote. "The key was to keep moving, set good picks, to cut off him and to be ready for the ball at any time. We were able to work at least one give-and-go every game. The entire Boston Garden crowd seemed to know when it was coming, but opponents never seemed to catch on." Walton especially impressed Bird during the team's first regular-season meeting with the Lakers that January: "Bill came into the game in the first period and completely dominated the game. He blocked a Kareem shot. He threw down a tremendous dunk. He finished with seven blocked shots in sixteen minutes. . . . Bill was getting into it because he knew what kind of team the Celtics were capable of being that year."[21]

Indeed, the Celtics became the basketball version of the 1927 New York Yankees, victimizing their opposition to the tune of a 67–15 record, the fourth best in NBA history. "If you were grading them for the season, your only conceivable mark would have been an A-plus," Bob Ryan later wrote.[22] The playoffs didn't present much of a challenge either. The Celtics lost only one game on their way to a third consecutive trip to the Finals. But instead of meeting familiar foe Los Angeles—the victims of a third-round upset—they faced the Houston Rockets and their famed "Twin Towers" frontcourt of Hakeem Olajuwon and Ralph Sampson. It didn't matter. They needed only six games to rub out the Rockets and bring home the franchise's 16th title. The only memorable highlight from the series was a fight that broke out between Sampson and feisty Celtics reserve guard Jerry Sichting in the fifth game. The 6–1 Sichting—acquired in a trade with the Indiana Pacers—spotted the All-Star big man over a foot in height and several pounds of muscle, prompting Bird to dryly observe that his girlfriend could beat up Sichting.[23] "It kind of flared up and ended," McHale said of the incident. "But, man, it became such a David and Goliath thing later on. Poor Ralph just wasn't going to win that one, you know."[24]

The Celtics were at the pinnacle of their success in the Larry Bird era and appeared destined to win several more championships with the selection of University of Maryland forward Len Bias as the second overall pick in that June's NBA draft. "This kid will make an impact quicker than almost anyone in the draft," Auerbach said. "He can play some off-guard, small forward and power forward. Some people say he won't get playing time because of our frontcourt situation, but you never know what's going to happen. Larry could get hurt. Kevin could get hurt. If that happens, you want someone that can step right in and do the job.

This kid will do that. And should we stay healthy, we'll just have a lot more power and flexibility with Bias."[25]

Bias, whose drafting rights had been acquired with the pick from the earlier Henderson swap with Seattle, averaged 23.2 points and 6.9 rebounds in his final season with the Terrapins. He hailed from the Greater Washington, D.C., area and was already drawing favorable comparisons to Michael Jordan, the 1986 NBA Rookie of the Year and future GOAT. "Back in the 80s there were three guys that stood out above the [collegiate] crowd," longtime basketball analyst Jay Bilas maintains. "Jordan, Ralph Sampson, and Bias. Bias was a complete player. There was nothing he couldn't do." Bias combined tremendous speed, strength, and athleticism with a silky smooth outside shot to make him nearly impossible to defend on the open floor. "Jordan, at that time, would have killed for that jumper," noted one contemporary.[26] Interestingly, in their only head-to-head encounter in college, Jordan's then top-ranked University of North Carolina Tar Heels had beaten Bias's Maryland squad, but Bias had bested MJ in the individual scoring department, 24–21. "[Bias] created things," Duke University coach Mike Krzyzewski said. "People associate the term 'playmaking' with point guards. But I consider a playmaker as someone who can do things others can't, the way Jordan did. Bias was like that. He could invent ways to score, and there was nothing you could do about it."[27]

The 22-year-old had long been a target of intense interest by the Celtics, as evidenced by Auerbach hiring him as a counselor at his annual summer basketball camp. "I know this kid well," Auerbach told reporters on draft day. "He's got good work habits, and most of all, he's drooling to play here." For sure, Bias had grown up an avid Celtics fan and relished the prospect of performing with Bird in front of packed Boston Garden audiences. "It's a dream come true," he said.[28] But the dream quickly turned into a nightmare. Two days after being drafted, Bias died of cardiorespiratory failure. He had ingested a large amount of cocaine in his Maryland dorm room with friends celebrating his selection by the Celtics. His reported last words were, "I'm a bad motherfucker."[29]

Bias's passing rocked Boston and the wider basketball world. "This is terrible news," an emotionally distraught Larry Bird told a reporter from his off-season home in French Lick. "This is one of the cruelest things I ever heard. I was looking forward to coming to rookie camp and working with him." Brad Daugherty—a hulking 7-foot center from North Carolina who was selected by the Cleveland Cavaliers just before Bias in the draft—was likewise unsettled: "He was a very good friend of mine, and it terrifies me to the point of depression."[30] The normally gruff, hard-bitten Johnny Most became so overcome with grief that he broke down and wept.[31] Auerbach, though, took the news the hardest. He had viewed Bias as the key to extending the dynasty another decade. Now those hopes were blasted. "I couldn't believe it when I heard it," he said. "The kid had his whole life ahead of him. He was one of the happiest people you'd ever want to see. His face was gleaming. He was the picture of health. At 6–8 in his stocking feet and 210 pounds, he was like the perfect physical specimen—the best athlete in the draft. He didn't have an ounce of fat."[32]

The death cast a pall over the entire 1986–87 campaign. The Celtics easily won their division again, but cracks began to show in their championship foundation. Although they remained nearly unbeatable at the Garden, they turned into proverbial pumpkins on the road, dropping below the .500 mark. "That bothers me," K. C. Jones said. "I don't want teams feeling too comfortable when they're playing us in their own building."[33] Injuries were a major factor. Bill Walton—who had provided such a big boost off the bench and in the locker room the year before—hurt his right ankle while working out on a stationary bike. He appeared in only 10 regular season games. "I wanted to be the best," Walton later confessed to author Michael McClellan, "but my body would not carry me where I needed to go or wanted to go."[34] Scott Wedman, Danny Ainge, Robert Parish, and Kevin McHale also experienced their own painful physical setbacks over the course of the year, prompting the *Boston Globe* to half-seriously compare the depleted club roster to the fictional U.S. Army mobile medical hospital depicted in the hit television series *M*A*S*H*.[35]

Nevertheless, Auerbach thought there was much to be proud of. "No team has ever given more," he claimed, "and that is all you can really ask of any team. Just give me everything you have. I have never seen a team give everything it had, until I saw this team."[36] And no one gave more than McHale. Playing with a misdiagnosed hairline fracture of his right foot after James Edwards of the Phoenix Suns stepped on it in early March, McHale still managed to submit an MVP-worthy performance: 26.1 points a game with a league-leading 60.4 field goal percentage. Remembered McHale, "People kept telling me, 'It's in your head.' I said, 'No, it's in my head. It hurts all the time, our medical staff would say, 'Ice it and forget about it.' But that was not going to work. I had played on it so long. I shouldn't have."[37]

McHale continued his dominant play in the postseason, helping the Celtics edge a rising Detroit Pistons team led by All-Star point guard Isaiah Thomas in a thrilling seven-game Eastern Conference Finals. Yet it was Bird who garnered the most attention with an improbable steal at the end of the pivotal fifth contest. With five seconds remaining and the Celtics trailing by one, Bird snatched a hurried inbounds pass by Thomas that was intended for Detroit center Bill Laimbeer and proceeded to feed a cutting Dennis Johnson for the game-winning layup. Move over, Gerald Henderson. "We found a miracle," Danny Ainge said. "That was the most unbelievable play I've ever seen in basketball."[38] A dazed Thomas was at a loss for words. "You can see I should not have thrown the pass," he dejectedly told the assembled media around his locker afterward. "You can see I should have thrown the ball harder or Bill should have come in. But all I can say is they stole the ball and they won the game."[39] For his part, Bird nonchalantly suggested he happened to be at the right place at the right time. "The ball just hung up there," he explained. "It seemed to take forever to get to Laimbeer. I kept going and got my left hand on the ball. I was thinking about shooting, but the ball was going the other way. Then I turned and saw Dennis. It was a lucky play. That was all it was."[40]

The Celtics' luck ran out against the Lakers in the Finals, their third such showdown in four seasons. Unlike the previous two encounters, however, this one was never really in doubt. The Lakers were clearly the superior team and won in six, including a come-from-behind 107–106 Game 4 victory at the Garden that turned on a Magic Johnson "junior, junior, junior skyhook" over the outstretched arms of Kevin McHale and Robert Parish with two seconds remaining. "The most frustrating part of that game was that we had played exactly the kind of game we needed to win," McHale said tearfully. "Everything was there except for the final score."[41]

One year removed from directing the franchise to a 16th banner, K. C. Jones struggled to find a silver lining. "We shouldn't have been [in the Finals]," the Boston coach said. "That's the thing to remember. This rag-tag team with the broken feet. These guys fought, hustled, grabbed, sat on the floor, did everything they could do." McHale was somewhat more wistful. "You think about how it could have been," he said. "You don't take anything away from the Lakers. You just wonder. What would we have done with a healthy Bill Walton, a 7-foot-3 guy off the bench who claims he's 6–11? What would we have done with Scott Wedman off the bench? What would we have done if everyone were healthy?" Bird had put aside such speculation after the final buzzer, preferring instead to focus on what he needed to do to improve his game in the off-season. "There are some things I want to work on," he said. "I know what I've got to do. I have to get a little stronger, stay in shape this summer, because I'm getting a little older and . . . I've just got to use my abilities a little better."[42]

Alas, there would be no additional championships, let alone Finals appearances for Bird and Company. Jones was forced out as coach after the 1987–88 season while retirements, poor health, and bad trades claimed key players like Johnson, Ainge, Wedman, and Walton. Unable to find adequate replacements, the team leaned even more heavily on an aging Big Three to carry the competitive load. It was too much to ask. McHale was never the same player after the foot injury; Bird suffered from Achilles and back problems that sidelined him for significant stretches. Indeed, the three-time MVP was no longer considered among the NBA's elite. "It was a rude awakening for [Bird]," noted Parish, who alone among the celebrated troika maintained relatively good health. "He had thought he was invincible. . . . There was a long readjustment period for him. And for a while, he was like a shell. He just could not believe he got hurt. I guess he started believing all his clips."[43]

Bird still had his moments. On May 22, 1988, he faced off against Atlanta Hawks forward Dominique Wilkins at home in one of the all-time greatest shootouts in league playoff history. "It was like two gunfighters waiting to blink," McHale enthused. "It was boom . . . boom . . . Larry would make one and Dominique would make one. Larry would make [another] one and Dominique would make [another] one. It was unbelievable . . . I tell you there was one four-minute [span] there that was as pure a form of basketball as you're ever going to see." Entering the fourth quarter of the deciding game of the Eastern Conference Semi-finals, the Celtics held the lead, but the blistering hot hand of Wilkins (a game-high 47 points) threatened to wrest it away. That's when Larry Legend went to work, single-handedly carrying the team by scoring 20 of his 34 points down the stretch and outdueling Wilkins, who amassed 16 points in the frame. The Celtics survived, 118–116. "I felt when he scored, I had to come back on the other end and keep our rhythm up, keep the tempo going," Wilkins said. "Our guys were pitching the ball to me off screens and my shots were going in—jumpers, bankers, top of the key." Yet in the end, it didn't matter. "The way I look at it," Bird explained, "the team goes to me a lot for the last-second shots throughout the year. And if it comes down to one shot or five shots or whatever, I think my teammates would rather see me have the ball and try to win the game for them."[44]

Bird enjoyed one final moment of hoops glory as a member of the 1992 U.S. men's Olympic basketball team in Barcelona. Proclaimed the "Dream Team" by *Sports Illustrated*, the team—which, in addition to Bird, boasted such extraordinary all-time talents as Michael Jordan, Magic Johnson, Charles Barkley, Scotty Pippen, and Patrick Ewing—marked the first time professionals were permitted to compete in the Olympics.[45] They did not disappoint, waltzing their way to a gold medal while demonstrating to the world America's total domination of the sport. Indeed, the average margin of victory in the eight games they played against top-flight international competition was an eye-popping 43.8 points. "It was like Elvis and the Beatles put together," gushed team coach Chuck Daly. "Traveling with the Dream Team was like traveling with twelve rock stars. That's all I can compare it to."[46]

Although Bird's on-court contributions were modest due to his bad back, he more than compensated for this fact with his off-court leader-ship. At 35, he, along with Magic and MJ, were the three veteran voices in the locker room that commanded the most respect. They made sure everyone remained focused on the task at hand, and woe to egocentric ballplayers like Barkley who were known for putting their own individualistic needs above team success. Recounted Pippen, "One of my favorite moments was when Barkley would come and shoot at our end [during practice], and Michael and Larry and Magic would tell him 'Shoot somewhere else. This basket is only for people who have rings.'"[47] All the same, the experience left a warm, lasting impression on Bird, who recalled his childhood in French Lick when his troubled father avidly followed the Olympics on television. The elder Bird would constantly update his family on how many gold medals the U.S. team won in track and field and other major events. "So when we stood on that platform in Barcelona to get our gold medals," Bird later told author Jack McCallum, "that was the most exciting thing for me. I was thinking back to my dad and remembering that when he heard that anthem he was happy. And I was happy too."[48]

Within days of his Olympic triumph, Bird publicly announced his retirement at a 45-minute Boston Garden press conference. He told the packed gathering that no one should feel sorry for him. He had enjoyed a satisfying and productive basketball career in spite of the crippling injuries he had endured. "I would have liked to play a little longer," he admitted, "but I've had enough pain to last me a lifetime."[49]

The tributes came pouring in. Hal Bock of the Associated Press wrote that the only comparable situation was "if they tore down the Green Monster at Fenway Park or turned the Boston Garden into a parking lot."[50] NBA Commissioner David Stern was less hyperbolic, believing there was no easy way to quantify Bird's impact on the game. "With his intensity, dedication, competitiveness and will to win," the Columbia University Law School graduate said, "he has been the ultimate team player in the quintessential team sport. Quite simply, Larry Bird has helped to define the way a generation of basketball fans has come to view and appreciate the NBA."[51] Red Auerbach found himself reminiscing about the time he had first met Bird more than a decade earlier. "He looked like a little country bumpkin," he said, "but when you talked to him and you looked into his eyes, you knew you weren't talking to any dummy. He knew what he wanted in life and he knew what it would take to get there."[52]

Pulitzer Prize–winning sports columnist Ira Berkow preferred to remember Bird as a selfless blue-collar athlete who always gave fans their money's worth. Bird "never had to score 50 points in a game to be sensational," he wrote. "One no-look, chest-high touch pass to a man cutting behind him was enough." But it was left to old rival and fellow Dream Teamer Magic Johnson, who had earlier announced his own retirement from basketball after being diagnosed with the human immunodeficiency virus (HIV), to pay him the ultimate compliment. "Larry Bird was the only player in the league that I feared and he was the smartest player I played against," he said. "I always enjoyed competing against him because he brought out the best in me. Even when we weren't going head-to-head, I would follow his game because I always used him as a measuring stick against mine."[53]

Meanwhile, the Celtics became an also-ran as McHale followed Bird into retirement in 1993, and Parish opted to sign as a free agent with the Charlotte Hornets the following season at 37. If that wasn't depressing enough, All-Star shooting guard Reggie Lewis—who had been selected 22nd overall in the 1987 draft—died from cardiac arrest after collapsing during an off-season workout. The shy, baby-faced Baltimore native had spent his college years at neighboring Northeastern University, where he became the school's all-time leading scorer. He continued to be an elite offensive force in the NBA and appeared on a path to superstardom. No less than Michael Jordan subscribed to this belief. Lewis "was a tough matchup," he said. "He had those long arms that really bothered me. I was trying to be aggressive with him. I was trying to take advantage of his passive demeanor, but he didn't back down. He never relinquished his own aggressiveness. He shocked me a little bit."[54] Likewise shocking were disturbing allegations first reported in the *Wall Street Journal* that Lewis's fatal heart condition may have been linked to cocaine abuse, which his widow and the Celtics vehemently denied. "A lot of people just knew Reggie was a basketball player, but the guys on the team knew him off the court," backcourt teammate Dee Brown said. "For something like this to come out to just tarnish an image, it doesn't even have to be true.

Just to throw that bone out there so people can think about it, I think that's not right at all."[55]

Regardless of the accuracy of the reporting, Lewis's tragic passing left the Celtics without a certifiable scoring threat and court leader. As a result, the team plunged further in the standings, bottoming out with a franchise-low 15 victories in 1997. Not that they were trying very hard to win. Future Hall of Famer Tim Duncan was projected to be available as the first overall pick in the following year's draft lottery, and the Celtics saw him as the answer to their rebuilding dreams. Thus, tanking would ensure them the best chance of securing the Wake Forest University forward/center in what popularly became known as the "Tim Duncan Sweepstakes."

Unfortunately, the bouncing ping pong balls went San Antonio's way instead, and the Celtics' string of ill fortune, which dated back to the unexpected death of Bias, remained unbroken. M. L. Carr, a coaching neophyte who had been brought back to lead the team in their race to the bottom, later characterized the experience as the toughest thing he had ever done in sports. "It was hard, but it was the right thing," he said. "For me, in terms of the decisions I was making, in the quietness of my home or in the wee hours of the night, you wrestle with some of the decisions. But you had to do what was right for the organization." Even if that meant not going with your best players in crunch time. "Guys would get upset not being in the game, which is natural in the NBA. . . . But . . . I'd say, 'The goal is to get Tim Duncan here. You guys are going to have a great ride. I had my Tim Duncan. His name was Larry Bird. I had Robert Parish. I got my ride. I'm trying to help you get your ride. So I'm going to need you to bear with me, work with me, come to practice and work hard, give me a great attitude.'"[56]

Carr was dismissed at season's end and replaced with former Knicks coach Rick Pitino, who had piloted the University of Kentucky Colonels to an NCAA title in 1996. Slick, erudite, overbearing, and self-confident to a fault, Pitino promised to restore the Celtics to their former greatness. "I came to Kentucky for a specific reason: to try to build a program in shambles to the championship level, and we've accomplished that," he said. "Now, I have a similar situation at the professional level . . .

something full of glory, full of tradition, full of wonderful pride that I'd like to see get back to the championship level."[57] But he soon learned painfully that turning around a storied college program was not the same as reviving an equally venerable NBA franchise, especially without a cornerstone impact player like Duncan.

The Celtics remained a pitiful outfit, never getting a sniff at the playoffs and losing more than they won during Pitino's underwhelming tenure with the club from 1997 to 2001. Fans and local media excoriated him for his lack of success, prompting Pitino to respond with an epic clubhouse rant. "Larry Bird is not walking through that door, fans," he thundered. "Kevin McHale is not walking through that door, and Robert Parish is not walking through that door. And if you expect them to walk through that door they're going to be gray and old. . . . People don't realize that, and as soon as they realize those three guys are not coming through that door, the better this town will be for all of us."[58] Bird DID walk through a different sort of door years later when he and Pitino crossed paths during the latter's enshrinement at the Naismith Memorial Basketball Hall of Fame in Springfield, Massachusetts. Pitino could not resist asking Indiana's most famous citizen what took him so long. "You don't want me now," Bird replied.[59]

In 2002, the Gaston family sold the Celtics to a private investor group led by local venture capitalists Wyc Grousbeck and Steve Pagliuca for $360 million, a then record sum for an NBA franchise. "I grew up wearing Celtics, Bruins, Patriots and Red Sox jerseys, season tickets to all four teams," Grousbeck said. "It's about as fun as it gets. [My favorite players] start with Bill Russell and goes on from there. I don't want to name any players and leave any out, but what a tradition." He added that the new ownership group's overarching goal was to "raise more championship banners."[60]

That objective would be achieved six years later when Paul Pierce, a prolific scoring small forward from Kansas whom Pitino had taken in the first round of the 1998 draft, teamed up with All-Star shooting guard Ray Allen and former league MVP forward Kevin Garnett. Allen and Garnett had been acquired via high-profile trades engineered by team Executive Director of Basketball Operations Danny Ainge, a popular hire made by Grousbeck and Pagliuca at the beginning of their regime. The new "Big Three" quickly jelled as a unit and propelled the Celtics into the 2008 NBA Finals, where they once again locked horns with the Lakers, spearheaded by the dazzling play of Hall of Fame guard Kobe Bryant. In six highly entertaining games, which drew comparisons to the two teams' legendary showdowns of the 1980s, the men in green prevailed, securing their 17th and second to last championship in franchise history. "This win is for Red Auerbach," Grousbeck said afterward.[61]

Sadly, Auerbach was not around to partake in the celebration. He passed away from a heart attack at 89 in 2006. "He was an original," reflected Tommy Heinsohn. "He left an indelible mark on the game of basketball and the NBA. He was a champion and he made champions."[62] Yet Auerbach's final years were far from happy. He suffered from declining health and the humiliation of having had his title as team president stripped away when Rick Pitino joined the organization. Pitino thought only he should hold that special distinction. Consequently, Paul Gaston, who succeeded his father as principal team owner in 1993, took it upon himself to personally notify Auerbach of the change. "The first words out of his mouth were, 'I've made a mistake,'" Auerbach later revealed to collaborator John Feinstein in their 2004 national best-seller *Let Me Tell You a Story*. "He told me how sorry he was but that he had made his commitment to Pitino. I wasn't going to make a big deal out of it, that's not my way. And I knew he was genuinely sorry." Nevertheless, the situation left a sour taste in his mouth. "It hurt me," Auerbach admitted. "And even though I tried not to think less of him for it, I did think less of Pitino. I simply couldn't understand why he had to have the *title*. He had the money, he had the power, why did he have to have the title too?"[63]

Auerbach was restored to the team's presidency after Pitino left town, but he had become more than just a name atop of an organizational chart by this point. He was now viewed as a certifiable hoops legend who had been present at the creation of the NBA in the 1940s. "Red Auerbach was the consummate teacher, leader and a true pioneer of the sport of basketball," David Stern said. "The NBA wouldn't be what it is today without Red."[64] Indeed, the great Celtics team Auerbach had assembled in 1984 played a crucial role in turbo-charging the league to soaring new heights of popularity, financial success, and national media exposure. But whatever happened to the other principals from that celebrated squad who made this outcome possible? In many respects, their stories and legacies are just as compelling as Auerbach's.

K. C. Jones did not stay away from the bench very long. After a brief unhappy stretch in the Celtics front office, where he was given little to do, Jones joined the Seattle SuperSonics in 1989 as an assistant to head coach Bernie Bickerstaff. When Bickerstaff quit a year later, Jones succeeded him and guided a talented but inexperienced team of underachievers featuring the explosive offense of third-year power forward Shawn Kemp to a respectable 41–41 record and a playoff berth. In remarks to reporters at his opening Seattle press conference, Jones conveyed that he would not abandon his low-key approach to coaching that had served him so well in Boston. "You won't see me yelling from the bench or giving long motivational speeches," he said. "That's not my personality."[65] Jones was unable to coax further improvement from the club, however, and was gone before the end of the 1991–92 season. "They're in a learning mode," he said. "It'll take some time. It just didn't happen quick enough."[66]

In later years, Jones would take up the clipboard again for the New England Blizzard, a Hartford, Connecticut-based women's pro team that played in the short-lived American Basketball League. When asked if the job represented "a step down" for someone of his stature, an irritated Jones responded that the question was "an insult to the profession—and to women who play the game."[67] Basketball was basketball, after all. As he once explained, "There's no real secret to coaching. Just be honest, fair and don't treat the players any differently than you'd want to be treated. Let them do what they do best and keep them happy and they'll usually make you look good."[68] Jones died of Alzheimer's disease at 88 in 2020.

Gerald Henderson never got over being traded from Boston. "Wasn't I their kind of guy?" he asked Joe Fitzgerald of the *Boston Herald*. "I mean, I tried to fit that mold because I really believed there was something special about the Celtics, about the mystique. And for five years it *was* special. But this . . . " He felt personally betrayed, especially after team management had inked him to a contract four days before dealing him to Seattle. He claimed that he never would have signed the deal if he had known what was coming. "It's like some poor guy finally figuring out that his wife's been fooling around on him," he explained. "It's a matter of truth, of trust. That's what any relationship is based on, whether it's your brother, your best friend, your mother, whoever. When you realize that trust has been abused, it's . . . what can I say? It's shocking."[69] Performing in a strange new uniform before sparse Seattle crowds also presented additional challenges as his new team struggled to reach the .500 mark. "More things are expected from me," Henderson said. "I've got the ball in my hands much more than I did in Boston. I'm expected to get more assists and penetrate more."[70]

Unfortunately, the situation was not a good fit, and Henderson spent what remained of his 13-year NBA career bouncing from one club to the next as a journeyman. It was a lonely, nomadic existence and one that made the Virginia Commonwealth graduate long for the close locker room camaraderie he had experienced with the Celtics. "In Boston, we all hung out with one another," he said. "We'd eat our meals together. We'd all kid around with each other, talking trash. Everyone looked forward to going to practice because we all loved to compete against each other. But, bottom line, during games we'd all root for each other to do well."[71] In his post-playing life, Henderson found success overseeing an energy consulting firm in Pennsylvania and mentoring his namesake son to an eight-year NBA career, mostly with the Charlotte Hornets. But mention of the Seattle trade that resulted in the Celtics' drafting Len Bias always riled him. "That deal wasn't right for anyone," he said.[72]

Unlike Henderson, Danny Ainge did not fault the Celtics for trading him. If anything, he thought the move made perfect basketball sense. "I just felt our team after the '87 season was just not the same," said Ainge, who had developed into a productive starter in the backcourt. "The health of Larry [Bird] and Kevin [McHale], those are guys who were two of the top five guys in the NBA and they weren't the same players. And the team, when they lost Len Bias, they needed to try to find a way to replace those guys."[73] So it came as no surprise when Ainge was dealt to the Sacramento Kings in 1989 for promising young center Joe Kleine, whom the Celtics incorrectly projected as a future frontcourt replacement for

Robert Parish. "I was excited about it," Ainge claimed.[74] But the Kings were in full rebuilding mode; and after the season, the 31-year-old was flipped to Portland, where he found himself on the losing end of the 1992 NBA Finals against Michael Jordan's dynastic Bulls. Ainge moved on to the Phoenix Suns as a free agent the following year and lost again in the Finals to Chicago. "I can't remember ever feeling as disappointed as I do now," he said.[75]

After unlacing his sneakers for good in 1995, he remained close to the game, coaching the Suns for three seasons and being an NBA color analyst for Turner Network Television—a job he relished. Yet when the new Celtics owners approached him with a lucrative offer to head team basketball operations in 2003, he enthusiastically accepted. "This guy will get it done," Red Auerbach said.[76] Indeed, apart from being the chief architect of the 2008 champions, for which he won NBA Executive of the Year honors, Ainge kept the club in regular playoff contention until he stepped down from the post in 2020. "Danny has meant so much to Celtics pride, the reinvigoration of the franchise," Steve Pagliuca said.[77] Not bad for a former washed-out major league baseball player who couldn't hit a curve.

Cedric Maxwell flourished in Los Angeles, having one of his finest seasons in 1986 (14.1 points and 8.2 rebounds per game) under the supportive coaching eye of old friend and mentor Don Chaney, who had introduced him to his first wife in the late 1970s. "I definitely felt that what the Clippers really needed was a championship player, and Max had proven he can win championships," Chaney recalled. "He could push his game up to another level and also set an example for the younger players who have not really had success at winning."[78] Yet Maxwell was still nursing a grudge about the abrupt, offhand way his departure from the Celtics was handled, especially when none of his former teammates bothered to contact him and offer consolation. "I don't know why, but players have never been able to leave Boston in good graces once they've been traded," he told Sam McManis of the *Los Angeles Times*. "It's like, Red Auerbach's this legend and no one else can be right. I couldn't win."[79] Nor could he make the Clippers a winner as they finished out of the playoffs for the eighth straight year of their undistinguished existence. Nevertheless, the perpetually warm and sunny LA clime held its own peculiar charms as Maxwell discovered when he was out house hunting one day. "I learned that if you see a peacock in the backyard," he recounted, "you need to find another place because they make an awful honky noise."[80]

Following a brief stint in Houston, Maxwell retired following the 1987–88 season. He was 32 years old and had no regrets. "There's nothing in my career I wish I could have done differently—even getting traded from the Celtics and getting hurt—because I feel like my whole career was just meant to be," he later wrote.[81] Maxwell was eventually persuaded to return to Boston in the early 2000s as a radio analyst for Celtics games, a position he has never left. He also had his old number retired by the team in 2003 with Auerbach's blessing. "Time heals a lot of wounds," observed longtime team PR man Jeff Twiss.[82] For certain, and from Maxwell's perspective the gesture represented an honor long overdue. "In some of the biggest games in this organization's history, among the Big Three, I played as well, if not better, than maybe some of those guys in particular games," he said. "I'm not saying I was better, or they did not deserve the honors they got. But to be a footnote to the greatest front line in basketball? . . . To me, that's like wow! How much can you be slapped around?"[83] As in his playing days, Max proved to be no pushover on defense.

Apart from his lackluster tenure as Celtics head coach, M. L. Carr served briefly as the club's GM in the mid-1990s. "I got that opportunity because I was trying to purchase the team from Paul Gaston," Carr recalled years later. "Paul didn't have an interest in the selling at that time, so he approached me about running the team. He said anyone who was chasing him as hard as I was in terms of trying to buy the team could definitely work for him running it."[84] Carr's most notable executive action during this period was a longshot attempt to put Michael Jordan in a Celtics uniform. Jordan had taken a sabbatical from basketball at the end of the 1992–93 season to play minor league baseball in the Chicago White Sox system. He would return to the NBA two years later when he discovered that he was about as adept at hitting off-speed pitches as Danny Ainge. During the interregnum Carr offered a high draft pick to the Chicago Bulls for the right to speak to Jordan about staging his hoops comeback with the Celtics. "I felt . . . it'd be worth laying out a first-round pick because I felt like I could convince him," Carr said. "Have an incredible new marketing path and make a fortune doing that. Tell him coming to the Celtics would be a good thing." In addition, Carr based his optimism on the their longtime friendship and shared North Carolina roots. "I've known Michael all his life," he said. "I've known his grandmother."[85]

But Chicago refused to go for the idea, and an empty-handed Carr was soon gone from the Boston front office. "The talent just wasn't there," he explained.[86] Carr moved on to become president of the WNBA's Charlotte Sting and work for a Massachusetts-based venture capital investment firm. Celtics fans still remember him best for his towel-waving antics against the Lakers in 1984. And that's OK by him. "I think that helped take the heat off Larry, Robert and Kevin," Carr said.[87]

Dennis Johnson entered the NBA coaching ranks after the Celtics declined to renew his contract before the start of the 1990–91 season. He had received offers from three other teams to continue playing but turned them down. "My pride wouldn't let me end my career like that," he said. "If I leave now, I still got all my credits."[88] He spent the next several years laboring as an assistant with the Celtics and Clippers before rising to the Clippers' head job on an interim basis in 2003. The experience did not go well, however, as Johnson compiled an 8–16 record and was summarily dismissed. Undaunted, he went on to coach the Boston entry in the NBA Developmental League, all the while hoping for another shot at the big time, which never came. He dropped dead of a heart attack at 52 on February 22, 2007, following a team practice. His '84 teammates were devastated. "That was my guy," Maxwell said. "We were very close. We were like two peas in a pod. As people would say, I'm shocked. It's like having a brother pass away. You win championships together, go through wars together, and to know he's passed away is amazing . . . I'm just numb."[89]

Bird preferred to remember him as one of the clutchest players from his era, citing an '85 Finals game against the Lakers as proof. "I got the ball on the right side of the top of the key," he said, "and they sent two guys running right at me. Out of the corner of my eye, I saw DJ was open and I said, 'Thank God.' I knew he'd hit it, and of course he did." Added

Ainge, "That was the thing about DJ. He found more ways to help us win than any other player I've ever played with. Whether it was hitting the shot, coming up with a steal, blocking a shot, or shutting down the team's best player, he would do it."[90] Johnson was posthumously enshrined in the Basketball Hall of Fame in 2010.

Robert Parish became the NBA's version of the Energizer Bunny— he kept on going and going. He became the all-time leader in minutes and games played and earned a fourth championship ring with the 1996–97 Chicago Bulls as a 43-year-old backup center in his final season. He also famously had a run-in with Michael Jordan in practice when the latter took exception to Parish's second unit beating His Airness's first. "He was at half court and I was at the top of the key . . . and I was talking trash," Parish recalled. Then things turned ugly as the two Hall of Famers squared off in a heated exchange. "I didn't back down," Parish maintained. "He said he would kick my butt, and I told him [if] he felt strongly about it, come and get some." Jordan wisely declined the offer, and that ended matters. "Michael has a tendency to test his teammates especially the new faces on the team," Parish explained afterward. "I think it was more than a threat. He was testing my reaction to his being a bully . . . I didn't read anything into it. I think it was just a test to see how I would respond."[91]

Parish may have finished his 21-year Hall of Fame career as a Bull, but he always remained a Celtic in spirit. "We came to play, no matter who we were playing," he said of his Boston teammates. "I'm interested in a lot of these teams today that they are pretty good. They go out and lose to the underachievers. We never lost to the underachievers. We punished them. Don't guys today understand? That's when you pad your stats, against the underachievers."[92] In retirement, Parish ran into financial problems that required auctioning off all his championship rings. "People shouldn't feel sad; they should help me get a job," he said. "I need a coaching job in the NBA." But no such offers were forthcoming, even from the Celtics. "Across the board, most NBA teams do not call back," he complained bitterly. "You need a court order just to get a phone call back from these organizations. I'm not part of their fraternity."[93] He still had his memories, though, especially from the '84 Finals. "That series against the Lakers was a war," he told author Michael McClellan in a 2018 interview. "Every game was a battle."[94] And the Chief was the most dependable foot soldier of all.

Kevin McHale headed back home to Minnesota and served as the general manager, coach, and vice president of basketball operations for the Minnesota Timberwolves, a young expansion team that had been founded in 1989. Prior to his arrival, the club had been a perennial loser, but McHale breathed new life into the organization, overseeing the club's transformation into an instant playoff contender. The key was McHale's bold decision to select Kevin Garnett as the Wolves' fifth overall pick in the 1995 NBA draft, thereby making the future Hall of Famer the first player in 20 years to be taken directly out of high school. "This was [my] first draft," McHale recalled. "The owner was also new. How do you tell him that the first thing he's going to do is sign this high school kid?"[95] McHale did anyway, and the Wolves flourished as a franchise. In 2004 Garnett was named league MVP and carried the team all the way to the Western Conference Finals.

Garnett's success illustrated the kind of crucial hands-on role McHale played in developing the maniacally driven Greenville, South Carolina, product into an elite power forward. "[McHale] was the Yoda to my young Skywalker," Garnett wrote in his 2021 memoir *KG: A to Z— An Uncensored Encyclopedia of Life, Basketball and Everything in Between.* "Kevin gave me all the one-on-one time I needed. He was always about 'Be a four that can handle the ball. Master the simple stuff: show the rock, come over the top, turn around and jump, now do it off the glass, pump fake, be creative, be in the moment, never settle for what you think you can do. Master what you think you *can't* do.' . . . He polished me in a way no one else could have."[96]

Unfortunately for McHale, Garnett became disenchanted with his situation in Minnesota by 2007, believing that team ownership was not committed to winning a championship. Garnett wanted out, and McHale reluctantly obliged him by working out a deal with Danny Ainge, then chief executive of the Celtics. "There are really no secrets between Kevin and I, we don't try to trick each other," Ainge said. "We've known each other way too long to ever do that."[97] Without Garnett, however, the

Wolves foundered, and McHale was fired. He eventually landed on his feet in Houston and coached the Rockets to an appearance in the 2015 Western Conference Finals before stepping down the following season. But his successful Houston tenure was marred by a devastating personal tragedy that befell his family in 2012. His 23-year-old college basketball-playing daughter, Alexandra, who sported the same number 32 on her game jersey that her father had worn in Boston, died of complications from lupus. "She was like her dad," her former high-school coach said, "everything rolled off her back."[98] McHale can be found these days dispensing incisive commentary for NBA TV and fielding endless questions about his still widely discussed "takedown" of Kurt Rambis 40 years ago. "The only regret I had," he says, "it wasn't a better player."[99]

Larry Bird had difficulty adjusting to his post-playing life. He was given a fancy job title with vaguely defined responsibilities in the Celtics front office and loathed every minute of it. He deemed his existence "boring" while privately seething that the team did not use him in a more substantial role that took advantage of his wealth of acquired basketball knowledge.[100] There had been some talk of Bird succeeding M. L. Carr on the Boston bench, but that subject became moot when Rick Pitino was hired. "[The owners] had already made up their mind what they wanted and it wasn't me," Bird said.[101] He longed for an exit ramp out of town, and that opportunity presented itself in 1997 when the Indiana Pacers approached him about taking over the team's vacant head coaching position. Bird was immediately intrigued. "I talked to 25 or 30 people," he revealed. "After I ran everything by them, I asked them directly, 'Do you think I should get into this or should I stay away from it?' It was probably 50–50. I had good input."[102]

Although the Pacers had finished below .500 and out of the playoffs the previous season for the first time in nine years, the club was not bereft of talent. The roster boasted explosive shooting guard Reggie Miller (21.6 points per game) and an All-Star caliber frontcourt consisting of Rik Smits and Antonio Davis. Bird was confident that he could get more out of the team, plus the job would allow him to return to his beloved Indiana. "The timing was perfect," he said. "I wanted to coach and the Pacers needed a coach. We both got what we wanted."[103]

Indeed, the team responded with a 58–29 record in Bird's first season at the helm, a turnaround that earned the former Indiana State Sycamore NBA Coach of the Year honors. Essential to his success was the buy-in he received from players who appreciated his calm, reassuring leadership style. "There comes a time in every game when you have to have the feeling that you're going to win," Indiana guard Mark Jackson said. "Last year we didn't have that. You could see it in our eyes, in our attitude. . . . Coach Bird has brought the confidence back. Sometimes it's not what he says; it's what he doesn't say. He doesn't have to tell you he has confidence in you. He shows it by not jumping up out of his seat when you turn the ball over, by not telling you that you made the wrong cut when you already know you made the wrong cut."[104]

The Pacers continued to benefit from Bird's sure hand over the next two seasons, winning a pair of divisional crowns and an Eastern Conference championship in 2000—a first in franchise history. But they were unable to get past Kobe Bryant's Lakers in the Finals, losing in six games. "I wasn't disappointed at all," Bird said afterward. "I thought we were playing hard."[105] The defeat marked the official end of Bird's coaching career. He had always told anyone willing to listen that carrying a clipboard had a limited shelf life. "Three years is the max," he posited. "Bill [Fitch] was a great coach, but at the end of that last year it started to get a little crazy."[106] Bird had no intention of seeing history repeat itself. He moved into the Pacers front office where he served two separate stints as team president before finally walking away from the NBA for good in 2017.

Although grayer and a few pounds heavier, a now 67-year-old Bird still looks as if he can walk into a gym, lace up a pair of Converse high-tops, and demolish anyone foolish enough to challenge him to a game of one-on-one. As he once said, "The way I see it, if I put two hours [of court time] in by myself, then someone who is working out with somebody else has to put in four hours in order to beat me."[107]

No truer words were ever spoken in basketball.

Notes

Chapter One

1. *Politico.com*, August 11, 2017.
2. Ibid.
3. Taylor Downing, *1983: Reagan, Andropov, and a World on the Brink* (New York: Da Capo Press, 2018), 222.
4. Ibid., 245.
5. Ibid.
6. *Washington Post*, October 24, 2015.
7. Ronald Reagan, *The Reagan Diaries* (New York: HarperCollins, 2007), 199.
8. Walter Mondale with David Hage, *The Good Fight: A Life in Liberal Politics* (New York: Scribner, 2010), 297.
9. Ibid.
10. Nancy Reagan with William Novak, *My Turn: The Memoirs of Nancy Reagan* (New York: Random House, 1989), 266.
11. H. W. Brands, *Reagan: The Life* (New York: Doubleday, 2015), 456.
12. Mondale with Hage, *The Good Fight*, 303.
13. *Los Angeles Times*, January 23,1985.
14. Ibid.
15. Graham Thompson, *American Culture in the 1980s* (Edinburgh: Edinburgh University Press, 2007), 12.
16. Paul Slansky, *The Clothes Have No Emperor: A Chronicle of the 1980s* (New York: Simon & Schuster, 1989), 221.
17. Michael Kranish and Marc Fisher, *Trump Revealed: An American Journey of Ambition, Ego, Money, and Power* (New York: Scribner, 2016), 3.
18. Ibid.
19. Craig Marks and Rob Tannenbaum, *I Want My MTV: The Uncensored History of the Music Video Revolution* (New York: Dutton, 2011), 185.
20. *Rolling Stone*, February 1983.
21. Ibid.
22. *Orange County Register*, June 25, 2009.
23. *Rolling Stone*, February 1983.
24. *New York Daily News*, January 28, 1984.

25. *Rolling Stone*, February 1983.
26. *New York Times*, July 19, 1984.
27. *New York Times*, July 20, 1984.
28. *Boston Globe*, July 21, 1984.
29. David Sirota, *Back to the Future: How the 1980s Explain the World We Live in Now— Our Culture, Our Politics, Our Everything* (New York: Ballantine Books, 2011), 88.
30. Nick de Semlyen, *Wild and Crazy Guys: How the Comedy Mavericks of the 80's Changed Hollywood Forever* (New York: Crown Archetype, 2019), 131–32.
31. *Los Angeles Times*, September 20, 1984.
32. *Rolling Stone*, October 8, 2014.
33. Walter Isaacson, *Steve Jobs* (New York: Simon & Schuster, 2011), 162.
34. *Los Angeles Times*, January 31, 2017.
35. Isaacson, *Steve Jobs*, 162.
36. *Washington Post*, May 9, 1984.
37. *The Guardian*, June 29, 2012.
38. Roland Lazenby, *Michael Jordan: The Life* (New York: Little, Brown, 2014), 229.
39. *Washington Post*, September 26, 1984.
40. Glenn Stout and Richard A. Johnson, *The Cubs: The Complete Story of Chicago Cubs Baseball* (Boston: Houghton Mifflin, 2007), 343.
41. Steve Silverman, *Who's Better, Who's Best in Hockey: Setting the Record Straight on the Top 50 Hockey Players in the Expansion Era* (New York: Sports Publishing, 2015), 9.
42. Peter Gzowski, "How Great Is Gretzky?," *Inside Sports*, November 1981.
43. Tom Callahan, "Masters of Their Game," *Time*, March 18, 1985.
44. *Edmonton Journal*, May 19, 1984.
45. David Cay Johnston, *The Making of Donald Trump* (Brooklyn, NY: Melville House, 2016), 54.
46. Drew Jubera, "How Donald Trump Destroyed a Football League," *Esquire*, January 13, 2016.
47. Ibid.
48. *New York Times*, January 1, 2020.
49. Bill Russell and Taylor Branch, *Second Wind: The Memoirs of an Opinionated Man* (New York: Simon & Schuster, 1979), 102.
50. Pete Croatto, *From Hang Time to Prime Time: Business, Entertainment, and the Birth of the Modern-Day NBA* (New York: Atria Books, 2020), 39.
51. David Halberstam, *The Breaks of the Game* (New York: Ballantine Books, 1981), 341.
52. Ibid.; Croatto, *From Hang Time to Prime Time*, 40.
53. Larry Bird with Bob Ryan, *Drive* (New York: Doubleday, 1989), 287.
54. *New York Times*, January 1, 2020.
55. Joshua Mendelsohn, *The Cap: How Larry Fleisher and David Stern Built the Modern NBA* (Lincoln: University of Nebraska Press, 2020), 275.
56. E. M. Swift, "From Corn Beef to Caviar," *Sports Illustrated*, June 3, 1991.

CHAPTER TWO

1. Jeff Greenfield, *The World's Greatest Team: Portrait of the Boston Celtics, 1957–69* (New York: A Sport Magazine Book, 1976), 21–22.

2. George Sullivan, *The Picture History of the Boston Celtics* (Indianapolis: Bobbs-Merrill, 1981), 8.

3. Ibid., 152–53.

4. *Boston Globe*, January 4, 1964.

5. Thomas J. Whalen, *Dynasty's End: Bill Russell and the 1968–69 World Champion Boston Celtics* (Boston: Northeastern University Press, 2003), 127–18.

6. *Boston Globe*, April 28, 1950.

7. Arnold Red Auerbach and Paul Sann, *Red Auerbach: Winning the Hard Way* (Boston: Little Brown, 1966), 66.

8. Terry Pluto, *Tall Tales: The Glory Years of the NBA* (Lincoln: University of Nebraska Press, 2000), 108.

9. Jack Ramsey, "The Red behind the Green," *The Final Game, Official Commemorative Game Program and Magazine*, April 21, 1995.

10. Greenfield, *World's Greatest Team*, 83.

11. Mike Carey with Jamie Most, *High above Courtside: The Lost Memoirs of Johnny Most* (Seattle: Sports Publishing, 2003), 90–91.

12. *Boston Globe*, November 26, 1989.

13. Dan Shaughnessy, *Seeing Red: The Red Auerbach Story* (Stoughton, MA: Adams Media, 1995), 109.

14. Pluto, *Tall Tales*, 128.

15. Tommy Heinsohn with Joe Fitzgerald, *Give 'Em the Hook* (New York: Prentice Hall, 1988), 86.

16. *Sports Illustrated*, February 3, 1958.

17. Greenfield, *World's Greatest Team*, 91.

18. Bill Russell and Taylor Branch, *Second Wind: The Memoirs of an Opinionated Man* (New York: Simon & Schuster, 1979), 168.

19. *Sport*, February 1963.

20. Sullivan, *Picture History of the Boston Celtics*, 195.

21. Robert W. Cohen, *The 40 Greatest Players in Boston Celtics Basketball History* (Camden, ME: Down East Books, 2017), 47.

22. Pluto, *Tall Tales*, 357.

23. *Boston Globe*, May 23, 2021.

24. *Christian Science Monitor*, April 20, 1966.

25. *Christian Science Monitor*, April 19, 1966.

26. *Boston Globe*, April 19, 1966.

27. Pluto, *Tall Tales*, 325.

28. Ibid., 363.

29. Sullivan, *Picture History of the Boston Celtics*, 89.

30. *Boston Globe*, May 23, 2021.

31. Bill Russell, "I'm Not Involved Anymore," *Sports Illustrated*, August 4, 1969.

32. Pluto, *Tall Tales*, 373.

33. Red Auerbach and Ed Fitzgerald, *Red Auerbach* (New York: Penguin, 1977), 151.
34. Sullivan, *Picture History of the Boston Celtics*, 91.
35. Dan Shaughnessy, *Ever Green: The Boston Celtics* (New York: St. Martin's Press, 1990), 133.
36. Sullivan, *Picture History of the Boston Celtics*, 94.
37. Ray Fitzgerald, *Champions Remembered: Choice Picks from a Boston Sports Desk* (New York: Penguin, 1983), 92–93.
38. *Grantland*, May 13, 2013.
39. Ibid., November 12, 2014.
40. Sullivan, *Picture History of the Boston Celtics*, 123.
41. Fitzgerald, *Red Auerbach*, 320.
42. Harvey Araton and Filip Bondy, *The Selling of the Green: The Financial Rise and Moral Decline of the Boston Celtics* (New York: HarperCollins, 1992), 73–74.
43. Heinsohn with Fitzgerald, *Give 'Em the Hook*, 145.
44. *Sports Illustrated*, November 22, 1976.
45. Ibid.
46. *Washington Post*, January 13, 1977.
47. Ibid.
48. *Sports Illustrated*, April 25, 1977.
49. Ibid.
50. Sullivan, *Picture History of the Boston Celtics*, 127.
51. Dave Bing, *Attacking the Rim: My Journey from NBA Legend to Business Leader to Big-City Mayor to Mentor* (Chicago: Triumph Books, 2020), 146.
52. John Powers, *The Short Season: A Boston Celtics Diary, 1977–1978* (New York: Harper & Row, 1979), 192.
53. Ibid.
54. *Boston Globe*, April 10, 1978.
55. Carey with Most, *High above Courtside*, 192.
56. Powers, *Short Season*, 212.
57. *Boston Globe*, April 10, 1978.
58. *South Florida Sun-Sentinel*, September 25, 1994.
59. *Sports Illustrated*, July 17, 1978.
60. Shaughnessy, *Ever Green*, 167.
61. *New York Times*, July 15, 1978.
62. Carey with Most, *High above Courtside*, 200.
63. *New York Times*, July 15, 1978.
64. Powers, *Short Season*, 221.
65. *New York Times*, July 15, 1978.
66. Araton and Bondy, *Selling of the Green*, 39.
67. Alan M. Webber, "Red Auerbach on Management," *Harvard Business Review*, March 1987.
68. Carey with Most, *High above Courtside*, 200.
69. Sullivan, *Picture History of the Boston Celtics*, 132.
70. *Chicago Tribune*, March 4, 1990.

71. Mike Carey, *Bad News: The Turbulent Life of Marvin Barnes, Pro Basketball's Original Renegade* (New York: Sports Publishing, 2016), 134.

72. *Boston Globe*, September 10, 2014.

73. Lee Daniel Levine, *Bird: The Making of an American Sports Legend* (New York: McGraw-Hill, 1988), 224.

74. Sullivan, *Picture History of the Boston Celtics*, 134.

75. Levine, *Bird*, 143.

76. *New York Times*, December 1, 1993.

77. Levine, *Bird*, 188.

78. Araton and Bondy, *Selling of the Green*, 115.

79. *Sports Illustrated*, October 15, 1979.

80. Shaughnessy, *Seeing Red*, 217.

81. Mike Carey and Michael D. McClellan, *Boston Celtics: Where Have You Gone?* (New York: Sports Publishing, 2012), 180.

82. Bird with Ryan, *Drive*, 83.

83. *Boston Herald*, February 15, 2018.

84. *Sports Illustrated*, May 15, 1980.

85. *United Press International*, October 1, 1980.

86. Bird with Ryan, *Drive*, 95.

87. *Boston Globe*, June 11, 1980.

88. Donald Hubbard, *100 Things Celtics Fans Should Know & Do Before They Die* (Chicago: Triumph Books, 2017), 16.

89. Shaughnessy, *Seeing Red*, 229.

90. Ibid., 227.

91. Red Auerbach and John Feinstein, *Let Me Tell You a Story: A Lifetime in the Game* (New York: Little, Brown, 2004), 154.

92. Ibid.

93. *Boston Globe*, May 15, 1981.

94. Bird with Ryan, *Drive*, 103.

95. Carey and McClellan, *Boston Celtics*, 181.

96. Sullivan, *Picture History of the Boston Celtics*, 150.

97. Levine, *Bird*, 266.

98. *Los Angeles Times*, May 29, 1986.

99. Levine, *Bird*, 267.

100. *Boston Globe*, May 28, 1985.

101. Carey with Most, *High above Courtside*, 284.

CHAPTER THREE

1. Russell with Branch, *Second Wind*, 82.

2. *Salem Evening News*, June 28, 1983.

3. Carey and McClellan, *Boston Celtics*, 64.

4. *New York Times*, June 28, 1983.

5. *New York Times*, June 22, 1983.

6. Peter May, *The Big Three* (New York: Simon & Schuster, 2007), 166.

7. *Salem Evening News*, June 16, 1983.
8. *New York Times*, June 17, 1983.
9. *Boston Globe*, July 22, 1983.
10. Levine, *Bird*, 273–74.
11. *New York Times*, September 28, 1983.
12. *Boston Globe*, September 29, 1983.
13. *Boston Globe*, August 9, 1983.
14. *Boston Globe*, August 4, 1983.
15. *Boston Globe*, August 6, 1983.
16. *Boston Globe*, August 9, 1983.
17. *Boston Globe*, April 17, 2022.
18. Author's interview, Dan Shaughnessy.
19. Ibid., August 11, 1983.
20. Ibid., October 8, 1983.
21. *Salem Evening News*, October 12, 1983.
22. May, *Big Three*, 171.
23. *Salem Evening News*, October 12, 1983.
24. May, *Big Three*, 171.
25. *Boston Globe*, October 14, 1983.
26. Ibid.
27. *Salem Evening News*, October 17, 1983.
28. *Beverly Times*, October 18, 1983.
29. *Washington Post*, October 18, 1983.
30. *Salem Evening News*, October 17, 1983.
31. Sullivan, *The Picture History of the Boston Celtics*, 38.
32. Ibid., 171.
33. Irv Goodman, "The Winning Ways of Red Auerbach," *Sport*, March 1958.
34. Russell and Branch, *Second Wind*, 125.
35. Araton and Bondy, *The Selling of the Green*, 40.
36. Bill Bradley, *Life on the Run* (New York: Vintage Books, 1995), 107.
37. Gilbert Rogin, "A Master's Touch," *Sports Illustrated*, April 5, 1965.
38. Ibid.
39. Pluto, *Tall Tales*, 272.
40. Ibid., 274–75.
41. Curt Gowdy with John Powers, *Seasons to Remember: The Way It Was in American Sports 1945–1960* (New York: HarperCollins, 1993), 113.
42. *Boston Globe*, January 5, 1985.
43. Ibid.
44. Frank Deford, "No. 2 in the Rafters, No. 1 in Their Hearts," *Sports Illustrated*, January 14, 1985.
45. Rogin, "A Master's Touch."
46. Pluto, *Tall Tales*, 270.
47. Bill Reynolds, *Rise of a Dynasty: The '57 Celtics, The First Banner, and the Dawning of a New America* (New York: New American Library, 2010), 234.

48. Joe Fitzgerald, "Mr. Celtics," *Boston Sunday Herald Magazine*, October 14, 1984.
49. Auerbach and Feinstein, *Let Me Tell You a Story*, 22.
50. Auerbach and Feinstein, *Let Me Tell You a Story*, 28.
51. *Beverly Times*, October 7, 1983.
52. *Salem Evening News*, October 8, 1983.
53. K. C. Jones with Jack Warner, *Rebound* (Boston: Quinlan, 1986), 177.
54. *Boston Herald*, June 8, 1983.
55. *Boston Globe*, October 18, 1983.
56. *Salem Evening News*, October 8, 1983.
57. *Boston Herald*, June 8, 1983.
58. Jones with Warner, *Rebound*, 43.
59. Ibid., 44.
60. Ibid.
61. *Los Angeles Times*, May 7, 1987.
62. *Boston Herald*, June 6, 1988.
63. James W. Johnson, *The Dandy Dons: Bill Russell, K. C. Jones, Phil Woolpert and One of College Basketball's Greatest and Most Innovative Teams* (Lincoln and London: University of Nebraska Press, 2009), 116.
64. Bruce Lee, "Bill Russell, K. C. Jones, Unstoppable San Francisco," *Sport*, April 1964.
65. Jones with Warner, *Rebound*, 55–56.
66. Ibid.
67. Ibid., 64.
68. Ibid., 65.
69. *Boston Record-American*, November 21, 1963.
70. Carey with Most, *High Above Courtside*, 118.
71. Pluto, *Tall Tales*, 253.
72. Joe Fitzgerald, *That Championship Feeling: The Story of the Boston Celtics* (New York: Scribner, 1975), 107.
73. Pluto, *Tall Tales*, 254.
74. Fitzgerald, *That Championship Feeling*, 107.
75. Sullivan, *Picture History of the Boston Celtics*, 187.
76. Jones with Warner, *Rebound*, 109.
77. Ibid.
78. *Washington Post*, December 26, 2020.
79. *Washington Post*, November 23, 1983.
80. Jones with Warner, *Rebound*, 170.
81. *Quincy Patriot Ledger*, October 28, 1983.
82. *Baltimore Sun*, March 31, 1991.
83. *Sports Illustrated*, October 31, 1983.
84. *Dallas Times*, November 15, 1983.
85. George Kalinsky, *The New York Knicks: The Official 50th Anniversary Celebration* (New York: Macmillan, 1997), 163.
86. *Sports Illustrated*, October 31, 1983.
87. *Sporting News*, October 31, 1983.

88. Ibid.

89. Roland Lazenby, *The Show: The Inside Story of the Spectacular Los Angeles Lakers in the Words of Those Who Lived It* (New York: McGraw-Hill, 2005), 226.

90. *Boston Globe*, October 29, 1983.

91. *Boston Herald*, October 29, 1983.

92. *Boston Globe*, October 29, 1983.

93. *Salem Evening News*, October 29, 1983.

94. *Boston Globe*, October 30, 1983.

95. *Boston Globe*, October 31, 1983.

96. *Boston Globe*, November 2, 1983.

97. Pat Jordan, "How the Bruins Flaunt Their Muscles," *Sport*, March 1970.

98. Leigh Montville, "Green Ghosts Saying Goodbye to Beloved Boston Garden, Old Celtics Relive a Half Century of Otherworldly Memories," *Sports Illustrated*, April 17, 1995.

99. *Boston.com*, November 6, 2015.

100. *Desert News*, May 24, 1998.

101. John Powers, *The Short Season: A Boston Celtics Diary, 1977–1978* (New York: Harper & Row, 1979), 4.

102. Montville, "Green Ghosts Saying Goodbye to Beloved Boston Garden."

103. *Boston Globe*, April 30, 1995.

104. Powers, *Short Season*, 3.

105. Montville, "Green Ghosts Saying Goodbye to Beloved Boston Garden."

106. *Boston Herald*, November 3, 1983.

107. *Boston Globe*, November 3, 1983.

108. *Beverly Times*, November 3, 1983.

109. *Salem Evening News*, November 3, 1983.

110. *Boston Herald*, November 3, 1983.

111. *Boston Globe*, November 3, 1983.

CHAPTER FOUR

1. *Boston Globe*, November 12, 1983.

2. Ibid.

3. M. L. Carr, *Don't Be Denied: My Story* (Boston: Quinlan Press, 1987), 115.

4. Robert Parish interview with author, February 26, 2022.

5. Leigh Montville, "Where's the Chief?" *Sports Illustrated*, July 12, 2004.

6. Carey and McClellan, *Boston Celtics*, 223.

7. May, *Big Three*, 166.

8. Ibid., 82.

9. Parish interview.

10. Ibid.

11. Bob Ryan, "The Chief Is So Much Better Than You Think," *Basketball Digest*, January 1983.

12. Carey and McClellan, *Boston Celtics*, 163.

13. Sam Moses, "Invisible in the Post," *Sports Illustrated*, December 8, 1975.

14. May, *Big Three*, 90.
15. Parish interview.
16. Ibid.
17. Ryan, "The Chief Is So Much Better Than You Think."
18. Alexander Wolff, "Still Going Strong," *Sports Illustrated*, March 11, 1991, 30.
19. Tony Kornheiser, "A Voice Crying in the Wilderness," in *The Sporting News Best Sports Stories 1984* (Charlotte: Sporting News Publishing Co., 1984), 147.
20. Parish interview.
21. Wolff, "Still Going Strong," *Sports Illustrated*, March 11, 1991, 30.
22. Parish interview.
23. McClellan, *Boston Celtics*, 225.
24. *Boston Globe*, April 24, 1982.
25. Parish interview.
26. Peter May, *The Last Banner: The Story of the 1985–86 Celtics and the NBA's Greatest Team of All Time* (New York: Simon & Schuster, 2007), 181–82.
27. *Boston Herald*, October 12, 1983.
28. Buck Harvey, "The New and Improved Robert Parish," *Basketball Digest*, April 1981.
29. *Boston Globe*, April 24, 1982.
30. Parish interview.
31. McClellan, *Boston Celtics*, 226.
32. *Boston Herald*, December 9, 1983.
33. *Boston Globe*, November 17, 1983.
34. *Boston Globe*, November 20, 1983.
35. *Boston Herald*, November 20, 1983.
36. Levine, *Bird*, 277.
37. *Boston Globe*, December 3, 1984.
38. *Boston Herald*, December 3, 1984.
39. Cedric Maxwell with Mike Isenberg, *If These Walls Could Talk: Boston Celtics: Stories from the Boston Celtics Sideline, Locker Room, and Press Box* (Chicago: Triumph Books, 2021), 108.
40. Carey with Most, *High Above Courtside*, 265.
41. Ibid., 272.
42. Ibid., 281.
43. Ibid., 282.
44. Ibid., 1.
45. Ibid., 2.
46. Ibid., 7.
47. *Boston Herald-American*, November 10, 1974.
48. *Boston Phoenix*, January 8, 1993.
49. *Boston Globe*, January 9, 1972.
50. *Sports Illustrated*, January 14, 1985
51. *Los Angeles Times*, January 4, 1993.
52. McCallum, *Unfinished Business*, 95–96.

53. Leigh Montville, "Green Ghosts Saying Goodbye to Beloved Boston Garden," *Sports Illustrated*, April 17, 1995.

54. *Boston Globe*, February 7, 1973.

55. Montville, "Green Ghosts Saying Goodbye to Beloved Boston Garden."

56. *Salem Evening News*, February 9, 1984.

57. *Boston Herald*, February 9, 1984.

58. Bruce Newman, "Together at Center Stage," *Sports Illustrated*, June 4, 1984.

59. Dan Klores, Jackie MacMullan, and Rafe Bartholomew, *Basketball: A Love Story* (New York: Crown, 2018), 214–15.

60. Larry Bird with Bob Ryan, *Drive* (New York: Doubleday, 1989), 63.

61. Larry Keith, "They Caged the Bird," *Sports Illustrated*, April 4, 1979.

62. Bird with Ryan, *Drive*, 64.

63. Earvin Magic Johnson with William Novak, *My Life* (New York: Random House, 1992), 91.

64. Ibid., 6.

65. Ibid.

66. *USA Today Weekend*, October 20, 1985.

67. Barry Ferrell, "It's the Magic Show," *Sport*, February 1980.

68. Bill Gutman, *Chairmen of the Boards* (New York: Ace Books, 1980), 168.

69. Ibid., 168–69.

70. Johnson with Novak, *My Life*, 25–26.

71. *Los Angeles Times*, June 5, 2002.

72. Johnson with Novak, *My Life*, 42.

73. *Los Angeles Times*, June 5, 2002.

74. Gutman, *Chairmen of the Boards*, 176–77.

75. Seth Davis, *When March Went Mad: The Game That Transformed Basketball* (New York: St. Martin's Griffin, 2010), 43.

76. Johnson with Novak, *My Life*, 59.

77. Davis, *When March Went Mad*, 77.

78. Johnson with Novak, *My Life*, 83.

79. Ibid., 97.

80. Larry Bird and Earvin Magic Johnson with Jackie MacMullan, *When the Game Was Ours* (New York: Houghton Mifflin Harcourt, 2009), 66.

81. Jeff Pearlman, *Showtime: Magic, Kareem, Riley, and the Los Angeles Lakers Dynasty of the 1980s* (New York: Avery Publishing, 2014), 44.

82. Marc Spears and Gary Washburn, *The Spencer Haywood Rule: Battles, Basketball, and the Making of an American Iconoclast* (Chicago: Triumph Books, 2020), 143–44.

83. Ferrell, "It's the Magic Show."

84. Kareem Abdul-Jabbar, *Giant Steps* (New York: Bantam Books, 1985), 314.

85. Johnson with Novak, *My Life*, 109.

86. Bruce Newman, "Doing It All for L.A.," *Sports Illustrated*, November 19, 1979.

87. Pearlman, *Showtime*, 97.

88. Johnson with Novak, *My Life*, 117.

89. *Boston Globe*, May 17, 1980.

90. John Papanek, "Arms and the Man," *Sports Illustrated*, May 26.

91. Ferrell, "It's the Magic Show."

92. Johnson with Novak, *My Life*, 147.

93. Pearlman, *Showtime*, 117.

94. Ibid., 120.

95. Johnson with Novak, *My Life*, 152.

96. Lazenby, *The Show*, 211.

97. Pearlman, *Showtime*, 129.

98. Ibid.

99. Lazenby, *The Show*, 211.

100. Johnson with Novak, *My Life*, 155.

101. Pearlman, *Showtime*, 128.

102. Johnson with Novak, *My Life*, 155.

103. Ibid., 155–56.

104. Pearlman, *Showtime*, 144.

105. Anthony Cotton, "Don't Blame Me, I Just Want to Have Fun," *Sports Illustrated*, November 30, 1981.

106. Ferrell, "It's the Magic Show."

107. *New York Post*, June 25, 1982.

108. Johnson with Novak, *My Life*, 157.

109. Ibid., 158.

110. *New York Post*, June 25, 1982.

111. Bruce Newman, "L.A. Needed a Pat on its Back," *Sports Illustrated*, June 21, 1982.

112. Roland Lazenby, *The Finals: The Official Illustrated History* (Lanham, MD: Taylor Trade, 1990), 220.

113. *New York Post*, December 17, 1982.

114. Ibid.

115. *Boston Globe*, April 16, 1984.

116. Ibid.

CHAPTER FIVE

1. *Washington Post*, April 17, 1984.

2. Ibid.

3. Bill Halls, "Ruland's Success Tribute to the Work Ethic," *Basketball Times*, January 1986.

4. Bob O'Donnell, "Jeff Ruland: He's More Than Just a Lot of Beef," *Basketball Digest*, April 1984.

5. Bryan Burwell, "Is Washington's Jeff Ruland Mean and Tough—Or Is He McFilthy?" *Basketball Digest*, January 1983.

6. *New York Times*, July 14, 1982.

7. *Boston Globe*, April 15, 1984.

8. *New York Times*, July 14, 1982.

9. Ibid.

10. Bruce Newman, "A Tough Man in a Scramble," *Sports Illustrated*, December 13, 1982.

11. Burwell, "Is Washington's Jeff Ruland Mean and Tough?"

12. O'Donnell, "Jeff Ruland."

13. Ralph Wiley, "A Master of Intimidation," *Sports Illustrated*, April 10, 1989.

14. *New York Times*, January 24, 1982.

15. Ibid.

16. Al Simon, "A Couple of Beefy Bullets," *NBA Today*, December 26, 1983.

17. *New York Times*, January 24, 1982.

18. *Washington Post*, April 13, 1982.

19. *New York Times*, January 24, 1982.

20. *Washington Post*, April 13, 1982.

21. *Washington Post*, April 18, 1982.

22. Ibid.

23. *Boston Globe*, April 18, 1984.

24. *Boston Herald*, April 20, 1984.

25. *Boston Herald*, April 22, 1984.

26. *Washington Post*, April 22, 1984.

27. *Boston Herald*, April 22, 1984.

28. *Boston Herald*, April 25, 1984.

29. *Boston Globe*, April 25, 1984.

30. *Beverly Times*, April 25, 1984.

31. *Salem Evening News*, April 25, 1984.

32. *Boston Herald*, April 25, 1984.

33. *Boston Globe*, April 25, 1984.

34. *Boston Globe*, April 29, 1984.

35. Bird with Ryan, *Drive*, 126.

36. *New York Times*, April 29, 1984.

37. Bruce Newman, "Hero of a Showdown in Motown," *Sports Illustrated*, May 7, 1984.

38. *New York Times*, April 29, 1984.

39. Bernard King with Jerome Preisler, *Game Face: A Lifetime of Hard-Earned Lessons on and off the Basketball Court* (New York: Da Capo Press, 2017), 3.

40. Ibid., 4.

41. Ibid., 9.

42. Ibid., 11.

43. Joe Klein, "Starting Over," *Inside Sports*, March 31, 1981.

44. Ibid.

45. *Boston Globe*, February 7, 1984.

46. King with Preisler, *Game Face*, 76–77.

47. Klein, "Starting Over."

48. King with Preisler, *Game Face*, 103.

49. Klein, "Starting Over."

50. Ibid.

51. *New York Times*, September 2, 1987; *Boston Globe*, January 4, 1978.

52. *Boston Globe*, January 4, 1978.
53. Klein, "Starting Over."
54. Joe Gergen, "The King Captures New York," in *1985 Season: The Complete Handbook of Pro Basketball*, ed. Zander Hollander (New York: Signet, 1985).
55. King with Preisler, *Game Face*, 181.
56. Klein, "Starting Over."
57. King with Preisler, *Game Face*, 193.
58. Klein, "Starting Over."
59. *New York Times*, February 3, 1984.
60. *New York Times*, April 25, 1984.
61. *Boston Globe*, April 29, 1984.
62. Maxwell with Isenberg, *If These Walls Could Talk*, 3.
63. *Boston Herald*, April 30, 1984.
64. Ibid.
65. *Salem Evening News*, April 30, 1984.
66. *New York Times*, April 30, 1984.
67. *Salem Evening News*, April 30, 1984.
68. Ibid.
69. *New York Daily News*, May 3, 1984.
70. *Boston Globe*, May 3, 1984.
71. Ibid.
72. *Boston Herald*, May 3, 1984.
73. Ibid.
74. *Boston Globe*, May 3, 1984.
75. *Beverly Times*, May 3, 1984.
76. *Salem Evening News*, May 3, 1984.
77. *New York Post*, May 3, 1984.
78. *New York Daily News*, May 3, 1984.
79. *New York Daily News*, May 5, 1984.
80. *Boston Globe*, May 5, 1984.
81. *Salem Evening News*, May 5, 1984.
82. *New York Times*, May 5, 1984.
83. King with Preisler, *Game Face*, 254.
84. *Beverly Times*, May 7, 1984.
85. King with Preisler, *Game Face*, 254.
86. Ibid., 255.
87. Maxwell with Isenberg, *If These Walls Could Talk*, 3.
88. *New York Post*, May 7, 1984.
89. *New York Daily News*, May 10, 1984.
90. *Boston Globe*, May 10, 1984.
91. *New York Times*, May 10, 1984.
92. King with Preisler, *Game Face*, 258.
93. *New York Daily News*, May 10, 1984.
94. *New York Times*, May 10, 1984.

95. *New York Post*, May 10, 1984.

96. *Beverly Times*, April 25, 1983.

97. *Boston Globe*, April 25, 1983.

98. *Boston Herald*, April 25, 1983.

99. *Boston Globe*, April 25, 1983.

100. *Boston Herald*, April 23, 2020.

101. May, *The Last Banner*, 97.

102. Paul Flannery, "Danny Ainge Goes Back to the Drawing Board," *Boston Magazine*, October 29, 2013.

103. *Toronto Star*, September 1, 2020.

104. *New York Times*, March 20, 1981.

105. *Eugene Register-Guard*, March 20, 1981.

106. Steve Barnfeld, "Danny Ainge Was Sitting Pretty—Now He's Just Sitting," *Basketball Digest*, April 1984.

107. *Toronto Sun*, September 1, 2020.

108. Michael Walker, "The Many Names of Danny Ainge," *Y Magazine*, Winter 2009.

109. Bird with Ryan, *Drive*, 106.

110. Flannery, "Danny Ainge Goes Back to the Drawing Board."

111. Barnfeld, "Danny Ainge Was Sitting Pretty."

112. Jackie MacMullan, "Trae Young, Kevin Love and the Future of Mental Health in the NBA," *ESPN.com*, August 24, 2018.

113. *Los Angeles Times*, May 29, 1985.

114. Ibid.

115. *Washington Post*, May 18, 1986.

Chapter Six

1. *Salem Evening News*, May 11, 1984.

2. King with Priesler, *Game Face*, 257.

3. *Salem Evening News*, May 12, 1984.

4. *Boston Globe*, May 12, 1984.

5. *Boston Globe*, May 12, 1984.

6. *Boston Herald*, May 12, 1984.

7. *New York Daily News*, May 12, 1984.

8. Bird with Ryan, *Drive*, 127.

9. Ibid.

10. *New York Post*, May 14, 1984.

11. *Boston Herald*, May 14, 1984.

12. King with Priesler, *Game Face*, 259.

13. Dennis D'Agostino, *Garden Glory: An Oral History of the New York Knicks* (Chicago: Triumph Books, 2003), 180.

14. King with Priesler, *Game Face*, 260.

15. *Boston Globe*, May 15, 1984.

16. *Boston Herald*, May 15, 1984.

17. Sam McManis, "Marques Johnson: Prodigal Son Returns," *Basketball Digest*, February 1985.

18. Ibid.

19. Jim Cohen, "Marques Johnson: Key to the Milwaukee Bucks' Future," *Basketball Digest*, December 1978.

20. Bob Wolf, "Marques Johnson, He Can Do It All—But How Far Can He Take the Bucks?" *Basketball Digest*, April 1980.

21. *Boston Globe*, May 15, 1984.

22. *Milwaukee Journal-Sentinel*, March 24, 2019.

23. Jeff Pearlman, "How One Draft Decision Changed the Fortunes of Two NBA Franchises," *si.com*, February 14, 2012.

24. John Rosenberg, "Sidney Moncrief: This Superman Works Hard," *Basketball Digest*, June/July 1984.

25. Bob Wolf, "Sidney Moncrief, The NBA's Newest Superstar," *Basketball Digest*, April 1982.

26. *Arkansas Democrat Gazette*, September 18, 2020.

27. Jaime Diaz, "He's Good All Over," *Sports Illustrated*, October 28, 1985.

28. Ibid.

29. Rosenberg, "Sidney Moncrief: This Superman Works Hard."

30. Anthony Cotton, "There's No Stopping the Bucks," *Sports Illustrated*, February 22, 1982.

31. Wolf, "Sidney Moncrief, The NBA's Newest Superstar."

32. Diaz, "He's Good All Over."

33. *Boston Globe*, May 15, 1984.

34. Ibid.

35. *Salem Evening News*, May 15, 1984.

36. John Lombardo, "Bob Lanier, the NBA's Inside Man," *Sports Business Journal*, February 22, 2016.

37. Ibid.

38. Ira Berkow, "The Buck Stops Here," *Sport*, February 1983.

39. Lombardo, "Bob Lanier, the NBA's Inside Man."

40. *New York Times*, May 11, 2022.

41. Ted Green, "The Frustrations of Bob Lanier," *Basketball Digest*, May 1978.

42. Dale Hoffman, "Bob Lanier: He Holds the Key to Milwaukee's Title Hopes," *Basketball Digest*, June 1980.

43. Berkow, "The Buck Stops Here."

44. *Boston Globe*, May 16, 1984.

45. *Boston Herald*, May 16, 1984.

46. *Boston Herald*, May 18, 1984.

47. *Salem Evening News*, May 18, 1984.

48. *Boston Globe*, May 18, 1984.

49. Ibid.

50. May, *The Last Banner*, 162.

51. Bob Hurt, "How Dennis Johnson Has Improved the Suns," *Basketball Digest*, May 1981.

52. Ibid.

53. Alexander Wolff, "D. J. Spins a Happy Tune," *Sports Illustrated*, May 26, 1986.

54. Ibid.

55. Hurt, "How Dennis Johnson Has Improved the Suns."

56. Ibid.

57. May, *Last Banner*, 166.

58. Charley Rosen, "The Greening of DJ," *Inside Sports*, June 1985.

59. McClellan, *The Boston Celtics*, 201.

60. Rosen, "Greening of DJ."

61. Aram Goudsouzian, *King of the Court: Bill Russell and the Basketball Revolution* (Oakland: University of California Press, 2010), 264.

62. Rosen, "Greening of DJ."

63. Ibid.

64. Wolff, "D. J. Spins a Happy Tune."

65. *Los Angeles Times*, June 9, 1985.

66. May, *Last Banner*, 168.

67. *Los Angeles Times*, June 9, 1985.

68. Ian Thomsen, *The Soul of Basketball: The Epic Showdown Between LeBron, Kobe, Doc, and Dirk That Saved the NBA* (New York: Houghton Mifflin Harcourt, 2018), 202.

69. *Boston Globe*, May 20, 1984.

70. *Boston Herald*, May 21, 1984.

71. *Salem Evening News*, March 21, 1984.

72. *Beverly Times*, May 21, 1984.

73. *Boston Herald*, May 21, 1984.

74. *Boston Herald*, May 22, 1984.

75. *Beverly Times*, May 22, 1984.

76. *Boston Herald*, May 24, 1984.

77. Ibid.

78. *Salem Evening News*, May 24, 1984.

79. *Beverly Times*, May 24, 1984.

80. *Boston Globe*, May 24, 1984.

CHAPTER SEVEN

1. *Los Angeles Times*, May 31, 1984.

2. Ibid.

3. *Boston Globe*, May 27, 1984.

4. Earl Bloom, "Move Over Wilt," *Sporting News*, April 16, 1984, 3.

5. Kareem Abdul-Jabbar, *Giant Steps* (New York: Bantam Books, 1985), 13.

6. Peter Knobler, "Not Just Another Pretty Face," *Inside Sports*, February 28, 1981.

7. Ibid., 25.

8. Abdul-Jabbar and Knobler, *Giant Steps*, 66.

9. Ibid., 67.

10. Kareem Abdul-Jabbar with Raymond Obstfeld, *Becoming Kareem: Growing Up On and Off the Court* (New York: Little, Brown Books for Young Readers, 2017), 160.

11. Bill Rhoden, "Kareem," *Ebony*, April 1975, 56.

12. Abdul-Jabbar with Obstfeld, *Becoming Kareem*, 261.

13. Rhoden, "Kareem," 56–58.

14. Abdul-Jabbar and Knobler, *Giant Steps*, 191.

15. Ibid., 193.

16. Ibid., 194.

17. Tex Maule, "Lew Turns Small Change to Big Bucks," *Sports Illustrated*, March 9, 1970.

18. Dave Klein, *Pro Basketball's Big Men* (New York: Random House, 1973), 144.

19. Richard Levin, "Kareem's Skyhook: The Greatest Shot Ever," *Basketball Digest*, December 1979, 31.

20. Gary Smith, "Now More Than Ever," *Sports Illustrated*, December 23–30, 1985.

21. John Papanek, "A Different Drummer," *Sports Illustrated*, March 31, 1980.

22. Abdul-Jabbar and Knobler, *Giant Steps*, 270.

23. Wayne Embry with Mary Schmitt Boyer, *The Inside Game: Race, Power, and Politics in the NBA* (Akron: University of Akron Press, 2004), 239.

24. Lazenby, *The Show*, 168.

25. Papanek, "A Different Drummer."

26. Randy Harvey, "He Remains Kareem of Crop," *The Sporting News 1982–83 Basketball Yearbook*, Fall 1982, 151.

27. Knobler, "Not Just Another Pretty Face," 26.

28. *Salem Evening News*, May 29, 1984.

29. *Los Angeles Times*, May 28, 1984.

30. Ibid.

31. *Boston Globe*, May 28, 1984.

32. *Boston Herald*, May 28, 1984.

33. Maxwell with Isenberg, *If These Walls Could Talk*, 5.

34. *Los Angeles Times*, June 1, 1984.

35. Maxwell with Isenberg, *If These Walls Could Talk*, 5.

36. *Salem Evening News*, June 1, 1984.

37. *Boston Herald*, June 1, 1984.

38. *Beverly Times*, June 1, 1984.

39. Carey and McClellan, *Boston Celtics*, 123.

40. Bird with Ryan, *Drive*, 130.

41. Carey and McClellan, *Boston Celtics*, 123.

42. *Boston Herald*, June 14, 1984.

43. Carey with Most, *High Above Courtside*, 238.

44. *Boston Herald*, June 14, 1984.

45. Carey with Most, *High above Courtside*, 238.

46. Larry Whiteside, "Gerald Henderson: Going from the Penthouse to Seattle," *Basketball Digest*, May 1985.

47. *Boston Globe*, September 25, 1980.

48. *Boston Globe*, June 15, 1984.
49. Carey and McClellan, *Boston Celtics*, 122.
50. *Quincy Patriot Ledger*, June 4, 1984.
51. *Salem Evening News*, June 4, 1984.
52. *Boston Globe*, June 4, 1984.
53. *Los Angeles Times*, June 4, 1984.
54. May, *The Big Three*, 180.
55. Dan Shaughnessy interview with author.
56. *Salem Evening News*, June 7, 1984.
57. Anthony Cotton, "Green and White and Red All Over," *Sports Illustrated*, June 26, 1984.
58. Roland Lazenby, *Magic: The Life of Earvin "Magic" Johnson* (New York: Celadon Books, 2023), 536.
59. *Beverly Times*, June 7, 1984.
60. Ibid.
61. *Basketball Times*, June 30, 1985.
62. Ibid.
63. *Los Angeles Times*, June 2, 1984.
64. Robert W. Cohen, *The Forty Greatest Players in Boston Celtics History* (Camden, ME: Down East Books, 2017), 94–95.
65. *Los Angeles Times*, June 2, 1984.
66. McCallum, *Unfinished Business*, 110.
67. *Los Angeles Times*, June 2, 1984.
68. Ibid.
69. Mark Ribowsky and Bill Feinberg, "The Pride of the Celtics," *Inside Sports*, March 1984.
70. *Los Angeles Times*, June 2, 1984.
71. May, *Big Three*, 135.
72. *Boston Globe*, September 10, 1980.
73. *Boston Globe*, September 17, 1980.
74. Donald Hall, *Fathers Playing Catch with Sons: Essays on Sport (Mostly Baseball)* (Berkeley, CA: North Point Press, 1984), 172.
75. Ibid., 173.
76. May, *Big Three*, 139.
77. Bird with Ryan, *Drive*, 97.
78. Paul Levy, "Kevin McHale; Fitting Nicely into the Celtics' Tradition," *Basketball Digest*, March 1981.
79. Mike Carey, "Kevin McHale: The Celtics' Working Class Hero," *Basketball Digest*.
80. Ibid., 39–40.
81. *Boston Globe*, May 2, 1981.
82. Bird with Ryan, *Drive*, 124.
83. *Boston Globe*, May 2, 1981.
84. Dan Shaughnessy, "The Most Wanted Man in the NBA," *Sport*, January 1984, 88.
85. Ribowsky and Feinberg, "The Pride of the Celtics."

86. Shaughnessy, "The Most Wanted Man in the NBA."
87. Ribowsky and Feinberg, "The Pride of the Celtics."
88. McCallum, *Unfinished Business*, 115.
89. May, *Big Three*, 162.
90. Robert Parish interview with author.
91. Shaughnessy interview with author.
92. *Boston.com*, February 19, 2018.
93. *Boston Globe*, June 9, 1984.
94. *Boston Herald*, June 9, 1984.
95. *Boston Globe*, June 9, 1984.
96. *Boston Herald*, June 9, 1984.
97. Ibid.
98. *Boston Globe*, June 9, 1984.
99. *Boston Herald*, June 9, 1984.
100. Ibid.

CHAPTER EIGHT

1. *Los Angeles Times*, June 11, 1984.
2. *Boston Globe*, June 11, 1984.
3. Ibid.
4. Anthony Cotton, "They Took It Down the Wire," *Sports Illustrated*, June 18, 1984.
5. *Los Angeles Times*, June 11, 1984.
6. *Boston Globe*, June 11, 1984.
7. Ibid.
8. *Los Angeles Times*, June 12, 1984.
9. Ibid.
10. Bird with Ryan, *Drive*, 134.
11. Levine, *Bird*, 47.
12. Bird with Ryan, *Drive*, 11.
13. Levine, *Bird*, 44.
14. Bird with Ryan, *Drive*, 15.
15. Ibid., 51.
16. Larry Bird with Dan Shaughnessy, "Why I Love This Game," *Indianapolis Monthly*, March 2000.
17. Diane K. Shah, "The Bird and the B's," *Inside Sports*, October 1979.
18. Bird with Shaughnessy, "Why I Love This Game," 83.
19. Gutman, *Chairmen of the Boards*, 67–68.
20. Bob Ryan, "Larry Bird: He's Happy to Be a Celtic," *Basketball Digest*, June 1982.
21. *Boston Globe Magazine*, September 21, 1986.
22. Levine, *Bird*, 79.
23. Bird with Ryan, *Drive*, 39.
24. Bob Ryan, "Larry Bird Player of the Year," *Basketball Digest*, June/July 1985.
25. Levine, *Bird*, 88.
26. Ibid.

27. Gutman, *Chairmen of the Boards*, 70.

28. Ryan, "Larry Bird Player of the Year."

29. Levine, *Bird*, 90.

30. Frank Deford, "A Player for the Ages," *Sports Illustrated*, March 21, 1988.

31. Gutman, *Chairmen of the Boards*, 71.

32. Bird with Ryan, *Drive*, 15.

33. Gutman, *Chairmen of the Boards*, 74.

34. Bird with Ryan, *Drive*, 47.

35. Richard O'Connor, "French Lick, You'll Just have to Wait," *Sport*, May 1980.

36. Diane K. Shah interview with author.

37. O'Connor, "French Lick, You'll Just Have to Wait.

38. Davis, *When March Went Mad*, 124.

39. Deford, "A Player for the Age," 75–76.

40. Levine, *Bird*, 108.

41. Gutman, *Chairmen of the Boards*, 76.

42. Bird with Ryan, *Drive*, 46–47.

43. Ibid.

44. Gutman, *Chairmen of the Boards*, 74.

45. Kent Hannon, "An Idea That's Gotten Off the Ground," *Sports Illustrated*, November 28, 1977.

46. *Ibid.*

47. Gutman, *Chairmen of the Boards*, 77–78.

48. May, *The Big Three*, 50.

49. Gutman, *Chairmen of the Boards*, 96.

50. *NBA Today*, March 25, 1983

51. Mike Carey, "Larry Bird; The Celtics' $15 Million Man," *Basketball Digest*, January 1984.

52. *TheAthletic.com*, April 9, 2020.

53. Steve Marantz, "The Real Larry Bird," *Sport*, May 1986.

54. *TheAthletic.com*, April 9, 2020.

55. Marantz, "The Real Larry Bird."

56. Ibid., 38.

57. Bird with Ryan, *Drive*, 221.

58. Ibid.

59. *Chicago Tribune*, April 5, 1987.

60. Bob Ryan, "The Greatest," *Basketball Times*, February 28, 1985.

61. *Los Angeles Times*, February 5, 1993.

62. *The Enterprise*, April 10, 2011.

63. *Boston Record*, November 21, 1958.

64. *Boston Globe*, September 3, 2023.

65. *Boston Globe*, June 15, 1988.

66. *Boston Globe*, December 25, 2022.

67. Araton and Bondy, *The Selling of the Green*, 56.

68. *Bostonmagazine.com*, December 21, 2007.

69. Howard Bryant, *Shut Out: A Story of Race and Baseball in Boston* (Boston: Beacon Press, 2003), 92.

70. Dan Shaughnessy, *The Curse of the Bambino* (New York: Penguin, 2004), 57.

71. Sullivan, *The Picture History of the Boston Celtics*, 18.

72. *The Guardian*, April 17, 2015.

73. *Boston Herald*, June 12, 1984.

74. Bird with Ryan, *Drive*, 134.

75. *Los Angeles Times*, June 13, 1984.

76. Ibid.

77. Ibid.

78. Maxwell with Isenberg, *If These Walls Could Talk*, 13.

79. *Los Angeles Times*, June 13, 1984.

80. *Boston Globe*, June 13, 1984.

81. *Boston Herald*, June 13, 1984.

82. Maxwell with Isenberg, *If These Walls Could Talk*, 18–19.

83. Ibid., 18.

84. Ibid., 21.

85. Larry Whiteside, "Cedric Maxwell: The Late Bloomer Made Good," *Basketball Digest*, March 1982.

86. Maxwell with Isenberg, *If These Walls Could Talk*, 19.

87. Whiteside, "Cedric Maxwell," 35–36.

88. Ibid., 36.

89. Maxwell with Isenberg, *If These Walls Could Talk*, 26.

90. Whiteside, "Cedric Maxwell."

91. Ibid.

92. McClellan, *The Boston Celtics*, 178.

93. Maxwell with Isenberg, *If These Walls Could Talk*, 30.

94. McClellan, *Boston Celtics*, 178–79.

95. Cedric Maxwell as told to Bert Rosenthal, "The Game I'll Never Forget," *Basketball Digest*, April 1986.

96. Embry with Boyer, *The Inside Game*, 260.

97. McClellan, *Boston Celtics*, 179.

98. Maxwell with Isenberg, *If These Walls Could Talk*, 43.

99. Powers, *The Short Season*, 65.

100. Larry Whiteside, "Cornbread Maxwell Looks Like a Celtic No. 1 Who Can Play," *Basketball Digest*, April 1979.

101. Maxwell as told to Rosenthal, "The Game I'll Never Forget," 91.

102. Maxwell with Isenberg, *If These Walls Could Talk*, 14.

103. *Boston Herald*, June 13, 1984.

104. *Boston Globe*, June 13, 1984.

105. Ibid.

106. L. Jon Wertheim, *Glory Days: The Summer of 1984 and the 90 Days That Changed Sports and Culture Forever*, 87.

107. *Los Angeles Times*, June 13, 1984.

108. *Salem Evening News,* June 13, 1984.
109. *Boston Herald,* June 13, 1984.
110. Johnson with Novak, *My Life,* 214.
111. Ibid.

CHAPTER NINE

1. *Boston Globe,* June 14, 1984.
2. Ibid.
3. *Boston Globe,* March 5, 2017.
4. Lee Daniel Levine, *Bird: The Making of an American Sports Legend* (New York: McGraw-Hill, 1988), 284.
5. May, *The Big Three,* 184.
6. *USA Today,* May 3, 2018.
7. *Boston.com,* December 7, 2017.
8. May, *Big Three,* 187.
9. Carey and McClellan, *Boston Celtics,* 123–24.
10. Ryan, *The Four Seasons,* 120.
11. *Los Angeles Times,* October 19, 1985.
12. Alexander Wolff, "Finally, A Happy Laker Ending," *SI,* June 17, 1985.
13. Levine, *Bird,* 292.
14. Bird with Ryan, *Drive,* 154.
15. May, *The Last Banner,* 22.
16. Ibid., 40.
17. *Los Angeles Times,* October 19, 1985.
18. *Chicago Tribune,* September 8, 1985.
19. *Boston Globe,* October 26, 1985.
20. Cohen, *The Forty Greatest Players,* 368.
21. Bird, *Drive,* 161–62.
22. Ryan, *The Four Seasons,* 132.
23. Levine, *Bird,* 303.
24. *Boston Herald,* June 5, 2020.
25. *Salem Evening News,* June 18, 1986.
26. *Washington City Paper,* May 7, 2020.
27. *Washington Post,* June 19, 2016.
28. *Boston Globe,* June 18, 1986.
29. Shaughnessy, *Ever Green,* 216.
30. *Boston Globe,* June 20, 1986.
31. Carey with Most, *High above Courtside,* 320.
32. *Salem Evening News,* June 20, 1986.
33. Carey with Most, *High above Courtside,* 326.
34. McClellan, *The Boston Celtics,* 218.
35. *Boston Globe,* June 16, 1987.
36. Ibid.
37. May, *Big Three,* 216.

38. *Salem Evening News*, May 27, 1987.
39. *Boston Globe*, May 27, 1987.
40. Ibid.
41. *Salem Evening News*, June 10, 1987.
42. *Boston Globe*, June 15, 1987.
43. May, *Big Three*, 249.
44. *Boston Globe*, May 23, 1988.
45. *Sports Illustrated*, February 18, 1991.
46. Lazenby, *Michael Jordan: The Life*, 457.
47. MacMullan, Bartholomew, and Klores, *Basketball*, 342.
48. McCallum, *Dream Team*, 330.
49. *Boston Globe*, August 19, 1992.
50. *Beverly Times*, August 19, 1992.
51. *New York Times*, August 19, 1992.
52. *Beverly Times*, August 19, 1992.
53. *New York Times*, August 19, 1992.
54. Cohen, *The Forty Greatest Players*, 203.
55. *Seattle Times*, March 9, 1995.
56. *Boston Herald*, November 18, 2018.
57. *Los Angeles Times*, May 7, 1997.
58. *ESPN.com*, September 4, 2013.
59. *Masslive.com*, September 9, 2013.
60. *Boston Globe*, September 28, 2002.
61. *Boston Globe*, June 18, 2008.
62. *Boston Globe*, October 29, 2006.
63. Auerbach and Feinstein, *Let Me Tell You a Story*, 182.
64. *The Guardian*, October 29, 2006.
65. *Los Angeles Times*, May 20, 1990.
66. *Washington Post*, January 16, 1992.
67. *Washington Post*, July 8, 1997.
68. *Washington Post*, December 26, 2020.
69. *Boston Herald*, October 18, 1984.
70. *Boston Herald*, January 22, 1985.
71. Carey and McClellan, *Boston Celtics*, 125.
72. Araton and Bondy, *The Selling of the Green*, 156.
73. *Boston Globe*, May 26, 2020.
74. Ibid.
75. *Chicago Tribune*, May 2, 2020.
76. *Desert News*, May 10, 2003.
77. *Washington Times*, June 2, 2021.
78. Maxwell with Isenberg, *If These Walls Could Talk*, 129.
79. *Los Angeles Times*, October 19, 1985.
80. Maxwell with Isenberg, *If These Walls Could Talk*, 135.
81. Ibid., 148.

82. Ibid., 155.

83. *Boston Globe*, December 14, 2003.

84. Cary and McClellan, *Boston Celtics*, 6.

85. *Masslive.com*, November 11, 2021.

86. Cary and McClellan, *Boston Celtics*, 6.

87. Ibid.

88. May, *The Last Banner*, 273.

89. *Boston Globe*, February 23, 2007.

90. Ibid.

91. *Masslive.com*, April 22, 2020.

92. *Sports Illustrated*, July 12, 2004.

93. *Boston Globe*, January 25, 2013.

94. McClellan, *Boston Celtics*, 226.

95. *Sports Illustrated*, May 3, 1999.

96. Kevin Garnett and David Ritz, *KG: A to Z—An Uncensored Encyclopedia of Life, Basketball, and Everything in Between* (New York: Simon & Schuster, 2021), 170.

97. *Sports Illustrated*, October 29, 2007.

98. *Bangor Daily News*, November 25, 2012.

99. *Boston Globe*, December 9, 2021.

100. Shaw, *Larry Legend*, 30.

101. *Sports Illustrated*, October 27, 1997.

102. Shaw, *Larry Legend*, 33.

103. Ibid., 35.

104. *Sports Illustrated*, January 12, 1998.

105. *Chicago Tribune*, June 4, 2000.

106. Shaughnessy, *Wish It Lasted Forever*, 72.

107. Shaw, *Larry Legend*, 121.

INDEX

AAU (American Athletic Union), 168–69

Abdul-Jabbar, Kareem: background, 141–43; Bird and, 152; Bucks drafting, 143; cameo role in *Airplane!*, 145–46; contract, 87; injuries, 85; Johnson (Magic) and, 84–85; 1983–1984 season, 77–78; 1984 NBA playoffs, 146, 150–51, 159, 163–64, 180, 187; religious conversion, 142–43; strengths, 60, 140–41, 143–44; traded to Lakers, 144–45

Ainge, Danny: background, 114–16; Bird and, 116–17, 160; Celtics signing, 116; ejection from Knick's game, 113–14; emotional displays of, 117; Fitch's criticism of, 117; Johnson (DJ) and, 134, 210; later years, 207; McHale and, 114, 212; 1981–82 season, 36; 1983–84 season, 40, 44; 1984 NBA playoffs, 109, 113–14, 179; 1985 NBA playoffs, 192; 1987 NBA playoffs, 197

Allen, Ray, 204

American Athletic Union (AAU), 168–69

Archibald, Tiny, 32, 36, 39, 71, 149, 173

Ard, Jim, 23

Atlanta Hawks, 191, 199

Auerbach, Arnold "Red": on Ainge, 207; background, 49–50; on Bias, 195, 196; Bird and, 31–32, 173, 190, 201; Brown and, 28–29; celebratory cigars, 46–47; on Celtics sale to Gaston, 43; coaching approach, 14–16, 49, 50; Cowens and, 22–26; driving skills, 47–48; on Johnson (Dennis), 40; Jones (K. C.) and, 51–52; Knicks team presidency opportunity, 28–29; later years, 204–5; Maxwell and, 184, 191; McHale and, 33, 34–35, 40–41; meeting Reagan, 189; on 1983–84 season, 91, 186; on 1986–87 season, 197; Parish and, 33, 34–35, 71;

Russell and, 16–18, 19–20, 21–22, 48; Sampson and, 35; Silas and, 23–24; understanding human behavior, 48; violent outbursts of, 45–46

Ballard, Greg, 94, 99
Barcelona basketball, 95
Barksdale, Don, 16
Barnes, Marvin, 30–31
Barnhill, Norton, 132
Barry, Rick, 70
Belkin, Steve, 42
Bias, Len, 194–96, 206
"The Big Three." *See* Bird, Larry; McHale, Kevin; Parish, Robert
Bing, Dave, 127
Bird, Larry: Abdul-Jabbar and, 152; Ainge and, 116–17; author's impression of, xi–xii; background, 78–80, 165–68, 169–73; on Bias, 196; on Bucks, 134; Celtics signing, 31–32; contract negotiations, 41–42; on Cowens, 34; on Eastern Conference Finals loss, 33; first seasons with Celtics, 173–76; injuries, 109–10, 198–99; on Johnson (DJ), 210; Johnson (Magic) and, 78–79; on Jones (K. C.), 50; later years, 212–14; leadership of, 200; Maxwell and, 192; McHale and, 156, 157, 158–59; on Moncrief, 125–26; 1983–1984 season, 61,

64, 65, 73; 1984 NBA playoffs, 98, 100, 109, 111, 112, 113, 119, 129, 136, 148, 151, 160, 164–65, 186; 1984–85 season, 190–91; 1985 NBA playoffs, 192; 1987 NBA playoffs, 197; not meeting Reagan, 189–90; on Parish, 43–44; Pitino and, 203; retirement and tributes, 200–201; as Rookie of the Year, 32; on 76ers, 101; on Stern, 164; strengths, 31, 174–75; talking trash, 173–74, 191; on Walton, 192–93, 194; work ethic, 166, 173
Borgia, Sid, 49
Boston Celtics: early years, 13–14; 1957–66 championships, 18; 1967–69 championships, 20–21; 1974 and 1976 championships, 23–24; 1977–78 season, 26; 1981–83 seasons, 35–37, 185; 1985 NBA playoffs, 192, 210; 1985–86 season, 192–94; 1986–87 season, 194–97; 1996–97 season, 202–3; origin of name, 13; sale of, 42–43, 203–4; season-ticket sales, 175–76. *See also* Auerbach, Arnold "Red"; Boston Celtics 1983–84 season; Boston Celtics *vs.* Lakers games; Fitch, Bill; Jones, K. C.; *specific players*
Boston Celtics 1983–84 season: *vs.* Bucks in playoffs,

on 1962 NBA playoffs, 139;
Russell and, 48
Cowens, Dave, 22–26, 30–31,
33–34, 70, 185
cultural and social history of
1984, 4–7
Cunningham, Billy, 45

Daly, Chuck, 65, 94
Detroit Pistons: Lanier and,
127–28; 1983–1984 season,
60, 65; 1984 NBA playoffs,
102; 1987 NBA playoffs, 197
Duncan, Tim, 202–3

Edmonton Oilers, 9–10
Erving, Julius "Dr. J," 58, 73, 190

Finkel, Hank, 22
Fitch, Bill: on Bird, 31; on
Henderson, 149; leader-
ship style, 36–37, 50–52; on
McHale, 155–56, 158; Parish
on, 71–72
Ford, Chris, 174–75
fouls, 23
Fox, George, 82

Garnett, Kevin, 204, 211–12
Gaston, Don F., 42–43
Gaston, Paul, 204, 208–9
Gernert, Al, 77
Glickman, Marty, 75
Gola, Tom, 54

Golden State Warriors, 69–70,
95, 107
Gretzky, Wayne, 9–10
Grousbeck, Wyc, 203–4
Gushue Joe, 48–49

Halberstam, David, 11
Havlicek, John: on Boston
Garden, 63–64; on Celtics, 20,
22; on Maxwell, 184; on Most
(Johnny), 76; playing last game,
27; in "sixth man" role, 18–19
Hawkins, Tom, 17
Hayes, Elvin, 95
Haywood, Spencer, 84
Heathcote, Jud, 82–83
Heinsohn, Tommy, 17, 22, 24,
26, 48
Henderson, Gerald: back-
ground, 148; Celtics signing, 149; 1983–84 season,
40, 61; 1984 NBA playoffs, 101,
135, 136–37, 147–48, 150, 152,
163; on Parish, 44; with Spurs,
148–49; strengths, 147–48,
149–50; traded to SuperSonics,
191, 206
historical perspective on
1984: baseball, 8–9; basketball
leading up to 1984, 11–12;
culture, 4–7; football, 10–11;
hockey, 9–10; Olympics, 7–8;
politics and economics, 1–4
Hodges, Bill, 169
Holzman, Red, 102

191; 1986–87 season, 196–97; 1987 NBA playoffs, 198; on Parish, 44; Rambis and, 151–52, 153; strengths, 156–57; on Walton, 193
Mears, Ray, 104–5
Michigan State Spartans, 79–80, 82–83
Milwaukee Bucks: leadership, 122; 1983–1984 season, 59, 61, 64; 1984 NBA playoffs, 121–22, 134–37. *See also* Nelson, Don; *specific players*
Minnesota Timberwolves, 211–12
"Miracle of Causeway Street," 147–48
Mokeski, Paul, 135
Moncrief, Sidney: background, 125; on Johnson (Magic), 83–84; 1984 NBA playoffs, 128–30; points per game, 122; strengths, 59, 124–25, 126
Most, Johnny: on Auerbach, 29; background, 74–77; "Fakers" reference, 180; on Havlicek, 27; Henderson and, 149; on Jones (K. C.), 56; reaction to Bias's passing, 196; rehabilitation after stroke, 74; on Ruland and Mahorn, 93

National Basketball Association beginnings, 13
Naulls, Willie, 18
NCAA Tournament, 79–80

Nelson, Don: on Bird, 134; Johnson (Marques) and, 123–24; on Lanier, 126, 128; 1969 NBA playoffs, 20, 140; 1984 NBA playoffs, 129; on Parish, 71
New England Blizzard, 205–6
New Jersey Nets, 59, 105–6
Newlin, Mike, 23
New York Knicks: interest in McHale, 40–41; King traded to, 107–8; 1983–84 season, 59, 101–2; 1984 NBA playoffs, 101–2, 107–14, 119–21. *See also specific players*
New York Nets, 143
Nixon, Norm, 60, 87

O'Brien, Larry, 11–12
Olajuwon, Hakeem, 194
Olympics, 142, 199–200
Ordway, Glenn, 77

Pagliuca, Steve, 203, 207
Parish, Robert: background, 66–69; on Bird and McHale, 158–59, 191, 199; on Bucks, 135; first year with Celtics, 70–72; Fitch and, 36–37; with Golden State Warriors, 69–70; on Henderson, 148; on Lanier, 126; later years, 201, 210–11; on loss to Detroit, 60; Maxwell on, 146; 1983–84 season, 64, 65–66; 1984 NBA playoffs,

98–99, 100, 109, 112, 129, 136, 150–51, 211; not meeting Reagan, 189–90; salary negotiations, 43–44; shunning spotlight, 66, 67; signing with Celtics, 33, 34–35
Philadelphia 76ers, 20, 33, 44–45, 58–59, 72–73, 101
Phoenix Suns, 133, 140
Pierce, Paul, 204
Pitino, Rick, 73, 203, 204–5
"point forward," 123–24
Pollin, Abe, 12
Portland Trail Blazers, 192–93

race-track business, 25
racism: Abdul-Jabbar and, 141–42; in Boston, 177–78; defusing, 78–79; Johnson (Magic) and, 78–79, 81; Jones (K. C.) and, 177; King and, 105; Maxwell and, 181; Moncrief and, 125; Russell and, 176, 178; Sanders and, 176–77; Smith (Reggie) and, 177
Rambis, Kurt, 151–52, 153, 163, 187–88, 212
Ramsey, Jack, 73
Rautins, Leo, 173–76
Ray, Clifford, 69–70
Reagan, Ronald, 1–2, 189
Rebound (Jones), 50–51
referees, 48–49
Reinhart, Bill, 50

Riley, Pat: on Celtics, 152, 160, 164; Lakers hiring, 88; 1984 NBA playoffs, 146; 1985 NBA playoffs, 192; as rookie head coach, 89
Roberts, Joe, 69
Robertson, Oscar, 56
Rodgers, Jimmie, 37
Rowe, Curtis, 24
Ruland, Jeffrey George, 94–96, 98–99
Russell, Bill: personality and quirks, 17–18; as player-coach, 19–21; racism faced by, 176, 178; retirement, 21–22; strengths, 16–17; on substance abuse in NBA, 11; as SuperSonics coach, 132
Russell, John "Honey," 14
Ryan, Bob, 71

Sacramento Kings, 207
salary negotiations: of Abdul-Jabbar, 87; of Bird, 41–42; caps in, 12, 40; of Johnson (Magic), 87; of McHale, 41, 155–56, 157–58; of Parish, 43–44
Sampson, Ralph, 35, 194
San Antonio Spurs, 148–49
Sanders, Satch, 26–27, 30, 176–77
San Diego Clippers, xi–xii
San Francisco Spurs, 26
scandals, 11, 95
Seattle SuperSonics, 129–30, 132–33, 205

About the Author

THOMAS J. WHALEN IS ASSOCIATE PROFESSOR OF SOCIAL SCIENCE AT Boston University and author of several books, including *Dynasty's End: Bill Russell and the 1968–69 World Champion Boston Celtics*. An expert in modern American politics, American foreign policy, and the American presidency, Whalen's commentary has appeared in the *New York Times*, WABCNews.com, *Wall Street Journal*, *Los Angeles Times*, *Chicago Tribune*, *USA Today*, *Newsweek*, *Washington Post*, *The Economist*, *The Globe and Mail*, and *Boston Globe*. He has also appeared in several national broadcast outlets including CNN, NPR, and Reuters TV. He is a resident of Boston's North Shore.

www.ingramcontent.com/pod-product-compliance
Lightning Source LLC
Chambersburg PA
CBHW030300100426
42812CB00002B/509